"In its largest sense, Christian service means bowing to the Lordship of Christ; being, following, and doing what He commands; and using the gifts He gives as He directs. Christian service is doing God's will, not man's and carries with it Jesus' beautiful assurance: 'Whoever hears the will of God and does it, the same is my brother, and my sister, and my mother.'"

Equal to Serve is a call to Christian men and women to yield their rights... their talents... their lives in totality to serving Jesus Christ.

"This book constitutes a challenge that cannot be dismissed or ignored to the bastions of inequality among Christian men and women."
Gilbert Bilezikian
Professor of Biblical Studies, Wheaton College

"Perhaps the most significant feature of the book is its dominant purpose: to free women from many impositions and limitations that impede their ability to *serve* others and supremely to *serve* the living God, their redeemer."
Roger Nicole, Professor Emeritus
Gordon-Conwell Theological Seminary

Gretchen Gaebelein Hull is the daughter of the late Frank Gaebelein, noted evangelical theologian. A Sunday-school teacher and elder in her local church, she also has been actively involved with the International Council on Biblical Inerrancy.

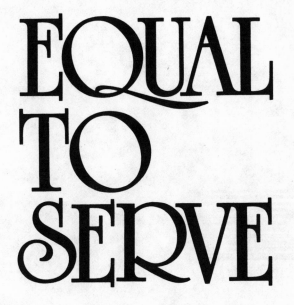

EQUAL TO SERVE

EQUAL TO SERVE

Gretchen Gaebelein Hull

Fleming H. Revell Company
Tarrytown, New York

Credit lines continue on page 5.

Library of Congress Cataloging-in-Publication Data

Hull, Gretchen Gaebelein.
  Equal to serve.

Bibliography: p.
  Includes index.
  1. Woman (Christian theology)   I. Title.
BT704.H85   1987   261.8'344   87-16323
ISBN 0-8007-5400-X

Copyright © 1987, 1991 by Gretchen Gaebelein Hull
Published by the Fleming H. Revell Company
Tarrytown, New York 10591
Printed in the United States of America

Contents

Publisher's Foreword

In a world that has become an interrelated global village of 4.5 billion men, women, and children, the problems of human existence have reached crisis proportions. People today are stretching to achieve new heights, but their very advances in technological and scientific realms sometimes threaten them with the loss of life's most precious gifts—and even life itself. In the midst of the crises, Christians believe the possibility for unprecedented good, for the flourishing of freedom, and for peace exists. This hopeful outlook is itself possible in a violent, threatened world because the Christian views the world from the center point of history, the Cross, where God dealt redemptively with the crux of the human problem.

While Christians do not doubt God's ability nor His final victory, they struggle to know and to implement God's plan. Thankfully, there is an ongoing discussion of contemporary problems as Christians wrestle with agendas for action. As the publisher of the Crucial Questions series, we earnestly hope that these volumes will contribute positively to that discussion. Although the viewpoints expressed by the authors in this series may not always be those of the publisher, we are grateful for the opportunity to present them to the public, and we trust that these volumes will serve to stimulate Christians to fulfill their role as salt and light in today's world.

I am not ashamed of the gospel, because it is the power of God for the salvation of every-one who believes. . . .

Romans 1:16

Jesus said: "The Spirit gives life; the flesh counts for nothing. The words I have spo-ken to you are spirit and they are life."

John 6:63

What God's Son has told me, take for truth I do; Truth himself speaks truly, or there's nothing true.

GERARD MANLEY HOPKINS

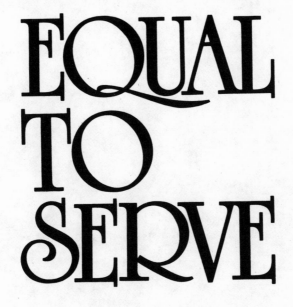

Chapter 1

The Journey Begins

In a crowded departure lounge at John F. Kennedy International Airport, in New York City, on the afternoon of August 13, 1985, I waited to board an airplane that would take me to San Francisco, where I would connect with a flight to Australia. My plane was scheduled to leave at 4:15, but 4:15 came and went, then 5:15. Many travelers saw their carefully planned time between flights ebbing away.

Nervously we passengers began to compare notes about our connecting flights. The man next to me asked where I was going, and when I responded "Sydney," he inquired what took me there. I told him that I was going to be speaking at a conference, and he asked, "On what?" My reply: "Equality of women, especially equality of women in Christian ministry."

He looked at me for a moment and then said, "Equality of women? You know, that's a subject that doesn't touch me at all. I just never have any occasion to think about it."

As we boarded the plane I thought, *It doesn't touch you at all? You never think about it? Don't you know any women? Don't you ever work with any women? After all, women make up half the human race!*

Well, this book is written for people who *are* thinking about some of the crucial questions regarding women today and who want to explore these questions within the context of Bible truth. This book is written especially for those who see these questions not just as women's concerns, but as *human* concerns. These questions relate to all humanity, because what concerns one half of the human race must of necessity involve and affect the other half. More and more people feel convinced of the need to deal with social issues at this most basic level—men and women as the two components of society—and they realize that if we do not have harmony here we cannot expect to solve problems on racial, economic, or political levels.

Even a superficial glance at newspapers or magazines shows us that tension and disharmony exist between men and women. We see increased incidence of divorce, that most visible evidence of severed relationships. We are increasingly conscious of violence between the sexes and of crimes like wife abuse and rape. We see exploitation and degradation of both sexes in the burgeoning pornography industry. These societal hurts touch us all, because when one member hurts, eventually we all hurt (1 Corinthians 12:26).

Over the years some people have sought to avoid dealing with such crucial questions by retreating into isolated communes, but most of us cannot afford the luxury of that sort of withdrawal from the contemporary scene. We have to live and work in the "real" world, where a societal acceptance of equality of persons, if only imperfectly implemented, confronts us.

We Americans are affected by Affirmative Action and Equal Economic Opportunity programs, and we must wrestle with the concept of comparable worth. We live in a society that finds many more women in the work force, most of them out of economic necessity, a society that includes more single women and sees more single women as heads of households. We are concerned with how best to use the vast, unused labor resource of older homemakers whose children are now grown. We read of women who feel called to enter fields formerly closed to them, such as the professional clergy. We are also aware that many men feel threatened by these changes as they ask, "But what of our place in this changing world? What will happen to what we have been taught is our role in life?"

When many Christians, especially evangelicals, think about these current issues, they may yearn for the "good old days."

That attitude reminds me of those people of Israel referred to in Ezra 3:12, 13, who wept for the past splendor of Solomon's temple, instead of picking themselves up, adjusting to the reality of their times, and working to build God's temple in their own day.

Hebrews 13:8 assures us, "Jesus Christ is the same yesterday and today and forever," but much we hear and read today seems to say, "Jesus Christ yesterday. . . . Oh, how good and safe it was in yesterday's world. . . . Oh, how ordered and traditional things used to be." But Jesus Christ must be for today, too, or how can He help us tomorrow? So it *is* appropriate to ask: *How does the Gospel relate to today's world? How does it speak to the needs of our twentieth-century church and society? Most important, how does it speak to our individual needs?* That is our first set of crucial questions, questions that all humanity needs to answer.

Our Need for Security

Although no country is entirely free from accident or violence, today we have become alert to places that might pose a higher-than-normal risk for the traveler. So as my plane finally started down the runway I thought how glad I was to be heading "down under." With so many terrorist acts being committed in Europe and the Middle East, I felt grateful that my journey took me to a politically calm part of the globe.

Today's world has experienced an alarming breakdown in security, and terrorism has become a sobering fact of life for the traveler. We all face the added threat posed by individuals or organizations that defy internationally accepted customs and laws by using violence to get attention for their cause or to force acceptance of their goals. Terrorism frightens us because it is evidence of irrationality and of anarchism.

Our instinctive abhorrence of terrorism tells us that we are more secure when we operate under a recognizable authority. Most of us feel more comfortable living and journeying in what we consider law-abiding and law-enforcing countries. Even such a simple illustration as a traffic light will prove this point. We obey the authority of the traffic light because we know that this does not represent a restriction of freedom to drive, but that it is necessary for the safety of all those who are free to drive.

We feel more secure when we know someone is in charge, and we are more secure when we have recognizable guidelines to follow as we interact with each other. Our need for security is really a need for authority. Yet while most people recognize this need and welcome various expressions of governmental regulation, many would reject any notion of divine authority either in their personal lives or in society.

Even in the so-called Christian nations many persons remain uncertain about accepting God's authority as it is transmitted through the Bible. Therefore they approach Scripture with reluctance and even fear. They may want Jesus Christ as Savior, but hesitate to acknowledge Him as Lord. Because they have only a casual acquaintance with the Bible, they have the idea that bowing to divine authority will have a negative impact on their life-style. They think that becoming "too religious" will mean "giving up things." These people do not want to look too closely at the Bible, in case it makes a demand on their lives. They will avoid discussing questions within a biblical context, preferring to discuss current issues in the light of political analyses, economic reports, or psychological, sociological, or anthropological studies.

Another group, made up of people who are completely ignorant of God's Word, in their ignorance have decided that they want no part of His authority. They base their ideas about Scripture on secondhand observations or hearsay. For example, after one introductory Bible class I taught, I recall a woman coming up and saying, "How can you expect me to be interested in studying a book that tells men to give daily thanks that they are not women?" I simply looked at her and asked, "Where is that stated in the Bible?" Of course it is not. Then I said to her, "Before you are so quick to reject Scripture as your authority, be sure you know what is in it. You may find that you are reacting against some human being's concept of God's Word that is not God's Word at all."

We must be very careful not to confuse God's authority with some human idea of it. Many people have assumed that God's authority aims to restrict or even oppress them, while all too many others consider it simply irrelevant. So we need to ask: What does accepting God's authority involve? Why do we need it? What is God's authority all about?

Our Need for "Something More"

When my husband and I moved back to New York City after years in the suburbs, we had difficulty finding a congenial home. In our first apartment we were not free to live what we consider a fulfilling personal life. This apartment was on the edge of a business district, and only after we moved in did we discover that at night the area was deserted and therefore unsafe. It was also far from shops, cultural centers, and our eventual new church home. In addition, the building had paper-thin walls. We could not play our piano, because our playing intruded on our neighbors, as did the noise of their stereos on us. We both love pets, but the rules said, "No pets," and while we got a variance, the building's management still had the power to demand at any time that we get rid of our dog and cat.

When we discovered these various drawbacks and felt their impact on our desired life-style, we began apartment hunting again. After some months, we settled on a condominium building that we selected because it had very thick walls between the apartments, approved of our pets, and was in a pleasant, safe, and convenient neighborhood. Why did we want to purchase a unit in this particular building? Because in the old building we found the restrictions diminished our quality of life, whereas in the new building we hoped to be free to live what we considered a fulfilling personal life-style.

This illustration highlights another human need, our need for "something more," that yearning we all feel for a better life. Even people indifferent to God experience the feeling, *There must be more to life than this.* Scripture puts it, ". . . He has also set eternity in the hearts of men . . ." (Ecclesiastes 3:11), and goes on to tell us that all our yearnings find their answer in Christ, in whom all the promises of God are "yes" (2 Corinthians 1:20).

God's Prospectus

How could we satisfy this need for "something more"? As we talked to the condominium's salesman we discovered that a crucial part of the entry process was accepting the sponsor's prospectus. Most readers have seen the ads that say, "Offering by prospectus only."

As Phil and I studied the condominium structure we found that the sponsor (or creator) of the condominium building had filed a prospectus, or plan, to which we had to respond. The sponsor owned the real estate and thus had the economic power to create the condominium building on that site and then to set forth the terms of the offering in his prospectus. Phil and I had to evaluate whether or not to accept the sponsor's plan, because only if we accepted it could we live in that condominium.

Yes, we perceived our projected purchase as a move to a freer and more fulfilling life-style—finding that "something more"—but paradoxically, to be liberated from past restrictions we first had to submit to the authority of the sponsor. To enter into the freedom we wanted, we had to accept the entrance requirements and agree to abide by the condominium rules. Acceptance of the terms in the prospectus not only guaranteed our place in that new building, but it was also an acknowledgment on our part that once in the building we would obey the condominium regulations, which were set up so that all residents could live together harmoniously. The paradox was that to achieve our goal of liberation from past restrictions, we first had to submit to the sponsor's authority.

The spiritual parallel is that only when we obey God's authority are we freed to function in right relation to Him and to our fellow human beings. We can think of God as the divine Sponsor of the universe and the Bible as His written Prospectus. For purposes of our illustration, we can think of God offering us a place in a "divine condominium," for to paraphrase John 14:2, Jesus told us that "In God's house are many rooms."

Our New York condominium sponsor was the only person who created our building and planned it for its future residents. The whole project was at his initiative. So God our Creator is in charge of the universe, and He alone has the perfect plan for us, its inhabitants. When we study His Prospectus, the Bible, we find the fantastic truths that for whosoever will accept God's plan there is no purchase price, that He wants to adopt us, and that we will live in the family home!

Fulfillment, Not Fear

As we contemplated our condominium purchase, my husband and I felt a little fearful about what we might get ourselves into, *until* we took the time to study the condominium document thoroughly. That removed our fear. But we had to study it for ourselves: This was too serious a matter for us to take someone else's opinion about it or for us to base our acceptance or rejection of the prospectus on hearsay.

Just as no one forced Phil and me to buy into our condominium building, God does not force humankind to accept His offer of new life. Yes, God's Prospectus offers the plan of salvation to whoever will accept it; but the wonder of divine love is that while God has the power to force obedience to divine authority, He lets us choose. The Bible tells us that the Gospel is the power of God to "whosoever believes," and Jesus said, "If you love me, you will obey what I command"—never "I'll force you."

Phil and I were not afraid of our human sponsor, because we knew that he wanted to create a pleasant place to attract us to live there. Likewise we need not fear God, because the Bible tells us that He loves us and wants us to live with Him. All through the Old Testament, God says, "I will be your God, and you shall be My people." Jesus assures us in John 6:37, ". . . Whoever comes to me I will never drive away." Therefore as we study the Bible carefully we find we need never fear the authority of the God of the Bible. God is truth, and He must always use His authority with integrity: God cannot lie, and His Word cannot lie. We can trust Scripture when it tells us that God is love and that perfect love casts out fear. God's Prospectus does not offer a place in a concentration camp!

Any fear that Scripture will oppress women or minorities does not come from God's Prospectus but from an imperfect understanding of it. God does not discriminate between His children. God is Savior, and for God's children all things work together for good. God's plan is to restore whoever will believe in Him to the wholeness of new life in Christ.

Perhaps another illustration will help us understand why we need never fear God's authority. I can remember my daughter screaming and hugging a toy to her bosom because I wanted to take it from her, but I wanted to take it because her toy was broken. I wanted to fix it and to give it back to her, whole. So God says, "Let Me use My authority as Creator to re-create your broken life and give it back to you, made whole." But we hug our lives and our pet ideas and even our man-made dogmas to ourselves; we do not hear God saying, "Give all that over to Me, and I will give it back to you, made whole." You see, God asks us to give over our lives to Him and to submit to His authority *not* to oppress any of us or to hurt us, but to make us new and to make us whole. In Jeremiah 29:11 God says, "For I know the plans I have for you, . . . plans to prosper you and not to harm you, plans to give you hope and a future."

Perfect Security

In the human situation, as a condominium fills up, a board of directors is elected, the sponsor's control decreases, and as soon as the condominium is sold out, the sponsor's involvement stops. The sponsor departs, and the unit owners are on their own. Suppose Phil and I want to retain an amenity that was spelled out in the sponsor's prospectus. We own only one of seventy-nine units, so once the sponsor has gone, if the other unit owners want to overrule that original prospectus, we would have no recourse.

But where an earthly condominium sponsor's activity ceases, God's perfect plan continues. God offers us a further security and protection that no human sponsor can ever match, because His sponsorship never ceases. In Matthew 28:20 Jesus said, ". . . I will be with you always, to the very end of the age." Our great God remains involved with His offering and always ready to help anyone who will accept His plan. He protects and sustains the new life of all persons who have accepted His plan—men, women, and children of whatever race or nation—and His Word is a continuing source of guidance for them on their journey toward their heavenly home.

Our Need for Approval

Another of the most basic human needs, and therefore a need of both men and women, is the need for approval. Approval is other people's favorable opinion of us, and we want it lifelong. Sometimes a person will put on a good front and say, "I could care less," but deep down we all *do* care what others think.

When we discuss this common human desire for acceptance, we often use the term *peer pressure* to describe the intangible force that molds acceptable thought or behavior. Actually we are discussing *peer approval*. The pressure we feel is simply the self-imposed strain of trying to decide whether or not to conform to the current standards of our peers, that is, whether or not we want to be part of the process of earning the approval of other human beings.

Often we can get so caught up in this process of "keeping up with the Joneses" that we can be in danger of losing sight of the true values in life. We have to be wary of buying into the latest fad or swallowing a popular philosophy just because "everybody's doing it." We also have to beware of blindly accepting traditions just because "people have always done things that way." We need to look beyond peer pressure, to see if what others pressure us to do is something good and if the way we respond to the pressure brings out the best in us.

Therefore anyone considering accepting God's Prospectus must ask: *What advice does the Bible have for us in our quest for approval? Whose approval do we really want, because—in the end—whose approval really matters?*

God's Approval

The Apostle Paul wrote to the church at Corinth (2 Corinthians 10:12) that people who measure themselves by one another and compare themselves only to one another are not wise. In contrast, Paul wrote in a letter to his young protege Timothy: "Do your best to present yourself to God as one approved, a workman who does not need to be ashamed and who correctly handles the word of truth." The New English Bible translates 2 Timothy 2:15 this way: "Try hard to show yourself worthy of God's approval. . . ." Therefore the Bible's advice about how to deal with peer pressure is to say, "Study to show yourself approved unto God." That's the bottom line.

Now we can ask: *Why is that the Bible's advice? Why is God's approval the real bottom line? Are we simply scared of a power that is obviously greater than that of our peers? Or do we fear that if we fail to please God, He will punish us for that in some way?*

No, for those of us who have accepted His offering and know Him as Savior and Friend, there is a different answer. We want to please God because His perfect love has indeed cast out all our fears. We love Him for what He has done for us, and we want to show our gratitude for His provision for our need for new life.

"If Only . . ."

For the Christian, God in Christ has dealt with all those inadequacies and imperfections that are at the heart of our fears of not measuring up enough to earn approval. We all have those fears. It is a fact of our humanity that, no matter how secure we may seem to our peers, all of us have thought, *If only. . . .*

We all yearn to erase these "if onlys" of life. We want someone to restore our inadequacies and our imperfections. We want someone to help us out of those personal shortcomings or problems or pain or—when we open the morning newspaper—someone to help us out of the despair of world confusion and injustice. If we are honest, we know that we all want someone to do for us what we cannot do for ourselves, someone with the power and authority to make things new and right again. Very simply, we all want a Savior, and we find Him in God's Prospectus.

Our Need for Renewal

Yes, common causes of contemporary anxiety are the realizations that "if onlys" mar our lives and we have not measured up either to our own expectations or to those that others have for us. The whole thrust of the advertising industry today plays upon our anxiety by telling us that we are not acceptable to our peers unless our hair is shinier, our floors cleaner, our cars newer, our money in a better bank. Yet most of us have begun to catch on to the rather dismal fact that no matter how hard we try or what products we buy or how we arrange our business affairs, we will never get to the top. We will all fall short somewhere.

God's Prospectus faces the reality of our shortcomings head-on and says: "True, you will never make perfection on your own." In the first chapters of the letter to the Romans, Paul talks about "the bad guys"—the obvious losers, those who go against God and society. Then Paul goes on to discuss "the good guys"—upstanding citizens, the genuinely nice people. The conclusion of Romans 3:23 is this: Whether good or bad in the eyes of our peers, we are all imperfect and have therefore come short of the glory of God.

In contrast to human imperfection, the Bible tells us God is perfect. In Romans 14:10–12 we also read that one day we will stand before that perfect God. Now this leaves us with an awful problem. It is not enough to hope that we will be acceptable when we meet God, and it is not enough to try to make ourselves acceptable, especially with all those ads dinning it into us that we do not even measure up to human ideals. So the Bible brings us right up against a question a child can understand, but that an adult hates to examine: "Are we sinful?" God does not ask us, "How good are you?" but He does ask, "Have you ever done anything—even just one thing—wrong?" Put that way, we join Paul in Romans 3 and sadly agree, "What shall we conclude? Are we any better than other people? Not at all! We are all alike—there is no one perfectly righteous" (*see* v. 9). None of us is good enough to meet the approval of the divine Sponsor.

Our First Crucial Question

In rebuttal someone might say, "This is quite unpleasant and unfair. I can't believe that I'm as bad in God's sight as a terrorist or some hardened criminal. I *am* good enough to be approved by God." That person needs to ask: "What will it mean to stand before a 100 percent perfect God, trusting only in my own merit?"

We must never make the mistake of concentrating on the horizontal comparison of ourselves to our peers. Remember Paul's admonition not to measure ourselves by each other. Only the vertical comparison counts, and this particular crucial question is: *How good are we in relation to God?*

Once we understand that the final standard is God's glory, we see that indeed we cannot save ourselves. Plagued by those shortcomings, those anxieties of not measuring up (even to our peers), those "if onlys" in life, we realize that the problem is not that we are as bad as possible, but that we are as "bad off" as possible. We cannot make ourselves perfect. Each of us needs a Savior who has the power and authority to make us new. There is no other alternative. Regardless of whatever other questions we may have about faith and life, first each one of us must answer this one: What will *you* do with Jesus?

Those of us who have accepted God's Prospectus and have found that Savior in Christ know the relief that comes from finally admitting: "I can't help myself, I can't fix up all those 'if onlys.' " Yes, the Good News of the Bible is to tell all humanity—"good guys" and "bad guys" alike—that when we accept His offer, Christ will credit His perfection to our account.

Those of us who now know Jesus Christ as Savior also know the relief of having Him take over our lives, share our burdens, and give us strength to cope in the here and now. Because of love for our Savior, who cared enough to die for us, we no longer want peer approval, but only His approval.

Our Need to Study

Phil and I initially studied the condominium prospectus to understand how to accept the offering and how to enter into our new life-style, but we also study it from time to time as we go along. So also a person who wants God's approval will not only accept His offer of salvation, but continue in lifelong study of His Word. This has been basic to Christianity, from the earliest days of the church. In Acts 17:10–12 (KJV) we read that when Paul preached and taught at Berea, new believers there were "more noble," because they "searched the scriptures daily," to see if Paul's words were true.

Unfortunately, during the Middle Ages, only a very few persons continued studying the Bible. Written material (which had to be hand copied) was in short supply and learning became a luxury restricted primarily to the clergy and nobility. An increasingly authoritarian church discouraged theological discussions by an increasingly illiterate populace, and eventually deemphasized personal Bible study even among the literate. One of the most important breakthroughs of the Renaissance was the invention of the printing press and the resulting dramatic increase in availability and affordability of the written word. Information about all fields of knowledge could now be more easily disseminated, and literacy rose. Scripture, too, became more readily accessible, not only in the centuries-old Latin version, but also in the vernacular. Martin Luther translated Scripture into German: courageous translators like martyr William Tyndale made the Bible available in English.

One of the hallmarks of the Protestant Reformation was a renewed emphasis on the authority of Scripture and the return to personal Bible study. Protestants were called "People of the Book." In recent years, since Vatican II, the Roman Catholic Church had also encouraged Bible study for its members. Today sincere Christians of all denominations can indeed be thought of as those who want to base their views on God's Word and who want to live their lives according to scriptural guidelines.

As a result of the renewed interest in Bible study, more and more people read God's Word for themselves. However, many of these people have very little knowledge of the history and background of Scripture as it comes to us in its present form. Not only are most churchgoers unfamiliar with the process that has produced the Bible in their own language, but they also remain unaware of the problems that can arise because the Bible as we read it in English is a translated book.

Yes, average churchgoers feel impressed when a minister or Sunday-school teacher refers to "the original languages." Most of them would also see the humor in the situation in which a person who wanted to shake up a class announced: "I like to read the King James Version, because I want to read the version Jesus read." But most of them remain unaware of the intense research into the Bible text as scholars of all theological persuasions struggle for a better understanding of that text, including, of course, the goal of working for more accurate translations.

As average churchgoers read their English Bibles they unconsciously assume, *What you see is what you get.* For these people the Bible in their favorite English version is "the last word" on every crucial question. In my Bible-teaching experience I have found that these people can become confused and even upset when one confronts them with the fact that their version may *not* be "the last word."

Further, because they have very little knowledge of the field of biblical textual criticism, they can even be uneasy with that very word *criticism*. They need reassurance that the word *criticism* is used here in a technical literary way and does not have a negative connotation. It simply indicates an investigative procedure, a digging into the background of the Bible text so that the text can be better understood and therefore more carefully and accurately interpreted.

A High View of Scripture

This book is written from the standpoint of what is called a high view of Scripture: The Bible is the inspired, trustworthy Word of God written and as such stands as the true revelation of God's message, regardless of any human reaction to it. As God's Prospectus, the Bible presents an accurate record of humankind's condition and offers us God's plan for redemption, the way of reconciliation between a holy God and fallen humanity—the way to become approved by the divine Sponsor.

In terms of our condominium-sponsor illustration, we can think of inspiration as God's action in initiating the writing-down process, and we can think of inerrancy as God's quality control over that process so that Scripture is reliable both for truth about God and for objective fact about humanity.

A high view of Scripture affirms that the Bible texts have been proven authentic and considers them completely reliable transmitters of God's message. However, a high view is not to be locked into wooden literalism. In interpreting the Bible we must take into account the wide variety of literary styles employed so that we pay proper attention to the use of poetry, allegory, parable, and apocalyptic literature. We must also be aware of the need to acquaint ourselves with the cultural background of the material.

In addition, we need not feel that right now we must have the answers to every difficult question, and we must allow for alternative interpretations of Scripture where the text is unclear to us. However, the bottom line for those of us who affirm a high view of Scripture is this: The Bible is absolutely trustworthy, both for objective fact and for revelation of God.

Therefore as those of us who hold such a view of the Bible seek to study to be approved by God our Savior, we will look to His inspired Word both for our overall world view and for specific help and guidance on our journey through this life. Within a scriptural context, we will examine the crucial questions that face us in the world of here and now, and by Scripture we will test our answers.

Our Need to Ask Questions

Honest and sincere questioning is part of any process of gaining that approval we all want and need. For example, the employee asks a supervisor at work: "How am I doing?" The entrepreneur must ask: "Does the consumer approve of my product?" The lawyer will ask: "Am I meeting the needs of my client?"

In family situations children feel appreciated and secure when they have their parents' approval. In a healthy family situation children want that approval because they love and respect their parents. Children will ask such questions as: "Did I do my chores okay?" or "Did you like the present I made you?"

In the classroom, teachers welcome the questioning student, because they know that through the question and answer process the student comes to a more thorough understanding of the particular subject. Of course when the student understands the subject, he or she will do well and will be approved by the teacher.

Since the Christian can think of God as Parent, Teacher, and spiritual Employer, it is not only acceptable but necessary to ask questions such as, "Do I know what God's Word says?"

and, "Is what I am doing meeting with His approval?" Our questions enhance our comprehension of God's Word, and by them we come to a better understanding of it so that our lives will honor Him.

I stress the validity of questions because some persons feel uncomfortable asking questions about Scripture. They feel they know so little about the Bible that if they ask a question, they will look foolish.

But others also feel uncomfortable asking questions, those who have grown up in a situation where they have heard: "*This* is exactly what you are to believe. No questions allowed." Such a dictatorial approach implies that everything in Scripture is crystal clear to the "right" or expert interpreters. It can also give the impression that there is no new thing to be learned about Scripture. People coming from such a tradition can feel threatened whenever they face any kind of discussion over an alternative way of looking at a passage or a verse, and they meet that threat by declaring their own interpretation to be the only orthodox one.

But Are the Answers Always Clear?

We have all heard people state: "God said it; I believe it; that settles it." Yes, in passages that are universally accepted as clear (such as John 3:16 or Ephesians 2:8–10) that is certainly an appropriate sequence to affirm. But in places that are not entirely clear, it can become very frustrating to try to affirm this sequence.

For example, think of that first point—"God said it"—in relation to 1 Peter 3:18–20, where the text tells us that after Christ's death, He ". . . preached to the spirits in prison who disobeyed long ago when God waited patiently in the days of Noah while the ark was being built." Now I certainly believe God's Word says this, but although I have pondered these verses and searched commentaries (where I found that the experts differed!) I do not understand what the passage really means. So it is very difficult to go on to say, "I believe it," because to say that implies a comprehension on my part that I do not yet have. Therefore it is impossible for me to continue the sequence and *honestly* say, "That settles it," because I am still sincerely questioning what God's Word said in the first place.

We must recognize that in some places Scripture is not completely clear to us. We need further light, such as a clearer rendering of the text or a greater understanding of the Bible background. On these unclear matters a rigidly dictatorial approach to Bible study must try to do too much, namely, give an answer to every question. It must lump together the clear and the unclear in its endeavor to give definitive answers in every situation. Thus it speaks out when it would more wisely have remained silent and awaited further light.

Unfortunately, people used to this kind of tradition find it hard to ask legitimate questions. They fear that such queries arising in their minds indicate lack of faith. This tradition presents the minister or scholar as such an expert on all scriptural matters that the ordinary man feels unable to discuss clear areas, much less question problem ones. In such a tradition women are often infantilized ("Don't you worry your pretty little head about these things"), so women especially do not dare to voice their questions or their concerns, but must accept "Father knows best."

Since rigid dogmatism considers any deviation from its specific teaching to be unorthodox, the potential questioner has a fear of being labeled not only disobedient but heretical. This demonstrates the force of peer pressure. That pressure can be a very powerful force indeed in crushing even the most honest and sincere questioner, because he or she hesitates to appear "different" or even rebellious to other members of the peer group.

However, most persons *are* honest, sincere questioners. Certainly Phil and I asked questions about our sponsor's prospectus, because we needed to understand the condominium plan more fully. Similarly, most people ask questions about Scripture because they do not understand something, and they sincerely want to find the answer.

Yes, sometimes a person will ask a question as a delaying tactic, in order to evade acting on a clear truth. That seems to be why, in Luke 10:29, the lawyer asked Jesus "Who is my neighbor?" right after Jesus had told him to love his neighbor.

He hoped Jesus would get bogged down in some intricate discussion of neighborhoods! But most people are not that devious. Most of us ask questions because we do not know the answers and we would like to know them. How sad that many people do not feel free to ask questions about what is not clear to them in God's Word!

What Does the Bible Teach About Questioning?

Scripture gives us many examples that show us that God approves of honest questioning. The Book of Job reveals the questioning heart as Job cries out to God in his agonized search for why such troubles have befallen him, a man who has tried to honor and serve God to the very best of his ability. The Prophet Jeremiah is another questioner, and in many places the writers of the Psalms ask such tough questions as "Why do the wicked prosper?"

One of my favorite questioners is the Prophet Habakkuk, who seems to have lived in an age much like our own. His prophecy begins with a heart cry to God as he asks how long violence and corruption will continue in Judah without God intervening to stop these awful injustices. But when God answers that He is indeed going to act and reveals that He will use the wicked Babylonians to punish Judah for her evil ways, the dismayed Habakkuk asks a much deeper question: How can a holy God use an evil instrument? Habakkuk retreats into an attitude of quiet expectation as he awaits God's next answer, and God reveals the great truth that the righteous is saved by faith, but that the person who persists in a God-defying attitude will not endure. The prophecy ends with Habakkuk's great vision of God and the assurance that no matter how the world falls apart, believers can rejoice in God's salvation.

Now what is fascinating about this Bible book is that God does not reprove Habakkuk's questioning spirit. Although He never answers Habakkuk's second question, God does give the prophet answers that he needs to know for day-to-day living. God tells Habakkuk that using evil is not the same as approving evil, and that regardless of how nations or individuals set themselves up against God, His purposes will never be thwarted. Finally, God gives Habakkuk the vision of His glory to assure the prophet that the Lord Almighty is indeed in charge of persons and events.

As we look at the many honest questioners in the Old Testament we see that the key to why God allows and approves of their questioning is in the manner of their asking. Their honest, tough questions are taken directly to God. In response, God does not squash them, but gives them answers to the extent that they can understand. Many of these questioners realize that they may never get complete answers in this life, but they affirm, as did Abraham in Genesis 18:25, that the Judge of all the earth will indeed act justly.

Further, in the New Testament we see that Jesus did not squelch the honest questioner or abandon the slow learner. He used the question-and-answer method in His teaching. He welcomed inquiries from His disciples, from individuals He encountered, and even from His enemies. The great discourses in John's Gospel show Jesus graciously and patiently dealing with questions from those who did not believe in Him, although we know from the synoptic gospels how these enemies tried to trap Him with trick questions such as "Should we pay taxes?" (Matthew 22:15–22).

Remember also that most inscrutable question Christ Himself asked from the cross in Matthew 27:46. It was evidence of the awful agony of soul and spirit that Jesus experienced in the suffering of His full humanity that He cried out those dreadful words: "My God, my God, why have you forsaken me?" Yet even here Jesus taught us that we take our questions to God.

In the accounts of the early church, we also see honest questioners encouraged. There was the eager question of the Philippian jailer in Acts 16:30: "What must I do to be saved?" Paul uses the question-and-answer method as a teaching device in Romans and Galatians, and it is obvious that his letters to Corinth answered specific questions that congregation had raised.

So we come back to the reason for honest, sincere questions. We ask them because we do indeed want God's approval and we earnestly want to know the answers to what is unclear to us in His Prospectus. When we face our questions about human relationships openly and are free to explore them within a biblical framework, we will all be stronger.

Chapter 2

Conflicting Signals

These were some of the things I thought about as my connecting flight left San Francisco, rose into the night, and flew on out over the Pacific Ocean. It seemed incredible to me that I was heading towards Australia, a continent I had never expected to visit, simply because it was so far away. I had certainly never expected that such a visit would involve lecturing and preaching about a biblical view of human needs and relationships. During that fifteen-hour flight, I had plenty of time to think back over the years to where my journey really started.

Looking Backwards

I grew up in the heart of the American fundamentalist movement. My grandfather, Arno C. Gaebelein, was a noted Methodist preacher, popular Bible expositor, and a colleague of C. I. Scofield in preparing the original *Scofield Reference Edition* of the Bible. Arno Gaebelein also had an extensive ministry to Jewish people and in the 1930s was one of the pioneers in warning Americans of the coming holocaust in Nazi Germany. From him I learned an appreciation of solid Bible teaching, and I also learned a concern for injustice and an awareness of human suffering.

In 1922 my father, Frank E. Gaebelein, became the founding headmaster of The Stony Brook School, a college-preparatory school for boys. His purpose was unique for the 1920s: to maintain the highest academic standards as well as to hold to conservative biblical belief.

This was a time when—in the flush of enthusiasm following "the war to end all wars"—scholars confidently set about creating a brave new world. Human intellect and especially science were almost deified, and most secular intellectual circles considered the Bible outdated. In Protestantism, this was the era of the fundamentalist-versus-modernist debate. Fundamentalists represented traditional orthodox Christianity. In contrast, the modernists were ridding themselves of what they considered antiquated ideas about God and emphasizing the historical Jesus as only one example among many for people to follow as they created the ideal society.

One result of the tension between fundamentalism and modernism was that some Christians began to mistrust the secular academic world and even to withdraw from it. It was both unique and courageous for Frank Gaebelein to come along in the twenties and say: "Conservative biblical faith is compatible with excellence in scholarship, because since all truth is God's truth, we as Christians need not fear any academic study." My father emphasized this search for God's truth not only in his work as an educator but also in his preaching, expository teaching, and writing. So from him I learned to keep an open mind and to be willing to "go where the evidence leads."

Our family lived right on the school campus. Both in the school chapel services and at the summer conference ministries held there I was privileged to hear some of the greatest preachers and missionaries of the thirties and forties, such as Harry Ironside, Clarence MacCartney, and Samuel Zwemer. These people stayed in our home, and I listened to their conversations. After a lecture I gave recently, someone asked if I were a graduate of a theological seminary, and an older minister present commented, "She grew up in one!"

During those summer conferences, I observed that some fundamentalists began to impose legalistic behavioral restrictions as criteria of orthodoxy. For example, swimming was thought to be too irreverent to be allowed on Sundays. Lipstick and nail polish were signs of wantonness, as was dancing, and of course smoking cigarettes and drinking fermented beverages were downright sinful. Today I often smile to myself when I see reviews of secular movies in magazines like *Eternity* and *Chris-*

tianity Today, because in my youth movies were labeled instruments of the devil. I can remember one well-known evangelist asking his audience: "How will you feel if you are in a movie theater when the Lord returns?" Then he went on with a graphic description of how a person would slink around heaven because, when Christ returned, he had been watching a movie and would not want to reveal this to any of the saints.

In contrast, my family emphasized the Bible as the authoritative Word of God, but they rejected the false human emphasis of legalism. When I was very young, I had trusted Jesus for my eternal salvation, and my parents always encouraged me to look to Scripture to guide me on my Christian walk and to search for God's truth within the whole range of ". . . whatever is true, honorable, right, pure, lovely, of good report" (*see* Philippians 4:8). My parents were not preoccupied with behavioral "dos" and "don'ts," but with serving Christ.

Nor were they preoccupied with role playing. They practiced mutual submission in marriage by each one considering the needs of the other greater than his or her own. My father was well-known, but he considered my mother, herself highly educated, as his partner in marriage and ministry. He always checked his sermons, lectures, and articles with my mother for her critical judgment. They planned and discussed school matters and prayed about them together. They were a team, and they laid the foundation of The Stony Brook School as a team. They were the embodiment of the biblical principle that in marriage the two shall become one.

The Real World of the Fifties

For my higher education I went to Bryn Mawr College, where I studied history and philosophy, and in 1950 I received my bachelor of arts degree *magna cum laude*. I then entered the Columbia University Graduate School, with the intention of getting an M.A. and then Ph.D. in philosophy. However, although the geographical distance between the two campuses was only about ninety miles, for me personally the distance between a women's college and a male-oriented and dominated academic environment made them light-years apart.

At Columbia, except for my transcript, I became invisible. For the first time in my life I was ignored in classroom situations, simply because I was a woman. In the department of philosophy two professors openly announced in their lectures, "No woman can think." Women friends of mine in the fields of architecture and medicine experienced the same hostility. At about this time I met my future husband, who was studying law, and he told me that one of the law professors enjoyed singling out the most retiring women students and asking them to expound the medical testimony in rape cases.

It is an indication of how far secular society has come in dealing with overt sexism that some younger readers may find it hard to believe such attitudes really existed. That these attitudes persisted is illustrated by the case of Dr. Sandra Gilbert, now professor of English at Princeton University. In a review of her new book, Columbia's alumni magazine made this wry comment: "Sandra Gilbert received the Ph.D. from Columbia in 1968. Although she had earlier been awarded a President's Fellowship, which carried with it the right to teach in Columbia College the year afterward, she was told she was not eligible to teach in the College because she was a woman."[1]

For me, back in 1950, those attitudes were most disillusioning, especially since my grade level on my written work was very good. I wondered: *What more do I have to do to prove my academic competence?* If I did get advanced degrees, how many openings would there be for a woman philosophy instructor?

In this soul-searching I also became increasingly disenchanted with studying only secular philosophy and engaging in some of the resulting mental gymnastics. I can remember one long and intricate discussion aimed at proving that the world was not round, but flat! Yes, that sort of thing was diverting, but as a follower of Jesus Christ I began to question: *Is this how I want to spend the rest of my life?*

During my last three years of college I had had complete responsibility for the Sunday afternoon maids' and porters' chapel services, including preparing the homily. At both Bryn Mawr College and Columbia University I was also active in InterVarsity Christian Fellowship. Yet when I asked older friends for career guidance, ironically, while I was considered a promising philosophy student, there was no question of anyone's suggesting that I enroll in theology. In the early 1950s no conservative Christian woman would be urged to consider the ministry as an option. I could pursue philosophy, but not theology. Looking backwards I wonder: What would the advice have been if I had been a son instead of a daughter?

To help pay my academic bills, I got a job as an editorial worker at the Oxford University Press. During the day I did copy editing and proofreading, and in the evenings I completed my M.A. thesis. But before I could plan the next academic step, Phil and I decided to get married. That decision effectively put an end both to my academic life and my intellectual soul-searching, because in 1952 it was a "given" in my conservative religious circle that wives did not have careers outside the home and that they would certainly never "work" once they had children. (Those of you with children can smile with me at the myth that mothers do not work!)

Shortly after my marriage, I shared with my minister my increasing desire to use my education and my publishing experience to serve God. His immediate reaction was to ask: "Can you type?" His secretary had just resigned, so his answer both to my desire to serve and his need was neatly resolved by my becoming the church's secretary, which post I filled until our first child was born.

Our family expanded rapidly—three children in twenty-seven months! When their needs became less demanding, I began to study again, this time concentrating on privately studying Bible and theology. My father often suggested books for me to read and was available to discuss any questions I had.

We also became active in our local church, a Presbyterian congregation we had chosen for its conservative theological stance. I was asked to become a Sunday-school teacher and over the next few years taught seventh grade, then ninth, tenth, and finally eleventh grade, where I settled in for ten years of teaching a church history survey course. Possibly because of growing up in a boys' school, I was used to "give and take" and really enjoyed interacting with older teenagers.

The Unrecognized Career

In the early 1960s my husband and I were asked to be cosuperintendents of the Sunday school. There were about 800 students and a staff of well over 100. The deliberate policy of

our local church was to search for a couple to head up the
Sunday school, because while the husband was away at his job,
the wife could take care of the many administrative details.

About this time I began to realize that I was working outside
the home. Not only was I teaching a large Sunday-school class,
with all the preparation that required, and being active in the
women's groups, but taking care of the Sunday school's administrative duties meant that I was down at our church many,
many hours a week. I would work at the church when the
children were in school, and often, after I picked them up from
school, I would bring them back to the church with me. Although we treated the overall responsibility for the Sunday
school as a family project, as a practical matter I really was
working outside the home.

When I attended a Bryn Mawr College reunion, the program
included a panel of four classmates who represented various
career fields: medicine, the arts, the academic world, and
volunteerism. I can recall what a revelation that last category
was for me, because up until then I had never thought of
volunteerism as the career it really is. As the panel discussion
progressed, I realized just how much volunteerism contributes
to our society in implementing programs in libraries, musical
organizations, museums, hospitals, and social-service areas,
not to mention the long hours spent by volunteers on school
boards or in the PTA. I thought of the many dedicated workers
staffing mental-health and family-service organizations on a
voluntary basis.

I also realized how much volunteerism has been devalued,
because it does not measure achievement in the usual currency
of success: money. But primarily I saw that for many women
volunteerism is indeed a bona fide career, particularly in the
case of women who are serving their churches or parachurch
organizations. It was true of my mother: Helping to build The
Stony Brook School was her lifework. It is also true of many
ministers' wives, because most congregations expect to get two
staff members for the price of one.

It was thought provoking to recognize that while traditional
conservative church circles held that wives and mothers should
not work outside the home, in actuality the Christian commu-

nity asked many of them to do just that as untold hours of woman power regularly staffed Sunday schools, nurseries, and Vacation Church School programs, ran church suppers, organized missionary conferences, and helped keep office costs down by volunteer clerical work. Think how often we say about some dedicated woman: "She just lives at the church." Persons glossed over this double standard, because these women were "serving" or "helping" and because they were not paid for their labor. But it was still a double standard: Church leaders said one thing but expected women to do something else. However, I was soon to become aware of another area in which a traditional position came into direct conflict with actual practice, and I found myself right in the middle of that conflict.

The Hidden Conflict

Our local church had the policy that women were not to be in positions of leadership or in positions where they would teach men. This policy reflected the view that human beings have definite roles in life and all human relationships are to mirror these roles.

Now as I have recounted, at the direct request of the senior minister, I had been in leadership in the Sunday school. I had been placed over men teachers and, in a few instances, had corrected and redeployed men. Since I was cosuperintendent, along with my husband, I had not given much thought to whether or not my actions contradicted church policy, but soon four things happened that made me give a great deal of thought to that policy.

First, in 1966 our Sunday-school building badly needed interior repainting, but no one was willing to coordinate the job. I discovered a local paint store that would give a substantial discount to the church, yet when I passed this information on to the house committee, everyone was too busy with other things, and no one volunteered to coordinate the classroom project. The rooms got dingier and dingier. Finally one of the trustees said to me, "Why don't you coordinate it?" so I did. I posted a sign-up sheet for the requisite number of Saturdays, bought the paint, collected newspapers and drop cloths, and the project became a reality. But on the final Saturday, as the work crew was winding up, exhausted yet filled with a sense of accomplishment, a male church member came in, walked up to me, and said: "Do you think it's been right for you to be in charge of this project and have men serving under you?" I recall feeling so let down, because I had thought of the painting crew as a team effort that simply needed a coordinator to get it off the ground. I also felt resentment at someone who would criticize instead of volunteering to do the coordinating himself.

Second, the elder in charge of Christian education asked me if I would teach a seminar on church history as part of a special Sunday-evening adult-education series. This happened over twenty years ago, but I can still remember how very diffident I felt the first evening, when I saw that my students were mostly men. I had been criticized for coordinating a painting team. What would happen when I taught men? At that first class I would not have felt surprised if someone had burst in and asked me to leave because I was a woman teacher, and I would have gone quickly. Yet no such thing happened. The men sat there, listened with apparent interest, and when the series finished, the elder who had recruited me thanked me in front of the entire congregation and presented me with a book in appreciation for my service. I rationalized to myself that perhaps my teaching of men was all right, because I only taught church history, although in the series I had also explained doctrinal points and made theological comments.

Third, the church had been growing, with well over 1,000 members, but it was short staffed. One day the senior minister called me into his office. He told me that the overburdened assistant minister simply could not keep up with the junior high school youth work. The senior minister knew I was a capable administrator, and he also knew I enjoyed working with teenagers. Since my own children were now of youth-group age, he felt that I would be involved anyway. His pitch was that it would be natural for me to lighten the load of the assistant minister by taking on the youth work myself. Yes, because my own three children participated, it *was* natural, because I would indeed attend most of the events. But at that point in the life of that particular church it was *not* natural to have a woman in charge of the entire program, including overseeing male youth-group advisors and deploying other men who volunteered to help. Our minister gave lip service to the thought, *I'm sure Phil will give you a hand,* but significantly he called only me into his office and made the pitch to me alone. He recognized that as a practical matter a woman would do most of the work, as indeed I did for the next three or four years.

Fourth, I served on the church nominating committee, of which the senior minister was a member ex officio. In our congregation there was a woman bank executive, and I proposed her name for trustee. In the Presbyterian form of government, trustee is not an ordained post, as are deacon and elder, but is a post required by state law, because for purposes of charitable giving, churches are considered nonprofit organizations run by a board of trustees. The woman I proposed was mature, exceedingly capable, and obviously knowledgeable about financial matters. But when I put forth her name, our minister announced: "Over my dead body will we ever have a woman in any position of leadership in this church."

Now I was filled with confusion upon hearing that. Up until that point in the late 1960s I had not questioned the system. I had grown up in it. I had accepted the fact that only men were ordained and only men filled the various church offices, and I had accepted the fact that women were simply tireless church workers. But in the light of how the church had asked me to serve, after that nominating committee the thought struck me: *What does the minister think I am doing? Furthermore I am doing these things at his request.*

In the early 1970s I was asked to repeat the adult church history seminar, and in this series one of my students was our new assistant minister. Then our senior minister became ill and asked me to substitute for him in a class he was teaching on church doctrine. These events increased my inner tension. How could people say one thing about the place of women when at the same time they asked a woman to do the opposite?

What About the Missionaries?

During this period of inner confusion, I began to observe more closely just how women were being used in the Christian community. As I knew from teaching church history, women—especially single women—were the backbone of the Protestant missionary movement. But I also knew about women missionaries firsthand.

From 1954 to 1971 I had served on the board of the Woman's Union Missionary Society of America. It had a unique ministry: to women and by women. It was founded in the middle 1800s by a group of American women concerned for the plight of women in the Far East. These American women had repeatedly asked the existing mission organizations to send single women to the field, but were told, "Women are too delicate." Finally the American women decided that if the male-organized boards would not send out women, the women would have to do it themselves, so they did. As I became familiar with this outreach I realized just how much Christian women contributed and just how able they were. The myth of the helpless little woman evaporated in the face of the tremendous contributions of these female missionary doctors, nurses, teachers, and administrators who ran hospitals, orphanages, homes for unwed mothers, and Bible-training schools. In the course of their duties, they had oversight of male staff, and they taught men students.

Yes, in Christian missions women indeed administered and taught both men and women on the foreign field and were even allowed to report these activities back home, at the nonthreatening Sunday-afternoon "missionary hour." (Maybe the pastors thought not too many people would come to hear about these women!) But the underlying assumption seemed to be that it was acceptable for these women to lead and teach overseas, where there was a different cultural situation, but that something else happened back home in the United States.

Yet now in the sixties and early seventies, here at home, I was being asked to administer and to teach both men and women, and I found the conflict between policy and practice very troubling. I wanted to accept the traditional position that in a church context women could not lead or teach men, but the very persons who stated this then requested me to do the exact opposite of what they said was prohibited.

Some people said that using women in positions of leadership was allowable if there were no qualified men available, but that as soon as there were such men, they should replace the women. This seemed to me to be situation ethics, similar to saying that until missions or churches could properly fund their programs, it would be allowable to use stolen money! So an increasing tension kept building inside me. I wanted to be under God's authority, and if women in leadership was not biblical, then what women missionaries did overseas and what women like me did here at home was wrong. If our actions were not in accord with scriptural principles, then they were wrong, and it did not make any difference who asked us to do these things or what the rationale was. If our actions were wrong, they were wrong. Period.

But because I am a question asker, deep inside me I wondered: *But are we doing something wrong?* So I kept on serving, and the tension increased.

Looking and Listening

Now I began paying close attention to things some Christian men so thoughtlessly said. To give examples: A visiting minister presented a family-life seminar in our church and stated, "It is a wife's duty to cater to any sexual demands her husband makes on her. He's a male animal, and if she doesn't give him sex whenever he wants it, he'll get it elsewhere." I thought: *Can this be a Christian view of the fidelity of the marriage relationship?*

Another man, who had grown up in a rural town, announced in our prayer meeting, "Women should suffer pain in childbirth. Their pain brings them closer to the Lord. I know, because during childbirth I've heard women cry out 'Oh, God.'" *Is this Christian compassion? Aren't we in the business of lifting the curse of pain?*

Then I had women from another church come to me for counseling, distraught because their minister had announced from the pulpit, "The husband's duty is to enforce his authority in the home, and if the wife won't obey him, he may use corporal punishment on her." I was appalled and thought: *That's not Christian marriage. That's a license for wife abuse.*

Another minister casually remarked, "I like the James Bond movies, because of the violence and the broads."

During this time of listening and observing, I was traveling home from a church-related conference and found myself with extra time in the airport. In the stationery store I noticed a minister I had met at breakfast, and I went into the store to ask if he would like to discuss the conference over a cup of coffee. As I came up behind him I saw that he was preoccupied with a pornographic magazine featuring naked women in provocative poses; disillusioned, I just walked out again. The message was finally getting through to me: To all too many Christian men, women were not even second-class citizens. Women were objects.

In the early seventies, I was asked to be the first woman on the executive committee of a denominational group. Here I experienced emotional hostility toward women. A strained meeting centered around a discussion of women's ordination, and possibly with the thought of defusing the tense atmosphere, one minister used the following illustration: "Trying to address the problems we have in our denomination with women's ordination is like a man climbing up the back leg of an elephant, intent on rape. How does he start? Where does he begin?" I cannot forget the laughter that greeted his words, nor can I forget my shock that a Christian minister would use an illustration both so crude and so insensitive to women. Nor can I forget my dismay that neither the chairman nor any other man censured that minister for his language, although a few men did look uncomfortable. When I protested the incident to the group's executive director, he did not fully understand why I took offense. The thought seemed to be that if I could not stand the heat, then I should get out of the kitchen. But rape is not a joke. Bestiality is not a joke. Our Lord *never* used coarse language to make a point.

I have recounted this biographical material so that the reader can see some of the stages in my journey toward awareness of problem areas in the church's perception of the position of women (which by definition will also include its perception of the position of men). By God's grace I grew up in a home that emphasized truth and integrity and social concern and where our family's desire was to be guided by God's Word and not by legalism or role playing. Having placed my own trust in Jesus Christ as Lord and Savior, I accepted His Word as the only trustworthy guide for my life. For me Scripture was—and is—God's utterly reliable revelation of His plan for humanity, and I believe that the Bible is the ultimate authority for all people.

However, as I myself became active in church work I became aware of the expedient use of women and also of the insensitivity of many Christian men toward women's personhood. The fact that these loveless actions and attitudes created increasing tensions and hurts both inside and outside the Christian community made it imperative to seek a biblical perspective on their underlying causes.

Yes, men and women do have differing traits and instincts, and we must not overlook or try to erase essential sexual differences. But men and women also share many common human traits and instincts (such as sociability and self-preservation) and many common human needs (such as the ones discussed in chapter 1).

Furthermore, any examination of relationships between Christian men and women must recognize the impact of our common salvation (Jude 3) on our behavior. In John 17:20–23 Christ prayed that we might be one in Him. The Book of Acts stressed the unity of believers. Paul not only urged mutual submission of believers (Ephesians 5:21), but one of his overriding concerns was their unity in Christ (Ephesians 2:11–22). Clearly any biblical study of both our distinctive sexuality and our common humanity must focus on concepts that bring us together, not on what divides.

However, when I began to look for answers to my questions about human relationships in church, home, and society, I found something surprising. I found the philosophical equivalent of a scarecrow, a device to frighten people away from examining these crucial questions. I found the straw woman.

Chapter 3

The Straw Woman

Undeniably, this *is* a hurting world. Yes, we human beings have made startling scientific discoveries and marvelous medical advances. Hardly a day goes by without the announcement of some tremendous technological breakthrough into hitherto uncharted areas of science or medicine. However, balanced against these evidences of human ingenuity, we hear about the stark facts of world hunger, constant wars and rumors of wars, natural disasters like earthquakes and volcanic eruptions, cataclysmic "human errors" like the Bhopal tragedy and the Chernobyl nuclear accident, violations of human rights like apartheid and the use of torture, the insoluble economic residue of people living at poverty level, the plague of AIDS, escalating crime rates, and alarming moral degeneration.

It is becoming increasingly difficult to think of the world as even a Dickensian combination of "the best of times and the worst of times." The balance seems to shift more and more in favor of the worst of times.

Although the United States has remained relatively untouched by many of the economic and environmental problems troubling other nations, most American readers will remember the 1960s and early 1970s as a time of social and political upheaval, a time of individual and national questioning. It became acceptable and even fashionable to question authority. Younger people rebelled against parietal rules, institutional regulations, and governmental laws. Demonstrations became the order of the day. There was also a reaction against religious authority, including the short-lived "God is dead" movement. The phrase "Do your own thing" became popular, and the general mood of "Nobody's going to tell *me* what to do" prevailed.

Some of this rebellion was understandable. The civil rights movement had made Americans sensitive to entrenched discriminatory attitudes and practices and to the need to correct overt injustices. Some persons felt impatient with what they considered to be the slow pace of reform, and they attempted to take matters into their own hands. But in addition, in the wake of the controversy over the tragic Vietnam War and then the scandal of Watergate, many people became downright confused about public policy and disillusioned by betrayal of public trust. In a climate of general cynicism many concerned citizens wondered: *Who can we trust?*

Some who found these issues too painful to confront retreated into forms of hedonism, seeking relief from contemporary problems by escaping through sex, drugs, or "alternate life-styles." A pop philosophy of "What feels good is good" developed. In despair, others dropped out of organized society by joining communes or drifting into what is euphemistically called the subculture.

On the positive side were those persons who wanted to be part of the solution to society's problems. Abroad, altruistic Americans reached out through organizations like the Peace Corps or the newly formed short-term foreign missionary programs. At home, concerned citizens grappled with the complexities of the civil rights movement, environmental crises, and issues of nuclear power. But the average citizen just plodded along, at times wistfully looking back to the 1950s or even to the 1920s and thinking, *Oh, how much less difficult things used to be.*

In any prolonged period of either individual or national uncertainty there *is* a natural tendency to look to the past, to a time when (for the people looking backward) society seemed to have been more stable and the world a less threatening place. But as those yearning for the past look back through the lens of their own experience they can sometimes overlook the fact that for others the past was not necessarily as pleasant or as safe.

An illustration of the ambivalent nature of the past was the reaction of many blacks to the Statue of Liberty centennial celebration in 1986. A *New York Times* article pointed out that among blacks this event evoked "mixed feelings and emotions well short of enthusiasm. Some say a celebration that focuses attention on the nation's immigrant heritage serves as a disquieting reminder of the way in which blacks arrived in America and how they have fared since. . . . Others view it as someone else's celebration." One black leader pointed out, "The statue's symbolism of liberty and opportunity was not universally viewed as a reality for all blacks" and that the celebration should "distinguish between those blacks who were in America as a result of choices made by their ancestors and those whose ancestors had no choice."[1] Certainly the American Indian population will also have intensely ambivalent feelings about the role of liberty in their past!

Unfortunately, people who yearn for "the good old days" can indeed overlook the problems of the past. They can ignore the toil and trouble of a society without labor-saving devices, a society in which diseases like tuberculosis and pneumonia were common killers (as were illnesses associated with childbirth), a society in which higher education was only for a privileged few, a society that limited the civil rights of minorities, and a society in which blacks and women did not vote.

Those looking back can also have a tendency to want to fix blame for their contemporary problems. For example, during the Great Depression of the 1930s a very convenient scapegoat was former President Herbert Hoover, although historians now recognize that this attitude was both simplistic and unjust.

The Straw Woman

In conservative Christian circles feminism has become the scapegoat for many societal ills. Some think: *If only women accepted their proper role in life and acted the way they used to act, then society would be stable.* This is a variation of the easy but superficial charge that women interested in equal rights have bought into a "secular humanist" outlook and therefore into a false world view. But as the dust of the upheavals of recent decades settles we must realize that complex forces have worked to cause the shifting of societal roles. Tensions between the sexes and the erosion of traditional family values cannot be laid solely at the door of the contemporary women's movement.

However, for many people, feminism has indeed become the

straw woman, the convenient but false target upon which to affix the blame for all problem areas in the realm of human relationships. The twentieth century women's liberation movement is charged with creating a new breed of irresponsible women who lead innocent men astray and wreck family values.

A letter to the editor of *Daughters of Sarah* magazine voiced this: "I've seen what 'feminism'—Christian or otherwise—has done to our society, producing divorce, abortion, latchkey children, teenage pregnancy, and pornography."[2] Such a sweeping indictment completely overlooks the fact that these problems long antedate the women's movement. Divorce was recorded in biblical times. Abortion was practiced in the ancient world. Latchkey children have existed throughout history and were certainly a feature of Dickensian London and O. Henry's New York, where both parents labored fourteen to sixteen hours a day in sweatshops. Teenage (illegitimate) pregnancy again is nothing new, nor—to anyone who has visited the ruins of ancient Pompeii or read ancient literature— is pornography. Some people have also tried to saddle feminism with causing the emergence of open homosexual and lesbian practices, but again this is historically inaccurate. Deviation from heterosexuality has been known from the beginning of time. Genesis 18:16–19:29 accounts for the origin of the term "sodomy." Judges 19 records blatant homosexual behavior. Romans 1:26, 27 recognizes the existence of homosexual and lesbian practices. Blaming feminism for these many problems is not only inaccurate but obscures the crucial point that *both* sexes have a role in the dynamics of these problems, including mutual responsibility for seeking their solutions.

People who throw the blame for latchkey children on feminism do not take into account the severe economic pressures on many families, where two incomes are needed to maintain even a modest life-style, nor does that simplistic accusation deal with the child-care needs of the single head of household. Instead of trying to fix blame for problems that arise in these situations, should not Christians look for creative solutions? The many Bible references to the economically disadvantaged and to widows and orphans indicate that God's people should be first in caring for those who have difficulty in caring for themselves. Christians should not look for scapegoats, but should be first in offering help.

In addition to disregarding economic and demographic reasons for latchkey children, turning feminism into the scapegoat also disregards any concept of mutual parenting. Both parents have responsibility for making provision for the welfare of children, and both must try to work out adequate child-care arrangements. Certainly in Christian marriage the decision to have children should be a mutual one, and the responsibility for the safety and well-being of these children is also accepted as mutual. Mutual responsibility for child care does not cease if the mother is a full-time homemaker. The father's responsibility does not end with simply providing the wherewithal for her to remain at home. He should also be concerned both with the conditions of her workplace and with his own continuing parenting responsibilities.

Critics unjustly blame feminism alone for the substitution of "living together" for legal marriage, because certainly the male partner always has the option of saying no. It is also unfair to blame feminism for the increasing number of unwed mothers, because for every unwed mother there is an unwed father. In my home area of Greater New York there is growing interest in programs that will heighten awareness of male responsibility for teenage pregnancies and deal with the complex psychological and social pressures that influence young women to choose premature motherhood.

And do we honestly face the fact that prior to an abortion there has been a male as well as a female action? Rarely do I read of anyone decrying the scandal of abortion urge that we concentrate on dealing with this problem at its *conception*. Allowing men to evade their responsibility has made abortion a "women's issue," even though what goes on in a pregnant woman's body results from a mutual act. As the phrase goes, "It takes two to tango," and except in cases of rape, incest, or incompetence *both* parties are accountable for their actions and for the result of those actions.

It is also unjust to blame only feminism for divorce, because both parties must accept the marriage commitment and both parties must work at maintaining the marriage relationship. Yes, it does take two to tango, and that metaphor must be enlarged to mean not just the opening steps but the whole dance, not just the sex act but the entire marriage relationship and any children issuing from that relationship.

Since the beginning of time people have wanted to evade responsibility by fixing blame on scapegoats: "The woman made me do it"; "the serpent made me do it." But setting up feminism as the straw woman ignores history, overlooks contemporary economic pressures and demographic realities, and condones male irresponsibility. Placing all the blame for human problems such as child-care needs, divorce, promiscuity, and abortion on women alone makes only women accountable for the actions of both sexes and the issue of those actions. Worse, putting all the burden for the resolution of these problems only on women ignores male responsibility altogether.

Special Pleading: For Men Only

The main reason for ignoring male responsibility for problem areas in male-female relationships is that from time immemorial men have claimed a "special dispensation" sexually, the rationale being that men have urgent sexual needs that women do not. Society has always tended to excuse men who "sow wild oats." (You may remember my account of the minister who warned wives that if they did not gratify their husband's every sexual desire, these male animals would stray elsewhere.)

In contrast to men's special dispensation, women have been expected to be "above reproach." Yes, in many parts of Western society today the "sexually active" woman is no longer ostracized, but she remains in a different category from the "sexually active" man: If she conceives out of wedlock or is raped, people say, "She asked for it." A continuing opprobrium attached to the "fallen woman" remains, in startling contrast to the fascination with the "dashing" bachelor or even subtle approval of the "rake." The man who "plays the field" is still considered sophisticated rather than promiscuous, and he is even, in some instances, thought more desirable. Brides may still hear the bromide that if their future husbands are "experienced," it "will make it easier" for them. Such notions beg the question: *Upon whom do these men practice?*

Since only men have ever received this "special dispensation," there has developed the idea that extramarital sexual activity is permissible in men, because men who lapse from chastity or strict monogamy cannot help themselves—they have merely fallen prey to those special temptations stemming from their more urgent sexual needs. In contrast, women who lapse are still thought of as "fallen women"—fallen because they could indeed have helped themselves stay pure. (Only recently have studies confirmed what most women have known all along, namely, that they, too, have strong sexual needs.) Ironically this all-too-easy acceptance of men's "baser nature" creates a demand for the "loose" or "fallen" women whose cooperation and existence society then self-righteously decries. What a vicious circle!

Acceptance of the "special dispensation" notion has also been used by some men to pressure "nice" women into premarital sex; then all too often the women who give in to that pressure are discarded as "used goods" when the men hypocritically decide they can only marry virgins. Psychologists are familiar with the "madonna/whore" syndrome.

Until the contemporary women's movement brought this subject under attack, even rape was downplayed, because most people assumed, "That is the sort of thing men who can't control their sex drive do." Even in this violent situation, men were absolved of responsibility. A very perceptive letter to the editor of *Newsweek* magazine pointed out this fallacy: "You stated in your rape article ('Rape and the Law,' JUSTICE, May 20, 1985) that if 'teen-age girls learn some basic self-defense, they might be able to give the word 'no' some force. I feel there are two tasks for parents—to teach daughters how to say 'no' and to teach sons to respect that 'no'."[3]

To that plea I would add: *Let us teach sons not even to ask in the first place!* Surely Christians should lead in teaching that men do not have a right to random sexual outlet, any more than women do. The biblical ideal is that humans express sexual activity within the marriage relationship.

We need to remember that biblical injunctions against immorality are sex blind—they apply to both sexes—and both sexes have a responsibility for obeying these biblical injunctions. Scripture tells us that we are each accountable for our actions and that we each will stand before the judgment seat of Christ. The Bible says to both men and women that God's will is their sanctification (1 Thessalonians 4:3–8), and God says to both: ". . . Be holy because I, the Lord your God, am holy" (Leviticus 19:2). Paul's words in 1 Corinthians 6:18–20 urge all Christians to sexual purity and the highest of moral standards, because their bodies are now the temple of the Holy Spirit. (*See also* Ephesians 5:3–20.) Peter reiterates these principles (1 Peter 1:13–16). Old Testament and New Testament teach personal, individual accountability and assure us that when we ask God's help in conforming to His standards, He has the power to keep us from stumbling.

Catch 22: For Women Only

Blaming feminism for all societal ills is simplistic, unfair, and unscriptural. It also places women in a no-win situation, what Joseph Heller's novel called "catch 22."

On one hand traditionalists say women are to be subordinate to men and to accept male leadership in all areas of church and society. Yet on the other hand they announce, "A nation is only as strong as the morals of its women," and proclaim, "The hand that rocks the cradle rules the world." Women are told they are "weaker vessels" at the same time that they are told they must have the strength to be the moral caretakers of all humanity.

We see this romantic elevation of women to the pedestal of moral superiority as a faulty generalization when we remember that accepting the notion of the baser nature of men will of necessity relegate some women to the gutter! But in addition, placing women on this moral pedestal by themselves begs the question: *If men so easily go astray, how can they be entrusted with verbal leadership* (pronouncements and policies that set the course of church, home, and society)? If we accept the notion that men are morally weak, and therefore inferior, why should they be allowed to head the family, steer the ship of state, or guide the affairs of the church?

A further problem with placing women on that moral pedestal is that this not only overburdens women but all too easily lets men "off the hook." For example, a popular daily devotional pamphlet said this: "Insight: The Hand That Rocks the Cradle Steadies the Nation . . . 'All the Hebrew prophets knew that for the temper and quality of a civilization, the women are greatly responsible. A country is largely what women make of it; if they are cruel or careless or unwomanly, the country is on the road to ruin.' Think about that!"[4] Well, when I did think about it, I realized that while the "Insight" seemed to place great power in the hands of women, it did so at the cost of implying that men's baser, cruder nature can only be restrained by women's civilizing influence. Again the greater responsibility was shifted from men to women, assigning to women that impossible task of being moral caretakers of all humanity and avoiding the concept of the mutual responsibility of *both* men and women.

So traditionalists cannot have it both ways. They cannot condone a double standard by continuing to declare only men the rightful leaders of home, government, and church, while subscribing to special pleading on behalf of the moral lapses of men. Traditionalists cannot put women in the no-win situation of not being taken seriously verbally (not considered able to lead, administer, do theology, and preach) yet hold them responsible nonverbally (in actions) for the moral direction of all of society.

Yes, setting up feminism as the straw woman might seem attractive at first glance, but it is fraught with these inconsistencies. We cannot relieve men of responsibility for their sexuality and any issue of their sexual activity and then blame women for falling off an artificial pedestal when society breaks down. It *does* take two to tango. Walt Kelly's insight in "Pogo" is particularly appropriate here: "We have met the enemy, and he is us." The true enemy of a just society is not feminism *or* chauvinism, but *us*—men and women as the two components of fallen humanity.

The most serious problem with burdening only women with the responsibility for setting sexual ethics and with being sole protectors of family values is that this thinking ignores the fact that for Christians the true source of moral strength must lie in God, not in other human beings. Both men and women have created society's problems; now both men and women must look to God for solutions to these problems. In God we *all* must trust, and apart from His help, no person of either sex can bear the burdens of leadership.

Facing the Flaws

Therefore we can see that setting up feminism as the straw woman has these basic flaws:

1. It reveals our common desire to simplify a complex issue by using a scapegoat, in this case lumping a variety of problems together and labeling feminism as their source.
2. It overlooks the fact that problem areas in human relationships are not new, but go back to the beginning of human history. The Bible sets forth the sad record of a fallen race.
3. It overlooks the fact that as the two components of human society, *both* men and women are responsible for the problems of that society. Scripture holds them both accountable, but Scripture also offers them both spiritual renewal and spiritual strength.
4. It overlooks women's desire to have their personhood treated with respect and women's need to be free to use their gifts and maximize their potential. Thus it overlooks the legitimate aims of the women's movement, and especially the aims of biblical or Christian feminism.

Time Out for Definitions

It is convenient to use various terms to designate ideological positions, but as our different denominational backgrounds and theological convictions come into play, words may mean different things to different people. Therefore this is a good place to define terms used in our continuing discussion.

First, we need to recognize the pitfalls involved in labels. It has always been difficult to categorize any religious position, as we know from the wide variety of terms in use today: *orthodox, fundamentalist, conservative, evangelical, liberal, neo-orthodox,* and even—in recent years—*neo-evangelical.* Someone aptly said that one person's orthodoxy is another person's heresy! However, to facilitate our discussion (and at the price of oversimplifying) I will define two general positions regarding male-female relationships and roles.

In this book, the words *traditionalism* and *traditionalist* are used to designate the view that women should not be in positions of authority or leadership over men, should not be ordained, and in religious matters should not teach men. This view also places wives in a position of subordination to husbands. As used here, therefore, the word *traditionalism* indicates a hierarchical, patriarchal view of church and society.

In contrast, many terms are used to describe the position that women are equal partners in ministry and marriage, and equal members of society: *egalitarian, equalitarian, Christian feminist, evangelical feminist,* and *biblical feminist.* At least one person I know uses the term *evangelical suffragette* to indicate that feminism is a justice issue. The emphasis among those who subscribe to equality of all persons is on servanthood rather than on assigned positions or prescribed roles in life. I myself am most comfortable with *biblical feminism.*

In making these two broad definitions, I repeat that they are made to help focus the discussion in this book. I recognize that in both Christian and secular thinking there is a breadth of views on these issues. Many Christians are in a state of transition. Others will consider themselves traditionalists but are open to reexamining knotty problems. Quite rightly, these people will not wish to be thought rigid on unclear areas in Scripture. At the other end of the spectrum, radical feminists might well consider a conservative biblical feminist like myself not much different from a traditionalist! However, in the interests of simplicity, such nuances have had to be sacrificed. For purposes of our discussion, *traditionalism* will indicate teaching subordination of women to men in both church and society, whereas *biblical feminism* will indicate teaching mutual submission and therefore equal opportunity for men and women to serve in both church and society.

The Challenge of Biblical Feminism

Historically the basic aims of the women's movement have been that women be accepted as equal members of society and be free to become full persons. A formal dictionary definition of *feminism* terms it "the theory of the political, economic, and social equality of the sexes," with the secondary meaning being "organized activity on behalf of women's rights and interests."[5] However, although the ultimate goal of both secular feminists and biblical feminists is to achieve full equality of persons, the two groups have vastly different orientations.

Secular feminism can take many different forms and be guided by many different philosophies as its supporters seek to achieve a society in which women can achieve their full potential. But persons who term themselves *biblical feminists* make an important break with the secularist approach. Secular feminism centers around gaining equal rights; biblical feminism centers around equal opportunity to serve.

The secular feminist says: "I want my rights. I want to be able to compete on an equal basis with men." The biblical feminist says: "I want to be free to be the person God created me to be and to have the privilege of following Christ as He calls me to do."

Feminism (or any other *ism*) without Christ is just another power struggle. But adding the word *biblical* to feminism indicates that these feminists want to explore their conviction about equality of women in a biblical way and implement their findings according to biblical guidelines. Therefore, within scriptural parameters, not an "anything goes" approach, biblical feminists will seek to promote a climate in which women are free to act as equal human beings and where Christian women can enter into their full inheritance as equal children of God.

Yes, as do secular feminists, biblical feminists see feminism as a justice issue, an issue of liberation, but they also see it as an issue of religious freedom. To the goals of political, economic, and social equality of the sexes, biblical feminists add religious equality.

Biblical feminists believe Scripture affirms the worth and value of men and women equally and all who have accepted Christ's offer of new life should have equal opportunity to serve Him as He calls. Biblical feminists want to bring the whole scope of the Bible to bear upon this justice issue as they submit the question of sexism to the light of God's Word. This is why biblical feminists advocate partnership and not competition, mutual submission and not domination by one sex or the other, the priesthood of all believers and not a male hierarchy.

The whole thrust of biblical feminism is to call all Christians to be biblical people, and by definition, when that happens, then the term *biblical feminism* will no longer be relevant. I know I personally yearn for the day when Christians will all be those biblical people, a day when there will be no sexism, racism, classism—no discrimination of any kind—and when we are all free to serve and worship God as He calls.

A Cruel Tool

Thanks largely to the secular women's movement, women are no longer routinely lampooned as nitwits who always drive into the garage door. But the caricature of women's liberation is still there in the straw woman—the exaggerated depiction of feminists as angry home wreckers or arrogant, "mannish" women preachers.

When I discuss these issues with an unfamiliar audience, I sometimes try to erase this caricature by telling my listeners that Phil and I have been married for thirty-five years and that we have three children and three grandchildren. I may also mention biblical feminist scholar Catherine Kroeger, pastor's wife and mother of five children, who has opened their home to over thirty foster children. It can be a revelation to those who have accepted the caricature to discover that many biblical feminists are both firmly Bible based and family oriented.

Yes, of course, any movement will have inadequacies of some sort, unwise policies, and persons and programs that are not to be emulated. However, it is not only unjust but intellectually dishonest and lazy to use caricature to write off a movement before asking: *Are the movement's* goals *legitimate?*

Compare treatment of the women's movement with how far we have come in our treatment of racial minorities. For example, today we would be shocked to see blacks caricatured as "shiftless darkies," contented with playing banjos and eating hunks of watermelon. We respect the desire of our black brothers and sisters to become full members of society. We would never want to hurt them by the cruel tool of caricature; therefore we would never trivialize their aspirations by calling programs to end racism "black lib."

Similarly (and irrespective of whether or not we agree with their ideological orientation) we have enough respect for the needs of emerging nations not to trivialize their struggles by saying, "Lib theology." Yet the use of the term *women's lib* is a subtle attempt to caricature the women's liberation movement as some sort of lightweight endeavor and to trivialize the aspirations of women to have their personhood respected, their request for equal opportunity accepted, and their status as full members of God's family acknowledged.

One reason for making feminism the scapegoat for societal ills is that people who promote rigid roles for men and women can feel threatened when these roles change, and they can react with hostility to any movement that promotes such change. Role-conscious people will often find it difficult to be open to new ideas. It is easier for them to caricature feminism and then to blame that caricature for various human problems than to be open to reexamining traditionalism.

Closed or Open?

A sincere Christian friend of mine was told: "If you support feminism, you have lost your faith." That critic had fallen for the straw-woman argument, but he also failed to see that because biblical feminists discuss these issues within a scriptural framework, they are retaining their faith, not abandoning it. Biblical feminists desire to be open to a better understanding of the Christian faith and how it relates to our twentieth century world. However, tension does occur when biblical feminists interact with people who place the highest premium on tradition, because often those people feel reluctant to reexamine their tradition to be sure that it is in harmony with Scripture.

We may properly question whether *traditional approaches and answers* are synonymous with *true approaches and answers*, because both Old Testament and New Testament make it clear that *tradition* does not automatically mean "truth." The strong words of Amos 5:21–24 and Isaiah 1:10–17 come immediately to mind. So whatever our denominations, we all need to ask ourselves: *Is our tradition scriptural?*

THE STRAW WOMAN

Remember Jesus' words in Mark 7:5–13 where the Pharisees asked Him why His disciples did not keep "the tradition of the elders," and Jesus replied, in effect: "You worship Me in vain, teaching for doctrines the commandments of men. . . . Full well you reject the commandment of God, that you may keep your own tradition . . . , making the word of God of no effect through your traditions." Those are harsh words indeed, but nothing could be plainer in warning us against blind acceptance of the accretion of traditions.

One of the saddest things about the dead hand of tradition is that it stifles discussion and encourages the closed mind. The person with the closed mind says, "We've always done things this way. We have no new thing to learn." What a tragedy!

The closed mind also tends to have a siege mentality—"us against them"—and will often try to simplify complex issues by the labels used for "us" and "them." But most questions are rarely that simple: Witness the many different Christian denominations and the divergencies of their doctrinal statements.

It can become very frustrating to try to discuss issues with persons who subscribe to that simple "us against them" dichotomy, because they give you no opportunity to say: "We agree on basic Christian doctrine, but we have severe disagreement in its application to contemporary issues. Let's talk."

I have felt that frustration when hearing or reading certain critiques of feminist writers. All too often the traditionalists lump all feminists together, treating them all as enemies of religious and family values. Little attempt is made to sort out the vast differences between feminist writers, including the vast differences among those writing from a Christian perspective. To many traditionalists, *all* feminists—of whatever persuasion—are "them" and are considered suspect and hostile to biblical truth and therefore not given a fair hearing. William Oddie took this tack in his book *What Will Happen to God?* However that technique is just as unsound as having a discussion of racism in which one connected the late Dr. Martin Luther King, Jr. with the Black Panthers or linked Bishop Desmond Tutu with the extremist Louis Farrakhan, simply because those people happen to be black.

Traditionalists who consider all feminists "them" will over-

look the important contributions of writers like Gilbert Bilezikian, Richard and Joyce Boldrey, Patricia Gundry, Richard and
Catherine Kroeger, Kari Torjeson Malcolm, Aida Besançon
Spencer, Elaine Storkey, Willard Swartley, and Don Williams,
all of whom write from a Bible-based, centrist point of view.[6]
Unfortunately those who subscribe to rigid roles for men and
women have often made little or no effort to distinguish between the variety of positions that differ from their traditional
one. It has been all too easy to group the Bible-believing egalitarian with the radical post-Christian, the centrist with the
extremist, and to label *any* person who questions the patriarchal, hierarchical view of human relationships as being unfaith-
ful to Scripture.

Such indiscriminate linkage effectively influences the uninformed person, but it is a tactic that lacks integrity. Some readers will justifiably draw a parallel with the McCarthy era in
American politics and recall how easily someone could be
blackballed by the unsubstantiated charge of "commie."

What is puzzling about this tactic is that evangelicals do address many other questions without fear of reprisal by fellow
believers. All evangelicals—both men and women—acknowledge that there can be hard problems in Scripture. We all struggle with that passage I referred to in chapter 1—1 Peter 3:18–20.
We all face the doubtful authenticity of Mark 16:9–20 and John
7:53–8:11. We study a section like James 4:1–6, where textual
problems make it difficult to get the exact meaning (scholars
call such a place an exegetical crux). Further, we graciously
allow the validity and acceptability of various modes of baptism
without breaking fellowship with those who differ from our
view; we do not "write off" people who diverge from our interpretation of the symbolism of Holy Communion; and we
certainly agree to disagree about types of church government.

Yet when fellow evangelicals holding a high view of Scripture suggest that the "hard passages" about women allow for
differing interpretations, then the dogmatists' reaction is more
and more to equate *any* differing opinion with a denial of the
authority of Scripture. More than puzzling and downright dis-
heartening is that this tactic has had the effect of squashing

legitimate inquiry and instead has created fear of any new understanding of the text.

Final Truth or More Truth?

As we study these crucial questions, could there be further insight as yet unknown to us? To ask that question is of course to answer it, because we who are only His creatures can never completely fathom God's truth. However, truth does open up to those who sincerely seek it, and we should be joyful and not fearful as we delve more deeply into it.

Asking questions about God's Word in no way compromises our acceptance of biblical authority. As we saw in chapter 1, we have a human need to ask questions, and the question-and-answer process enhances our comprehension of a topic. Scripture itself encourages the honest questioner to take those questions to God. Remember Habakkuk, whom some commentators have called "the prophet of honest doubt"!

No one who acknowledges biblical authority needs to fear "going where the evidence leads." Only insecure persons might get panicky at not having all the answers to every difficult question right now, but those of us whose security is in God will never find it threatening to say, "Let's reexamine an issue." We who have accepted God's plan know that God is in charge and that His Word will stand the closest scrutiny. As we explored in chapter 1, we never need to fear studying the divine Prospectus. Our divine Sponsor is the God of truth, who wants only good for us. Only His abundant life will satisfy our need for "something more."

In 2 Corinthians 3:6 we read, "He has made us competent as ministers of a new covenant—not of the letter but of the Spirit; for the letter kills, but the Spirit gives life." Life is not rigid: Life breathes, moves, learns, matures. God's offer of abundant life is contained in the living Word, inspired by the living God, through the agency of the living Holy Spirit, written down by living human writers, telling us about a living person, Jesus Christ, who is the same yesterday, today, and forever.

The Bible is not rigid. This vital Book of books offers us a changing, everexpanding experience of new life in Christ. That is one reason why Paul wrote in 1 Corinthians 13 that our present knowledge will one day be superseded. "We know in part and we prophesy in part" because we experience the limitations of this earthly life, "but when perfection comes, the imperfect disappears. . . . Now we see but a poor reflection; then we shall see face to face. . . ." Yes, as long as we remain in our mortal bodies, there will still be more to know; therefore it is arrogant to assert: "I have final truth on all matters." The person open to the leading of the Holy Spirit's illuminating presence must humbly say, "I will ask God to guide me further into more of His truth."

My father, Frank Gaebelein, warned about the danger of the closed mind when he wrote these words in *Christianity Today* magazine: "Sometimes evangelicals tend to be afraid of newly discovered truth. If so, they may have been equating some cherished doctrinal formulation or historical position with final truth. So when some hitherto unrecognized truth, some breakthrough into wider knowledge, faces them, it may seem a threat and they may react in fear or anger."[7]

But opening ourselves to more truth does not indicate any compromise with untruth. Retaining an open mind about an unclear passage is not the same as compromising on a clear passage. Rather, persons who close their minds to the possibility of new light being shed on an unclear passage make themselves liable to the criticism that they are using the presuppositional approach they so decry in liberal biblical scholars. Oswald Chambers has these cautionary words for all of us: "It is a dangerous thing to refuse to go on knowing."[8]

Think of the many centuries when the collective Christian conscience was dulled to slavery, prison reform, child labor, inhumane mental asylums, and callous treatment of orphans. Looking backward, with our consciences awakened, we abhor those abuses, yet at the time even "good Christians" needed a fresh vision of the Gospel to combat such social ills and inequities.

Then, in more recent years, during the fundamentalist-modernist controversies, fundamentalists did not have final truth when they suppressed or ignored social concern, when to be "pure" many thought that biblical preaching should be devoid of social consciousness. I can remember when the phrase *social gospel* was a derogatory epithet.

Nor did certain segments of the church have final truth when they restricted certain spiritual gifts to the Book of Acts and labeled, as they did in my youth, any contemporary gift of tongues as demented or even satanic. This is why I have recounted my own background. I know the stands various church groups have taken and the claims for final truth that have had to be reevaluated—often because those groups simply could no longer deny the experiences of other Christians.

Discerning truth takes hard work. Discernment is an ongoing process in places where what Scripture says is not entirely clear to us, or where the text cannot be rendered exactly or interpreted uniformly, or in areas where valid Christian experience differs. Therefore biblical feminists lovingly ask those who differ with them not to be deceived by the straw-woman argument and not to accept a caricature of biblical feminism as the reality, but to be open to reevaluating their conclusions about subordination of women and the restrictions of women's sphere of service.

Just as in recent years the evangelical wing of the Christian church has rediscovered social concern (although of course it was never lost, we just were not heeding the whole counsel of God) and just as in recent decades the church at large has come to accept and appreciate the validity and practice of all the gifts of the Spirit, so now we need to move toward including all believers equally—female as well as male—in all areas of life and ministry. As we do, we must call men and women alike to individual accountability and mutual responsibility for their actions. The Body of Christ must become sensitive to the yearning of all its members to live and serve as God directs. As long as one member hurts, we all hurt, and the Body cannot get on with its main business of proclaiming Christ to a lost world.

Chapter Four

Equal Ambassadors

Many traditionalists assert that people who question subordination of women have been influenced by the secular feminist movement, but my own journey shows that my questions arose from within the context of the Christian community. These questions resulted from the conflict I saw between the traditionalists' theory and what they asked me to do in practice.

As an active laywoman, I was being sent a very confusing message: "You are doing things women should not do, but we are asking you to keep on doing these things anyway." This message produced conflicting pressures within me. On one side, I felt pressure to perform services for the church, but on the other was pressure to conform to a teaching that in effect condemned my performance.

After I had put aside the straw woman, I was in an attitude of openness, not chafing at some restricted role in either home or church. In our marriage, Phil and I had always acted as equal partners, so I had no personal reason to bridle at any reference to "women's place." My economic circumstances allowed me to be a full-time homemaker, and I was busy raising three closely spaced children. I experienced intellectual challenge and fulfillment in using whatever gifts God had given me in teaching, administering, and leading church programs. True, in my own home congregation (although not in my denomination) any ordained post was closed to me, but I had never considered such a post. I had also never espoused any position on "the women issue" and therefore had no face to save and nothing to defend. Initially I tended to accept the traditional position, because I was so used to hearing it. Still, because of how my church called upon me to serve, I had to inquire: "Will you explain the traditional position to me so that I will feel free and comfortable continuing doing the things you are asking me to do?"

I received varied answers. "Women were created to be subservient to men." "Women, like Eve, are easily deceived and can't be trusted to lead or teach properly." "Women are simply not suited to do these things." The last one was particularly puzzling in view of the ways I had been asked to serve!

In their answers to my questions people most often referred to three Bible passages as their reason for restricting women's activities: 1 Corinthians 11:2–16; 1 Corinthians 14:33b–38; and 1 Timothy 2:8–15. But when I turned to commentaries and learned journals, I discovered a surprising fact! There is no scholarly consensus on the meaning or interpretation of these passages. Most translators resolve (sometimes arbitrarily) the intricate textual problems as best they can so that in most English versions the verses read clearly. However, in the original Greek these passages are not "clear sailing," even to the most knowledgeable exegetes or interpreters.

Practical evidence of this lack of consensus on the Pauline "hard passages" is apparent in the vast divergence of views within the Christian church. Some denominations allow no participation of women at all, but require female believers to be silent observers in worship and Christian education. Others allow women to teach only women and children, while some groups allow women to teach any group and hold any committee post as long as there is a male "authority figure" over them. Still other congregations concentrate on the gifts and not the sex of the gifted person, and many of these congregations have women ministers.

Parachurch organizations also vary in their practices, which range from no women in teaching or leadership to full participation of women. There is also a difference of opinion about women's place in seminary training: Some seminaries accept women in all degree programs, and some do not. However, many seminaries have women on their faculties and on their boards, and at least one conservative seminary even has had a woman chairperson of its board of directors. As I read and studied, I also found similar divergence of views with respect to women's place in marriage, ranging from those that teach complete subordination to those that proclaim the mutuality of equal partnership.

It soon became apparent that "the women issue" was very complicated and that there were no easy answers. Although most laypeople remain unaware of the textual difficulties, the three Pauline passages many regard as definitive cannot be uniformly translated, exegeted, or interpreted at this time. So, as I have had to do with 1 Peter 3:18–20 (as mentioned in chapter 1), I put these Pauline passages temporarily aside. Rather than concentrating on passages that even the experts are sharply divided over, it seemed sensible to continue the search for answers to my questions by first studying Scripture scholars agree upon as clear.

A Central Truth

As we have seen, so many of our problems stem from the "if onlys" in life. If only there were no divorce, or latchkey children, or promiscuity, abortion, or pornography. If only there were no wife or child abuse. If only there were no tensions, disharmony, or competition between the sexes. If only men and women just plain got on better with each other.

These "if onlys" are another way of saying that we human beings have that common need for renewal. In answer to that need, God's Prospectus offers us what Jude 3 (KJV) calls our "common salvation"; that is, the same offer of renewal is made to all persons who accept God's plan, regardless of race, creed, color, national origin, sex, or station in life.

But after the wonder of renewal, another central truth applies to all Christians. God's Prospectus plainly tells us that all persons who trust in Jesus Christ as Savior are new creatures with a new mission in life. The Bible passage that most clearly explains what this involves is 2 Corinthians 5:14–21, where Paul writes:

. . . We are convinced that one died for all, and therefore all died. And he died for all, that those who live should no longer live for themselves but for him who died for them and was raised again. So from now on we regard no one from a worldly point of view. Though we once regarded Christ in this way, we do so no longer. Therefore, if anyone is in Christ, he is a new creation; the old has gone, the new has come! All this is from God, who reconciled us to himself through Christ and gave us the ministry of reconciliation; that God was reconciling the world to himself in Christ, not counting men's sins against them. And he has committed to us the message of reconciliation. We are therefore Christ's ambassadors, as though God were making his appeal through us. We implore you on Christ's behalf: Be reconciled to God. God made him who had no sin to be sin for us, so that in him we might become the righteousness of God.

All believers in Christ are new creatures who are called to be Christ's ambassadors. What does this clear truth tell us about our relationship to God? What does it tell us about our relationship to one another?

The New Life

Sometimes, when I share my faith with someone, the person will say: "You don't mean to tell me you are born again, do you?" Because of the publicity given to the words *born again* by people like Billy Graham, Jimmy Carter, and Chuck Colson, some think that it is a contemporary concept and probably the mark of a religious fanatic. They can be surprised to learn that Jesus Himself used the phrase to explain God's re-creative work in the lives of those who accept the plan of salvation as found in His Prospectus, the Bible.

Revealing this mystery to Nicodemus, in John 3 Jesus flatly stated: "I tell you the truth, unless a man is born again, he cannot see the kingdom of God." Jesus went on to explain that this process is accomplished by the mysterious activity of God as the Holy Spirit works in the life of the believer to make that person acceptable to enter God's kingdom and become part of God's family.

Paul's way of expressing this truth is found in 2 Corinthians 5:17: ". . . If anyone is in Christ, [that person] is a new creation: the old has gone, the new has come!" Paul felt so keenly about this truth that he wrote in verse 20: "We implore you on Christ's behalf: Be reconciled to God." Why? Because of the marvel of the substitutionary atonement, that re-creative process as explained in verse 21: "God made him who had no sin to be sin for us, so that in him we might become the righteousness of God." This is yet another way to express the answer to our human need for renewal, our need to have God's perfection replace our puny efforts to measure up to His standards.

So the new birth experience, that re-creation of the believer in Christ, lies at the heart of Paul's teaching about Christian life and service. Obviously, a person must become a Christian before living the Christian life or engaging in Christian service! Then Paul goes on to challenge these new creatures called Christians not to live for themselves, but to consider themselves representatives of the resurrected Christ.

The New Power Source

The Resurrection is the basis for our new life and our new service and the A note to which all the New Testament is tuned. In preparation for His resurrection, all during Christ's earthly ministry He challenged His hearers to expand their minds and to think of Him in larger terms than simply good teacher or exemplary man.

In verses like Matthew 20:17–19, whenever He spoke about the coming cross, He also looked ahead to the Resurrection. Jesus wanted His followers to get the larger picture and to grasp the fact that He was greater than they could ever imagine. When they accepted Him as Savior, they would enter into a life greater than anything they had ever known. That they finally understood this truth is evident, because after His resurrection, they became new people with a new outlook. Nothing but the reality of the Resurrection can account for the change in Jesus' followers from timid and weak to bold and courageous!

Now in 2 Corinthians 5 Paul urges his readers not to limit Christ to the historical Jesus, but to accept the reality of His resurrection power and to recognize the implications of that power in their own lives. The wonder of it all is this tremendous parallel: Just as since His resurrection we no longer think of Christ as simply an extraordinary person but as Very God, transcending forever the human limitations of the Incarnation, so now we Christians must expand our concept of ourselves and understand that we are not limited to what we once were either.

This teaching complements Romans 5:12–6:14, where Paul's thought is "as with Christ, so with the believer." The Resurrection has shown that the divine Sponsor has the power to make the offering in His Prospectus. Now we, too, must reach out and claim our new life as set forth in His plan.

The Berkeley Version reads this way: "Consequently, from now on we think of no one just in terms of his human nature. Even if we had thought of Christ in that way, we now no longer know Him just in terms of His human nature. Accordingly, if any one is in Christ he is a new creation. The old has gone; lo, the new has come" (5:16, 17). We can properly say, "The new has come with us, just as it has with Christ." In 2 Corinthians 5:17 the New International Version even has an exclamation mark: ". . . The new has come!" These glorious verses assure us that when we are converted from our old energy source of self to the new power source of life in Christ, all life becomes a new experience. Yes, the old *has* gone, the new *has* come!

The New Emphasis

Nothing could more plainly tell us that we who have accepted God's Prospectus are in a new situation and no longer limited by our earthly "houses." This emphasis on newness lifts us above the usual human way of looking at other people.

Most persons tend to concentrate on factors like race, sex, or class distinctions when they evaluate others, but the Bible tells us in 1 Samuel 16:7, ". . . The Lord does not look at the things man looks at. Man looks at the outward appearance, but the Lord looks at the heart." Yes, the biblical emphasis on newness transcends our usual human way of thinking and fixes our minds upon spiritual realities, which are the true realities.

The emphasis in our new life is no longer on our humanity.

It may reassure some readers to know that in the Greek the language used for human beings in our key passage is inclusive and that if *anyone* is in Christ he *or* she is a new creation. In 2 Corinthians 4:7 Paul has already pointed out that our new spirit is simply "encased" in our human body and that the power source for our new life does not come from its imperfect human container, but from God. Thus any teaching that would put some sort of merit, even "appointed" merit, on a human attribute like gender would place an unscriptural value on that human container.

So that we do not miss his point, Paul goes on in 2 Corinthians 4:16 to tell us that while our outer container wastes away, our inner nature is being renewed day by day. Paul triumphantly concludes in verse 18, "what is unseen is eternal." This is the ultimate answer to our universal need for renewal, because God's power effects renewal where it really counts—renewal in our inner self, the "real me."

Here again Paul expounds a truth that Jesus taught first. Jesus challenged any preoccupation with earthly distinctions. In John 8:31–58 He urged a Jewish audience not to be engrossed with pride of ancestry, but rather to concentrate on their relationship with God. In Matthew 22:23–33, in answer to an intricate question about a woman's marital status, He said: "At the resurrection people will neither marry nor be given in marriage . . ." (v. 30). In John 6:63 He stated: "The Spirit gives life; the flesh counts for nothing. The words I have spoken to you are spirit and they are life."

The New Unity

In Ephesians 2 Paul explores another facet of our new creation, when he emphasizes our new unity, telling us that Jesus came to unite us and make us one in Him, to the end that we have peace with one another and not alienation. We new creatures are to make up one new Body. We are not to be fragmented.

Again, the Savior Himself taught the initial truth of the unity of believers. In John 17:20–23 Jesus prayed that all who believe in Him be one, and this passage of His prayer concluded: ". . . May they be brought to complete unity to let the world know that you sent me and have loved them even as you have loved me."

God's design for the unity of believers reverses the confusion of Babel. God's ideal is that a harmony of spirit should exist among Christians, transcending race, sex, language, culture, family background, and social and economic status. This new spirit will be a compelling witness to the force of the new life within us. Jesus made this clear in John 13:34, 35: "A new commandment I give you: Love one another. As I have loved you, so you must love one another. All men will know that you are my disciples if you love one another."

Only Christ-like love is the antidote for the sin of disunity. When we are divided, we fall into the trap of thinking, *My way is better than yours,* and then we find it all to easy too slide in believing, *I am better than you.* The sure corrective will be to concentrate on the finished work of Christ. When we focus on Him as Savior, we *must* see ourselves as only fellow sinners for whom Christ died.

Probably the most familiar verse expressing the new unity of fellow believers is Galatians 3:28: "There is neither Jew nor Greek, slave nor free, male nor female, for you are all one in Christ Jesus." Because of the interest today in male-female relationships, we have tended to overlook the significance of that first group: Jew/Gentile. Ironically, because most Christian churches are mostly composed of Gentile members, we have forgotten that in the early days of Christianity the Gentiles were the "outsiders." Full acceptance of Gentiles into one Body became such a crucial question that the first church council was called to deal with this matter. At that council Peter made an impassioned plea for full acceptance of Gentiles: "God, who knows the heart, showed that he accepted them by giving the Holy Spirit to them, . . . for he purified their hearts by faith" (Acts 15:8, 9). Peter's words made it clear that no one could consider Gentiles second-class Christians. The key to their equal spiritual standing with Jewish believers was in God's great power, not in their physical differences. Peter concluded: "We believe it is through the grace of our Lord Jesus that we are saved, just as they are."

Paul comments on this new understanding of the unity of believers in Galatians 6:15, where he writes: "Neither circumcision nor uncircumcision means anything; what counts is a new creation." Yes, the difference between Jew and Gentile is as physical and psychological and sometimes even as social a difference as gender can be. But in Acts 15 and Galatians 6 Scripture teaches that the God who can transform Jew and Gentile into one new Body can indeed unite all believers so that we transcend looking at each other in terms of our human nature, our physical "houses."

God's Prospectus does not offer different redemptive plans, different new birth processes. God does not present one set of entry requirements for Jews and one for Gentiles, or—to make our discussion more relevant—one set of requirements for men and another set for women. Referring back to our condominium analogy, God does not say that all women must live in rooms with no view, nor does He say that minorities must live in the basement, to run the laundry machines. No, in James 2:8, 9 God's Word assures us that God is not a respecter of petty human distinctions. All Christians are equal members of the one Body. As the familiar chorus puts it "We are one in the Spirit, we are one in the Lord."

In the Old Testament the Psalmist confirms that God will bless those who fear Him ". . . small and great alike" or as the Jerusalem Bible has it, ". . . without distinction of rank" (Psalms 115:13). In the New Testament Jesus assures us in John 6:37, ". . . Whoever comes to me I will never drive away." When we do come to Him, Hebrews 7:25 affirms, "He is able to save completely those who come to God through him, because he always lives to intercede for them."

So our security is in a God great and powerful enough to effect our complete renewal, and He wants to do so. A clear and compelling truth about our redemption is that all persons are equally redeemed and become equal children of God, now united into one new Body. All Christians have equal spiritual standing and equal eligibility to serve as ambassadors of Christ. Our common bond of new life makes us all candidates for God's diplomatic corps.

The New Mission

In 2 Corinthians 5:18–20 Paul explains that Christians have a special mission—the ministry of reconciliation. This is Paul's metaphor for sharing the Good News of salvation. We newborn Christians must now present Christ's saving grace to those still outside His family: God, as it were, making His appeal through us.

Yes, many crucial questions fill our agenda, such as those regarding a Christian view of marriage and the family. But not all men and women marry, and not all men and women have children or families to care for. All Christians *do* have the privilege of representing Christ, and all Christians are to serve their Savior as He calls.

Of course, individual situations will differ, so we will serve in various ways. Some persons will be "tent makers" and others will be in "full-time service." Some will have an interior mission of prayer and intercession, and still others will mirror their Lord by Christ-like actions in un-Christ-like circumstances. But however or wherever we do it, all Christians are commanded to serve Christ. There is no question about our new mission: We are called to be Christ's ambassadors, members of God's diplomatic corps.

Nor is there any question about the basis of this new ministry. We do not live and serve Christ in our old self, our old nature, preoccupied with our old ways of looking at life. Only because He has made us new are we now fit to enter God's service. It is only because we are new creatures that we are entrusted with our new mission.

Second Corinthians 5:18–21 beautifully expresses God's love and patience in offering us a second chance to serve as He created us to serve. Back in Genesis 1:26–28 God charged both man and woman equally with the mutual responsibility of caring for this world, with being God's equal representatives, using His delegated authority to rule His creation together. Tragically, as a result of the Fall, we men and women became adversaries, competitors, and even oppressors, instead of co-operators and joint administrators of our inheritance. Now, Paul says in 2 Corinthians 5:19, God in Christ offers us re-creation and therefore complete renewal and restoration—a second chance, not counting our sins (our first failure) against us. God's Word tells us that all who accept God's offer now have a new mission, the privilege of transmitting this Good News to others.

That all believers are equally redeemed and therefore equally eligible to serve forms the basis for any philosophy of Christian life and service. God makes no distinction based on race, class, or gender. The Jew is not more or less redeemed than the Gentile. The rich person is not more or less redeemed than the economically disadvantaged; the Westerner is neither more or less redeemed than the Third World citizen. The woman does not have a different new-birth process from the man's. *All* believers are made new, and *all* are called to be Christ's servants.

On the basis of our new spiritual status all Christians are fit for God's diplomatic corps. All believers are called to be Christ's ambassadors, channels through which God makes His appeal today to those still outside His Body. He has made us His agents in publicizing and explaining His Prospectus to that hurting world, proclaiming His plan as the only answer to our human need for renewal and that "something more."

Paul's recurring theme of the newness of the Christian's life lies at the heart of His call for us to become ambassadors for Christ. To paraphrase 2 Corinthians 5:16 and 17: "Just as now [post-Calvary] we see that the resurrected Christ is so much more than merely an historical personage, so we must see ourselves as so much more than what we were before our new birth. The resurrected Christ is the first fruits, and in Him we are now new—completely new!" All those "if onlys" are erased! We have a completely fresh start in life, and this is exciting! This is what Christianity is all about! We have something tremendous to celebrate!

Yet . . .

Yet when I went back to share my excitement about the message of 2 Corinthians 5 with my traditionalist friends, I received a mixed reception. "Yes," they said, "it is true that we Christians do indeed have a new spiritual standing, but that does not come into full effect in this earthly life. During our human life span, we are still housed in our physical bodies, and our human society is set up in ways that reflect the gender of those physical bodies. Yes, men and women do have equal spiritual status, but in the present reality of their humanity, women have a functionally subordinate place. In this life men fill one role, and women fill another."

This reaction puzzled me. If the things that are not seen are the true realities, as Paul taught in 2 Corinthians 4:18, why would we want to operate as though limited by our transient bodies? If the Good News of the Gospel is that we are indeed new creatures, why would our opportunities to serve God in this present life be restricted according to attributes of the perishable flesh—especially since Jesus Himself said "the flesh counts for nothing"? Again I came up against the problem of people who taught one thing in theory but another thing in practice.

It became evident that I needed to explore the reason for the practice. What basis did my friends have for teaching gender restrictions? Did this practice indicate ingrained factors in the fabric of human society? What does Scripture say about the social framework of our human life and about how God uses men and women during their human lives? This, too, would be part of the task of discerning truth and "going where the evidence leads."

Chapter Five

True or False?

At the beginning of our journey together, exploring these crucial questions, we set forth various common human needs. Both men and women have a need for security and feel a need to be guided by some authority. Both men and women experience a need for "something more," and both yearn for renewal, an answer to those nagging "if onlys" of life. Both have a need for acceptance and approval of their actions.

Our need to know truth underlies these needs. We are only free from anxiety when we trust in a true authority. We only feel secure when we ground our need for renewal in a true solution. Ultimately only true answers to our need for "something more" satisfy us. We only experience inner peace when we base our lives on a true foundation, and we are only sure of approval if we have done true actions.

Our need to ask questions is part of the lifelong process of discovering true answers to these problems, of discerning on what values to base our lives and by what standards to guide our actions. So whether he asked it in jest, in perplexity, or in frustration, Pilate's question still rings in our ears, too: "What is truth?"

Christians believe the person of the Savior, who said "I am the truth," best expresses the answer. We affirm the words of 1 Corinthians 3:11: "For no one can lay any foundation other than one already laid, which is Jesus Christ." He satisfies our need for "something more," because as 2 Corinthains 1:20 puts it, in Him all the promises of God are yes. We hear Him say that

God's Word is truth (John 17:17), so we look to Scripture to find God's truth for us in the world of here and now.

During His earthly ministry, Jesus constantly expanded human ideas of truth. As the legalists tried to defend and promote their system of salvation by works, with its emphasis on human effort and human merit, Jesus kept pointing out that God's ways are different and that His kingdom means a new era and a new way of looking at life. To a people obsessed with trying to win God's and man's approval by keeping rules and rules upon rules, He said in effect: "The problem is deeper than that. Look into your very hearts and see if you have even wanted to keep all those rules." He constantly challenged them: "Do you want to cling to human tradition, or do you want new life?"

We read in John 2:24, 25 that Jesus did not seek human support, as would a politician, because He knew that in our hearts unregenerate human beings are out for Number One. He knew that we need a complete change of heart, that new birth, before we can begin to understand God's truth. Until we undergo that radical change, that conversion from our old energy source of self to the new energy source of Christ, we will all be variations of the rich young ruler in Luke 18:18–30, unwilling to trust only Jesus for our every need.

However, once we are born again, or converted from our old energy source to His perfect new one, we become more and more open to looking at life from God's perspective. Now as we ask our questions we want only His truth for our answers. We understand that only when we operate according to His guidelines will we have true security, and only then will we have His approval and hear His "Well done, good and faithful servant" at the end of our journey. For this reason we search the Scriptures when we face the need to discover truth in the area of human relationships.

Equal Value, Equal Truth

In the Book of Genesis, Scripture presents the creation of human beings as the culmination of God's creative act. Only after the creation of humankind in His image did God see that all He had made was "very good" (Genesis 1:31). The final and deliberate setting apart of man and woman as created "in the image of God" determines that we cannot treat human beings as merely the highest of many animal species.

Even a superficial reading of the Bible shows that God's Word affirms the worth and dignity of all men and women. The many genealogies, the two censuses in the Book of Numbers, the individual names of real people in real-life situations that God caused to be recorded all show His interest in human individuals. Human life is not cheap, but precious in God's sight, so precious that He entered our world Himself, in the person of Jesus Christ, to offer us a second chance to be what He created us to be.

Thus the fact of the Incarnation (God come in the flesh) also supports the uniqueness of human life: Because Christ was fully human, He bestowed worth upon human life from its very conception; because Christ interacted with fallen humanity, He gave dignity to humankind; because Christ died for our sins, He placed the highest possible value on human life; because Christ rose again, He makes possible the re-creation of all who believe in Him and gives to them new spiritual life, that renewal of the "real me."

As we focus on Scripture's teaching that God considers each human life equally important, we must recognize that, however flawed in implementation or in the execution of their goals, all movements seeking to support and protect the personhood of the individual are (even unconsciously) based on the truths that all human beings are made in the image of God and all persons have equal value in His sight. *Therefore traditionalists cannot inveigh against all social changes that spring from secular sources without first asking if these changes are in accord with the scriptural truth of the worth and value of the individual.* For example, regardless of denominational background, I would hope that no reader would deny the validity of universal suffrage or the importance of programs to end racial discrimination.

Christians must remember that all truth is God's truth. There exists no "secular truth" that is lesser than "scriptural truth," although of course not every true thing or every true idea will have the same weight or impact on our lives. An abstruse mathematical equation will not have the same bearing on our daily activities as the truth that God is love. However, everything or every idea that is true is equally true, and because God's Word calls us to be "doers of the truth," we must recognize truth wherever it appears.

No responsible person will condemn secular movements across the board, but must recognize the many good changes that have come from these sources, because, whenever there is truth in society, it is God's truth. Thus we must acknowledge whatever is true and just and right in the women's movement, just as the Christian community (albeit belatedly in some instances) has had to face the truth, justice, and rightness of the black liberation movement. Truth is truth wherever we find it.

In a sense we can also say that truth is sex blind. When we consider the academic world, we can clearly see this and that the notion that certain subjects have a gender is a cultural phenomenon. In reality the worth of these subjects is independent of the student's sex, although to become meaningful in a given life situation, a person of one sex or the other has to utilize them.

For example, when I was in high school, the home-economics courses were only available to girls, although today it is perfectly acceptable for men to cook, and men who aspire to be chefs vie for the privilege of attending a school like the Culinary Institute of America. Stenographic courses were considered feminine, yet today any man who wants to use a computer efficiently must have excellent typing skills. When I was in college, English literature was considered to be an appropriate major for girls, while mathematics or physics was more suitable for boys. Today we freely acknowledge that to label these subjects masculine or feminine places artificial restrictions on their study and usage.

Truth in the arts or truth in the sciences exists completely apart from the gender of the persons studying or using these disciplines. Two plus two equals four, regardless of whether a male or a female adds the numbers. One of the greatest mathematical minds of the twentieth century was that of Emmy Noether, a founder of modern algebra. A woman like Jane Bryant Quinn is a nationally respected financial analyst, and physicist Sally Ride is eminently well-qualified to be an astronaut.

Turning to theology, we see that our creation in the image of

God is also a sex-blind truth. Men are not "more" in the image of God than women. Because God created both sexes in His image, both have equal worth and value. There was no sexual discrimination in creation; rather, in Genesis 2 we see a completeness and a mutuality in the male-female relationship. When Adam said of Eve, "This is . . . flesh of my flesh," the words connoted oneness, not separation, and certainly not inequality, lesser gifts, or limited role. Genesis 1:26–30 tells us that as originally created, both men and women were to rule the earth mutually and cooperatively.

God's Prospectus goes on to tell us that His re-creation of all who accept His offer of new life is also an equal and therefore a sex-blind truth. As we saw in chapter 4, both men and women are equally redeemed. The Bible does not present one set of redemptive truths for males and another set for females. This principle of equal, sex-blind truth lies at the core of Paul's teaching that both men and women are called to be ambassadors for Christ.

The True Record of the False Idea

"But," someone asks, "what about the sexual disharmony we find in the Bible? What about the accounts of male domination and the acts of sexual violence? Aren't these records evidence of the inequality of the sexes?"

Yes, Scripture portrays human discord and discrimination—not because these things are God's ideal, but because Scripture is so accurate. The Bible is a true record, and that means it truthfully records sinful actions and false philosophies.

After recording the Fall, humanity's loss of innocence, the Bible presents an accurate picture of an imperfect world, a world marred by sin. As the poet Gerard Manley Hopkins put it, we live in a "bent world," and we see that bentness in the accounts of murder, theft, tyranny, torture, rape, pillage, extortion, broken treaties, betrayed friends, lies, cheating, greed, laziness, selfishness, immorality, idolatry, blasphemy, and apostasy. In its accurate reporting the biblical list of human failings goes on and on and includes the record of tension and competition between the sexes. God's Word portrays both sexes equally in all their frailty: Both men and women are described fairly, "warts and all."

An understanding of the fact that the Bible contains the paradox of the true record of the false idea is vital to proper understanding of Scripture. The person who interprets the Bible with wooden literalism might say, "The Bible is inspired by God; therefore every word is true." However, that can mislead us, because where the Bible presents a true record of something false, we need to distinguish the falsehood. So we might better phrase our affirmation of the trustworthiness of Scripture: "The Bible presents truth and is always reliable in its presentation as it gives us an accurate record both of God's revelation and of humanity's imperfect fallen condition." Part of the true record of the results of the Fall is to set forth an accurate record of a lie, a true recording of a falsehood, an accurate depiction of a false human philosophy. Yes, the Bible is completely trustworthy, but that does not mean everything in the Bible reflects God's will.

One of the tremendous by-products of the paradox of the true record of the false idea is that we can contrast humanity's reasoning and humanity's answers to our crucial questions with God's perfect answers. When we do that, we can see how much better God's answers are than ours.

For example, the purpose of God's Prospectus is to present His plan of redemption, a plan for imperfect humanity to return to fellowship with a perfect God. In Matthew 27:1–5 we can contrast God's loving offer of redemption with the callous indifference of the worldly leaders to Judas's remorse. This tragic passage tells us that after Judas betrayed Christ, he returned and in agony of spirit wanted to give back the blood money. Listen to the false answer the legalists gave Judas: "What is that to us? That's your responsibility." In effect they said, "You go deal with your own problems—save yourself." That false human reasoning contrasts starkly with the tremendous first words Jesus spoke from the cross, those great words of intercession for His enemies: "Father, forgive them, for they do not know what they are doing" (Luke 23:34). When I compare the world's answer to my need for renewal to Jesus' actual words of forgiveness, there is no doubt in my mind as to which answer I need to erase the "if onlys" in my life.

This illustration is obvious, but in many places the paradox of the true record of the false idea does not come across so directly. For example, the speeches of Job and his friends truthfully record those persons' ideas, but we must use great care to discern God's truth as we read and study the Book of Job. The same is true of the Book of Ecclesiastes. One of the points of both these Bible books is that a human traditional teaching does not always have "the last word" on a subject.

As we go on to examine the scriptural record of human relationships, we become aware that tensions and disharmony between the sexes fall into the category of the true record of the false idea. Therefore we need to understand the important point that while the Bible accurately sets forth sexual discord and discrimination, it does not approve, condone, or ever make those sins God's norm. We must not confuse factual accounts of relationships between fallen individuals in both Old and New Testament culture with God's Word for men and women for all time. First Corinthians 10:11 tells us: "These things happened to them as examples and were written down as warnings for us. . . ." Thus the Bible uses tragic accounts of rape or sexual abuse as bad examples, but they do not indicate that rape is ever a permissible course of action or that sexual abuse is justifiable.

We cannot take any one verse indiscriminately and out of context and use it as a proof text for a pet idea, nor can we pull random passages about human relationships and assume that these passages automatically give us God's view of human relationships. We must subject all passages to the light of redemptive truth, and where the Bible records fallen humanity's view, we must see it as such.

Patriarchalism: True or False?

One of the areas of keenest debate today is patriarchalism. Anthropologists, sociologists, psychologists, and also historians are busy researching ancient and modern cultures to try to determine if male domination and female subordination are traits inherent in human nature.[1] Christians also hotly debate the issue. As more and more women seek equality in the church as well as in society it is important to explore what Scripture has to say about patriarchalism.

First, a definition. Webster's New Collegiate Dictionary defines *patriarchy* as "social organization marked by the supremacy of the father in the clan or family, the legal dependence of the wife and children, and the reckoning of descent and inheritance in the male line."[2] The secondary definition is "a society organized according to principles of patriarchy."

Now there is no question but that Scripture records a patriarchal society. The crucial questions are: *Is patriarchy a true record of a false idea? Is male domination a true idea, or is it simply an account of fallen man's discrimination against a fellow human being, woman?*

Interestingly we have no problem answering that set of questions in the negative if we substitute racism or classism for sexism. Scripture uses many illustrations of subject peoples or classes, yet it is readily apparent to us today that neither the Christian community nor society at large should emulate these examples or perpetuate the discriminatory practices behind them. We find the Egyptian oppression of the Hebrews and Haman's cruel actions aimed at mass extermination of the Jews abhorrent. Not only the Roman institution of slavery, but also rigid Roman class structure is abhorrent. No sincere Christian today would allow the biblical factual accounts of racism or classism to be held up as God's norm. They are false human philosophies and we recognize them as such. There is no scriptural basis for anti-Semitism, discrimination against blacks, or an institutionalized class structure like the caste system.

Yet many persons seem to accept patriarchy, with its resulting discrimination against women, as a "given," without asking our crucial question: *Does the fact that Scripture records patriarchy teach that it is* God's *plan for society?*

At this point in our discussion we must bring something out in the open: Any espousal of patriarchy is an espousal of male domination. The very definition of patriarchy presents a male-dominated and male-controlled society and therefore means a philosophy of male supremacy.

Today justice issues like discrimination and human rights very much concern us, and we shrink from baldly pronouncing the words *male supremacy*. Yet if one group is forever subordinate, then the group to which it is forever subordinate must be forever dominant. No matter how many teaspoons of sugar one puts in the medicine of patriarchy to try to make it go down easily, it remains bitter medicine for the people who see it for what it is—male supremacy. We may find contemporary evidence of this in the plight of women in openly patriarchal societies, such as some Islamic countries.[3]

One popular argument for the validity of patriarchy runs that it has existed from the beginning of time. So has murder, but we understand that murder is not God's will. And what about slavery? Slavery has been known since the most ancient eras, yet today we decry using people as chattel, and we denounce slave labor.[4] The Book of Philemon has been called an emancipation proclamation, not because Paul wrote, "Slavery is wrong and slaves should be freed," but because of the principles he set forth. The spiritual equality of Philemon and Onesimus, which originated in their common humanity, made them fellow children of God, and no family member has the right to enslave another—nor would want to.

We could go on to mention polygamy, adultery, cruelty, and torture, but who today will try to argue that these ancient abuses are God-ordained societal norms?

We come back to the paradox of the true record of the false idea and recognize that simply because the Bible tells of an idea or an action does not mean God approves of it. Since Jesus asked His disciples to look beyond tradition, it is indeed crucial to discover whether subordination of women is a biblical concept or a product of human custom and tradition. For someone to support patriarchalism as God's norm by saying "We've always heard it expounded this way," is not a convincing argument. We cannot evade our crucial question: Is patriarchy a true record of a false idea, a true record of false actions?

What steps will we take to find our answers? First, we can compare patriarchy to clear truth. Second, we can look at the fruits of patriarchy as found in the scriptural case histories of real people in real-life situations.

Patriarchy and Human Rights

The Bible not only presents humanity as a unique life form, the only one created in the image of God, it also gives guidelines for the treatment of this life form. Because each human individual has worth and value in God's sight, each individual also has certain human rights—rights necessary for the preservation and enhancement of God's gift of life.

The Bible also presents a God of justice and righteousness, who is concerned about violations of human rights. God did not create the world and thereafter ignore it. Remember our condominium illustration: Our divine Sponsor remains involved with His creation, and His Prospectus inveighs against unjust and inhumane actions.

The Old Testament gives specific commands about fair dealing, which indicate that God not only expects us in all situations to treat our fellow human beings impartially and compassionately, but also that He expects us to give special care to those who cannot help themselves. Most significantly the Bible language repeatedly emphasizes the need to preserve the rights of the widow, the orphan, the alien, the poor, the oppressed. God is deeply concerned with justice issues and expects His people to be so also. In Micah 6:8 God gives a tremendous challenge to all human beings: ". . . What does the Lord require of you? To act justly and to love mercy and to walk humbly with your God."

We see the divine ideal of justice embodied in the life of Jesus. In His own announcement of His mission, by quoting Isaiah 61:1, 2 He indicated that the Good News of the Gospel incorporates the ending of injustice and oppression. Although the Incarnate Christ lived in a society dominated by discrimination, He Himself showed none. He said, "Whoever comes to me I will never drive away." He treated all persons with respect, regardless of their race, sex, age, physical condition, political preference, economic status, or educational level. By touching the untouchables and interacting with "the least of these," He told all persons, "You have worth and value, and there is rejoicing in heaven when you as an individual become part of My family" (Luke 15:1–10).

Jesus overturned the social and cultural mores of His day and challenged legalistic traditions. He came to meet human need, whether that need was embodied in a hated tax collector, an alien Roman, a mixed-race Samaritan woman, an outcast leper, a homemaker, a lawyer, or a dying girl. He mingled with "sinners" and accepted the homage of a prostitute. He offered His deepest teaching to the scholars of His day, to fishermen, and to women, thereby treating both the educated and the uneducated as intelligent and responsible human beings. He did not seek to curry favor with the powerful and influential, but constantly called to account those in authority with words like Matthew 23:23: ". . . You have neglected the more important matters of the law—justice, mercy and faithfulness."

When questioned about the most important commandment, Jesus joined belief with compassion and reinforced this with the parable of the Good Samaritan (Luke 10:25–37), to teach us that the criterion for social concern is human need and not some discriminatory practice. Such was Christ's view of the sanctity of human life that He did not discriminate in picking His disciples, but offered himself freely to the "worst case" when He said: "Have I not chosen you, the Twelve? Yet one of you is a devil!" (John 6:70).

The record of the early church in Acts continues to underscore the fact that God does not discriminate against any person. Old Testament and New Testament join in telling us that God is no respecter of persons, with the supreme revelation of this truth in the Person and work of Jesus Christ and in His new commandment that we love others as He had loved us. Therefore no person who desires to be obedient to Scripture can engage in or condone discriminatory acts.

In seeking to apply these truths, we must always use the scriptural affirmation of the worth and value of the individual human being as the standard by which we evaluate whether or not acts are discriminatory. Discrimination means treating oneself or one's group as entitled to certain human rights and other persons as unentitled or not entitled to the same degree and basing this unequal treatment on the proposition that the unentitled have different characteristics or belong to a different group from the entitled. Usually the societally empowered practice discrimination against the societally unempowered.

Institutionalized Discrimination

In the light of these biblical principles, we can see patriarchy for the false idea that it is: Patriarchy is institutionalized discrimination. Its own definition condemns it: "Patriarchy is a social organization marked by the supremacy of the father in the clan or family; a society founded on that principle."

Patriarchal groups do not affirm the worth and dignity of women to the extent that they do that of men and therefore go against the biblical truth of the equal value of both sexes. In rigid patriarchalism a desire for sons as heirs not only puts a premium on a particular woman's childbearing ability, it also quickly leads to the acceptability of many wives and concubines. In addition, marriage becomes an economic and/or political tool—a means to gain additional wealth and property and/or a means to cement political alliances. Women cease to be partners in a "one flesh" union and become possessions, treated as objects to be picked up or discarded at the will of the men who control their destinies. Perpetuating the family or the clan or even the institution of patriarchy itself becomes the overriding consideration, not justice—and certainly not the human rights of women.

Patriarchalism also encourages sexual irresponsibility in men. By rejecting women as equal partners and by fostering in men a sense of entitlement to the dominant position, the system shortcircuits any accompanying sense of sexual accountability men might have. A person is not accountable to an inferior.

A further vice is that patriarchalism encourages women to become manipulative. Because persons in such a system perceive women's worth and value in their relationships to men (either as wives or mothers of sons), women must resort to "feminine wiles" at best—and deceit or treachery at worst—not only to achieve a sense of personhood, but all too often for their very survival.

Patriarchy fosters continuing discrimination against women, denies their human rights, and encourages less than truthful conduct in both men and women. These conclusions become evident as we look at the fruits of patriarchalism as found in actual scriptural case histories.

The Early Patriarchs

Someone has rightly called the Old Testament the dark continent of Scripture, because the average Christian so infrequently explores it, but we go there to find the beginning of patriarchy. Irrespective of when it was actually written down, the Book of Job probably contains some of the earliest material in the Bible. In Job 31:7–11 we read words that indicate a low view of the value of women:

> If my steps have turned from the path,
>> if my heart has been led by my eyes,
>> or if my hands have been defiled,
> then may others eat what I have sown,
>> and may my crops be uprooted.
> If my heart has been enticed by a woman,
>> or if I have lurked by my neighbor's door,
> then may my wife grind another man's grain,
>> and may other men sleep with her.

As Job defended his integrity it did not occur to him that he devalued another human being, his wife, by treating her as an object on a par with agricultural produce.

Abraham's expedient use of Sarah as a bargaining chip also reflects this attitude. In Genesis 12:11–13 we read: "As he was about to enter Egypt, he said to his wife Sarai, 'I know what a beautiful woman you are. When the Egyptians see you, they will say, "This is his wife." Then they will kill me but will let you live. Say you are my sister, so that I will be treated well for your sake and my life will be spared because of you.' "

For Abraham the worst scenario was "they will kill me but let you live." That Sarah might become "fair game" (as indeed happened when she was taken into pharaoh's palace) did not figure in Abraham's reasoning. The fact that Abraham repeated this cowardly and expedient deception in Genesis 20:1–17, and that his son Isaac copied it with his wife in Genesis 26:1–11, shows the expendability of women. Neither Abraham nor Isaac showed sacrificial love; they did not show true caring for the other person. In all these instances the Lord had to intervene to save Sarah and Rebecca.

When Abraham and Sarah ran ahead of God's timetable, in Genesis 16, and used Hagar merely as a device to get an heir, they both encouraged the use of a woman as an object. In Genesis 25:6 we are told that Abraham had more sons by his concubines (multiple common-law wives). In his use of women, Abraham's example was not a good one. Nor is Sarah blameless: She succumbed to the patriarchal system with her manipulative use of Hagar and lived to regret it.

Isaac's son Jacob continued to use women as objects. On his wedding night Jacob did not notice that he had married Leah instead of Rachel. The Jerusalem Bible coyly notes "The bride was veiled until the wedding night," but this is hardly an adequate explanation for Jacob's inability to distinguish Leah from Rachel when they were alone together and had sexual relations. Most probably Jacob was drunk, but what a sad way to begin marriage with your supposed beloved. After marrying Rachel also, Jacob willingly had sexual intercourse with both wives and with their maidservants as the two sisters sought to gain self-worth through procreation. The overriding compulsion was the desire for male heirs; women were simply means to this end. Jacob's callous use of women not only undermined the biblical concept of marriage as "one flesh," but also had an impact on successive generations. With such a stage set by the earliest and most revered patriarchs, no wonder the Old Testament period is a sad record of mistreatment of women, with the women themselves all too often cooperating in their own oppression, in order to gain recognition or survival. (*See also* Genesis 19:30–38; 29:31–30:24; 38:1–26.)

Samson the Womanizer

Ironically, most people think of Samson in connection with his betrayal by Delilah, with Delilah as the villainess in the piece. Yet a careful reading of Samson's story shows that he brought about his own disgrace, and the circumstances leading up to his fall reveal a ghastly set of events from a woman's point of view.

In direct disobedience of the Mosaic law, which prohibited intermarriage with non-Jews, Samson demanded a certain Philistine woman as his wife (Judges 14:1, 2). She was manipulated by her family and then abandoned by Samson at their wedding feast. When Samson's anger cooled, he returned, only to hear his erstwhile father-in-law tell him: "I was so sure you thoroughly hated her . . . that I gave her to your friend. Isn't her younger sister more attractive? Take her instead" (Judges 15:2). In his wounded pride, Samson destroyed the Philistines' property, and they in turn burned Samson's wife and her father to death.

In all of this where was there any genuine concern for that woman? How little her father thought of her and her sister. How poorly Samson used her and how casually she went in and out of his life, simply a transient object of sexual desire. (Further evidence of Samson's sexual intemperance is Judges 16:1–3, which records Samson being ambushed after openly spending the night with a prostitute.)

The more familiar part of the story is found later in Judges 16. Again disobeying Mosaic law, Samson picked another Philistine woman, Delilah. One wonders what sort of loyalty he expected from her, for she surely would have known of his treatment of her people and also of his abandonment of his first wife! Like that wife, Delilah also resorted to manipulation to try to protect herself. Women were reduced to that in a society where ". . . everyone did as he saw fit" (Judges 17:6).

What factual reporting—but of such false ideas and actions! What image of God did Samson the womanizer project to the Philistines? Who would ever want to emulate Samson's personal life?

The Treatment of "Everywoman"

Judges 17–21 records the depths of social depravity in possibly Scripture's clearest depiction of the flaws of a patriarchal society. These chapters truly show the ultimate in degradation: idolatry, pride, selfishness, moral perversion, and insensitivity to human life. Chapters 19–21 also reveal the most awful violations of the human rights of a nameless woman. This frank reporting removes any vestige of courtesy or civility from patriarchy, revealing male dominance at its very worst.

One key to the passage is that phrase ". . . everyone did as he saw fit," which occurs in Judges 17:6 and finally in 21:25, bracketing the story. Another key to this section is patriarchal preoccupation with clan, because that idea also brackets the story. Chapters 17 and 18 put clan loyalty over pure worship of God; chapter 21 puts clan survival over human rights. Thus preservation of both the male-dominated group (clan) and the individual male became the guide for action.

The dreadful "centerpiece" of these appalling chapters is found in chapter 19, where we learn that a Levite, his servant, and his concubine spent the night in Gibeah. Verses 22–26 read:

> While they were enjoying themselves, some of the wicked men of the city surrounded the house. Pounding on the door, they shouted to the old man who owned the house, "Bring out the man who came to your house so we can have sex with him."
>
> The owner of the house went outside and said to them, "No, my friends, don't be so vile. Since this man is my guest, don't do this disgraceful thing. Look, here is my virgin daughter, and his concubine. I will bring them out to you now, and you can use them and do to them whatever you wish. But to this man, don't do such a disgraceful thing."
>
> But the men would not listen to him. So the man took his concubine and sent her outside to them, and they raped her and abused her throughout the night, and at dawn they let her go. At daybreak the woman went back to the house where her master was staying, fell down at the door and lay there until daylight.

As a result of this horrible treatment the concubine died.

What a perversion of the custom of hospitality! Not only was this custom considered more important than the rights of women, but it is questionable whether it even applied to women. Following a pattern already set in Genesis 19:8, there was no attempt to defend the house and its occupants. No, the men who cast out the nameless concubine thought: *Here is an object that will satisfy the lust of the attackers. Abuse of a man must be prevented, but gang rape of a woman is inconsequential, because she is only a bargaining chip.* Remember that the host in this story would willingly have thrown away his virgin daughter, not only denying her human rights but also doing so in direct violation of Leviticus 19:29: "Do not degrade your daughter by making her a prostitute. . . ." Such a father would have no compunction in sacrificing another man's woman (read "possession") on the altar of male pride and perversion. The heartless offer of the nameless daughter and the bestial abuse of the nameless concubine represent the potential treatment of every woman in a society that places man's lust over God's law.

How does the ghastly case history conclude? Intertribal warfare, decimation of the tribe of Benjamin (to which the men of Gibeah belonged), and the kidnapping of women to provide new wives to keep that clan viable. Judges 21:17 gives the reasoning of the elders of Israel in encouraging such kidnapping: "The Benjaminite survivors must have heirs," they said, "so that a tribe of Israel will not be wiped out." The rights of every woman were subordinated to the preservation of the clan, although in Matthew 18:8, 9 Jesus said that it would be better to be maimed by cutting off a member of the body that offends than to go to perdition whole.

Yes, when patriarchy ruled, every man did as he saw fit—and treated every woman as he wished.

David and Solomon

By the time of the kings of Israel, the idea of women as objects devoid of human rights had become firmly entrenched. Many persons are familiar with the story of David and Goliath or with David the Psalmist, but for our discussion we must look at David's encounters with the women in his life.

When King Saul was jealous of David's increasing popularity and sought ways to undermine David, 1 Samuel 18:20, 21 tells us, "Saul's daughter Michal was in love with David, and when they told Saul about it, he was pleased. 'I will give her to him,' he thought, 'so that she may be a snare to him. . . .' " Although Michal probably knew she was a political pawn, she nevertheless bravely aided David's escape from Saul's wrath (1 Samuel 19:11–17). Saul disciplined her by marrying her off to a man called Paltiel (1 Samuel 25:44).

During his period of wandering to escape from Saul, David married both Ahinoam and Abigail, then added four more wives. Obviously these six women were primarily important for their childbearing abilities, because we can wryly note that in 2 Samuel 3:2–5 their identity is secondary to that of their sons. Very possibly David passed on to a new wife as soon as the prior wife delivered a boy.

Now Michal reentered the picture. To solidify his position as king over all Israel, David needed to quell Saul's former followers. Saul's general Abner offered to hand over the dissidents to David, and in 2 Samuel 3:13 we read: "Good," said David, "I will make an agreement with you. But I demand one thing of you: Do not come into my presence unless you bring Michal daughter of Saul when you come to see me."

Michal had been married to David only briefly, but now she was forcibly returned to him in a power play to salve his wounded ego and to help consolidate his political position. Obviously he did not truly care for Michal personally, because he had been so easily solaced with his six other wives. The account continues: "So Ish-Bosheth gave orders and had her taken away from her husband Paltiel son of Laish. Her husband, however, went with her, weeping behind her all the way to Bahurim. Then Abner said to him, 'Go back home!' So he went back." I have always had a soft spot for Paltiel, the only man who cared for Michal and who was loyal and open enough to show it.

What of Michal? We can imagine her dismay, not only at being wrenched from a loving husband (to whom she had now been married for about ten years) but upon finding herself back in David's household, part of an evergrowing list of wives and concubines (2 Samuel 5:13–16). Is it any wonder that when Michal saw David exuberantly dancing in a religious celebration, she despised him? Was she thinking: *You, who care so much for your God, don't care much for human beings He made.* Is it so surprising that she greeted him with sarcasm when he returned? There was no relationship between these two, no "one flesh" union. The story of this unfortunate woman's life concludes on a bitter note. Michal's punishment for her lack of respect for the man who treated her as a possession was to be deprived of the ancient world's female status symbol: "And Michal daughter of Saul had no children to the day of her death."

But there is more to come in David's case history: He was not content with his many wives and concubines. Second Samuel

11:2–27 tells us David's roving eye lit on the beautiful Bathsheba, another tragic cipher. Well aware that she was Uriah's wife, David now had *her* brought to him. We cannot give David's sordid and eventually murderous actions any overlay of romantic love. He simply lusted after a pretty woman, forcibly seized her, and when she became pregnant, cold-bloodedly arranged for the murder of her husband. When male supremacy ruled, might made right and people were throwaways. God disciplined David, but not Bathsheba, although of course she, too, suffered when their first child died.

An overlooked woman in David's life is his daughter Tamar. When David found out that her half-brother Amnon had raped her, David reacted with anger, but nothing more. Such was the moral climate of the court that Amnon received no punishment, although under Mosaic law he should have been "cut off from the people" (*see* Leviticus 18:29) for his crime. However, preserving his firstborn son seemed more important to David than the defilement of his daughter. In these dark days another son, Absalom, took matters into his own hands and dispatched Amnon himself.

During the ensuing civil war between David and Absalom, women again became pawns. Second Samuel 16:20–22 tells us: "Absalom said to Ahithophel, 'Give us your advice. What should we do?' Ahithophel answered, 'Lie with your father's concubines whom he left to take care of the palace. Then all Israel will hear that you have made yourself a stench in your father's nostrils, and the hands of everyone with you will be strengthened.' So they pitched a tent for Absalom on the roof, and he lay with his father's concubines in the sight of all Israel." There was no pretense of affection or even attraction in this cruel treatment, only a physical act—an animal act, the strong preying on the weak. Second Samuel 20:3 records the conclusion of this unsavory incident: "When David returned to his palace in Jerusalem, he took the ten concubines he had left to take care of the palace and put them in a house under guard. He provided for them, but did not lie with them. They were kept in confinement till the day of their death, living as widows." What gross injustice: A life sentence of house arrest for the crime of being powerless women in a patriarchal society!

TRUE OR FALSE?

The last woman in David's life was Abishag the Shunammite (1 Kings 1:1–4). Who she was and why she was chosen we do not know, except for the usual requirement that she was "beautiful," but she probably didn't volunteer for the job of warming the aged king. After David's death, she, too, became a political tool, valuable as his former attendant, and thus the focus of a power struggle between Adonijah and Solomon (1 Kings 2:13–25).

None of these women in David's life were valued for themselves alone. While they may have gratified a passing fancy and, in the case of Abigail, been briefly admired, David's possession of multiple wives and concubines sent the unspoken message that women were objects. Therefore we need not feel surprise that his son Solomon used his first marriage as an occasion to cement a political alliance with the Egyptian pharaoh (1 Kings 3:1). However, David's many wives and concubines were minor peccadillos compared with Solomon's extravagant immorality.

Solomon had 700 wives of royal birth and 300 concubines, a total of 1,000 women to gratify his sexual appetite. First Kings 11:1, 2 records the facts: "King Solomon, however, loved many foreign women besides Pharaoh's daughter—Moabites, Ammonites, Edomites, Sidonians and Hittites. They were from nations about which the Lord had told the Israelites, 'You must not intermarry with them, because they will surely turn your hearts after their gods.' Nevertheless, Solomon held fast to them in love." Such was the moral slippage that we have no mention of any prophet, priest, or royal advisor brave enough to remonstrate with Solomon about his actions. Not surprisingly, the sad account concludes: "As Solomon grew old, his wives turned his heart after other gods . . ." (v. 4). However, although I have heard sermons blaming Solomon's depravity and idolatry on these women and their "feminine wiles," Solomon himself was responsible for his apostasy. The text indicates that he knew these women were from forbidden countries, and he also would have known the admonition of Deuteronomy 17:16, 17: "The king . . . must not take many wives, or his heart will be led astray. . . ."

Solomon's great wisdom must not blind us to his great fail-

95

ings. Yes, the bulk of the Book of Proverbs is attributed to Solomon, but these sections are filled with injunctions against immorality, which Solomon himself did not heed. He is a practical example of the person who says one thing but does another. His power, power inherent in a male supremist society, corrupted him. As absolute monarch he had the power to collect these women; when he copied the polygyny and polytheism of other nations, he alone had responsibility for those acts. In the area of male-female relationships, we cannot admire Solomon's case history.

Courageous Women

The true record of male domination as a false idea also occurs in the Book of Esther. In this account King Xerxes wronged Queen Vashti, her successor, Esther, and a host of nameless virgins.

Chapter 1 tells us that the Persian king deposed Vashti after she refused to parade before a drunken orgy. King Xerxes' advisors concluded that he must discipline Vashti in order to send the message that women could never disobey their husbands. A royal edict was sent ". . . proclaiming in each people's tongue that every man should be ruler over his own household" (Esther 1:22).

Now I have heard expositions of the Book of Esther laud this edict, but we need to think carefully about the incident. Is it sensible for Christians seriously to suggest that men today should simply dump a wife who refuses to display herself to a stag party? Would any Christian seriously suggest that Vashti's defense of her personhood and her modesty could undermine traditional family values? Hardly. Rather than teaching subordination of women, this bizarre tale simply reinforces the conclusion that male domination is a false idea, especially since the account informs us that in Xerxes' next move he ordered hundreds of beautiful girls brought to him so that on the basis of a "one-night stand" he could pick the next queen.

I have also heard people speak of Xerxes' choice of Esther for queen as Esther's reward for her obediently subordinate conduct. Reward? No, degradation—degradation for a devout Jewish virgin to be conscripted by this cynical and depraved monarch.[5] Xerxes had slept with one girl after another, examining their bodies and then discarding them. He picked them up and threw them down like a man pawing over items in a bazaar, occasionally calling one back for a second look (Esther 2:14). How could *anyone* think that a godly Jewish woman would consider union with such a man a reward? That Esther allowed God to use her in this difficult situation and that she behaved honorably and courageously is a tribute to her godliness, but we cannot believe that she herself considered being queen a "reward." Rather the way she conducted herself with dignity in front of this patriarchal autocrat and acted fearlessly to save her people measures her inner strength. What a contrast to those cowardly actions of Abraham and Isaac, who placed self-preservation over the preservation of their wives.

Rotten Fruit

Looking at the outcome, or fruits, of a philosophy is one measure of estimating its truthfulness. A true proposition will have integrity, and a true system will yield just and fair actions. A system that consistently produces injustice and fear cannot be true.

Even such a brief overview as our consideration of the words and deeds found in these Old Testament case histories shows that the fruits of patriarchy condemn it. Patriarchy fosters discrimination and abuses of human rights. The treatment of women in a patriarchal society contradicts the biblical principle of the worth and value of all human life and falls short of God's ideal that all persons be treated justly and fairly.

Inherent in patriarchy is male retention of power, so that one group of human beings feels permanently entitled to control the destiny of another group. Patriarchy encourages in men, the empowered, a sense of entitlement to a position of dominance over women, the unempowered. The spoken or unspoken rationale of "I am ordained to be over you" results in paternalistic programs that have effectively infantilized women. The subsequent male conclusion "it is right that we be over you, because you obviously cannot manage your own affairs" fails to see that by its very continuing existence, the patriarchal system hinders the unempowered group, women, from maturing into responsible adults. If father *always* knows best, why bother to grow up?

A further vice is that, in addition to remaining immature, women also become manipulative. In order to maintain a sense of personhood, not to mention often merely trying to survive, the unempowered group has had to resort to manipulation and duplicity.

Patriarchalism also undermines the biblical ideal of the "one flesh" union in marriage. A system built on a dominant/subordinate concept of male-female roles in life will by its very nature discourage any deep relationship between man and wife. Truly meaningful relationships only occur where both parties participate equally in all aspects of their relationship. Mature relationships can only develop when the personhood of both parties is of equal worth.

Compare David's friendship with Jonathan to his liaisons with women. David had severe difficulty forming a marriage relationship, but he formed the deepest friendship with Jonathan, a friendship so deep that on Jonathan's death David mourned:

> I grieve for you, Jonathan my brother;
>   you were very dear to me.
> Your love for me was wonderful,
>   more wonderful than that of women.
>   2 Samuel 1:26

Such a close friendship was possible because David and Jonathan were equals, whereas David's use of his wives and concubines indicates his inability to accept their equal personhood. Such inability to consider women equal partners all too easily leads men to consider the women in their power to be in the same category as material possessions. Remember Job's equation of his wife with agricultural produce. In Numbers 31:32–35, women prisoners of war were listed after animals as "plunder remaining from the spoils." (*See also* Deuteronomy 20:14; 21:10–14; Judges 5:30.) The parallel accounts of Joshua

15:16, 17 and Judges 1:12 also tell us that Caleb's daughter was parcelled out as a sort of prize of war.

There is another reason why patriarchalism undermines the biblical concept of the "one flesh" union. When society does not accept women as equal partners, then women's worth is primarily related to biological functions. It follows that such a system reduces women to utilitarian devices that have the primary usefulness of satisfying men's sexual needs and producing male heirs; then the number of women a man has will become a matter of personal desire, and polygyny will be commonplace. We have just discussed some ancient examples of this; in recent times the point was graphically illustrated by the late Shah of Iran as he publicly discarded one wife after another in his quest for a son.

In addition, a dominant/subordinate patriarchal practice will discourage any thought of mutual accountability. There is no thought in patriarchy that men are responsible to women and thus no way to call men to account for any casual or even abusive treatment of women. In a rigidly patriarchal society women simply become a form of currency whose market value rises and falls depending on the needs and perceptions of men, forcing the women themselves to measure their self-worth in terms of their attractiveness to men, their economic value (dowry or earning power), their possible political importance in terms of family alliances, but most of all in terms of their childbearing ability (especially of sons). The whole system devastates the self-esteem of the single woman, the poor woman, the childless wife, and the mother of daughters; it marginalizes and depersonalizes half the human race.

Possibly worst of all, with the highest premium being placed on male heirs, patriarchy has its own built-in mechanism to perpetuate the system—but what a system! At its crudest, as Judges 19–22 proved, patriarchalism spawned the most inhumane actions, because of its overriding compulsion: "Anything to keep the clan name going." Yet the Bible makes it clear that there is no merit in a clan or a family name. As John 1:12, 13 tell us, our standing before God is not by will of man, by blood inheritance, or by some priestly pronouncement, but by God's will we become children of God when we believe in Him.

Yes, the Mosaic law did lift women above the contemporary cultural usage and gave women some measure of protection within the harsh framework of Old Testament society and ancient world mores. But in many ways the Mosaic law made concessions to culture, and therefore while it did offer some relief to unempowered women (as it did for slaves), it was not a perfectly satisfactory solution to women's needs. Significantly, when Jesus commented on one aspect of Mosaic law, divorce, he said: "Moses permitted you to divorce your wives because your hearts were hard" (Matthew 19:8). And the New Testament clearly teaches that only when there is a complete change of heart will all persons—of whatever sex, race, or social class—be treated as individuals created in the image of God and therefore of equal worth and value, whose human rights must be protected in all situations.

"Texts of Terror"?

Although today most of us do not live in a rigidly patriarchal society, we must still come to terms with our patriarchal past and how it influences contemporary thinking. As Americans have done in the civil rights movement, we must face the injustices of the past and must begin to apply the lessons of the past to the future.

In so doing, it will be obvious that not all men are tyrannical oppressors of women! Except for the deliberate wife beater, very few American men arise each day with the thought *Now I will act as a male supremist,* anymore than before the days of desegregation most whites arose with the thought *Now we will oppress blacks.* But to the extent that whites failed to recognize that they were part of a system of discrimination, they perpetuated that system, and in the same way those who ignore the abuses of patriarchy will help perpetuate its injustices.

The Bible tells us in 1 Corinthians 10:11 that God inspired the many scriptural case histories to be written down for our instruction. We must closely study these lessons from the past, to see which are the good examples to follow and which are the bad examples to avoid. We must be alert to discern the difference between truth and falsehood in the human history recorded in the Bible. This is why it has been important to look at case histories relevant to our questions about the validity of patriarchalism.

Theologian Phyllis Trible has written a book entitled *Texts of Terror*, a critical examination of four Bible women: Hagar, Tamar, "Everywoman" in Judges 19, and Jephthah's daughter. One does not have to agree with Professor Trible's every conclusion to be sympathetic to her title. These frightening texts are indeed "tales of terror, with women as victims."[6]

However, these texts only remain texts of terror today if we uphold patriarchy as God's ideal for human society. They only remain texts of terror for women if we consider male supremacy the norm for human social structure. But if we see patriarchy for what it is, institutionalized discrimination, and if we reject male supremacy for what it is, a false human philosophy, then these do not continue as texts of terror, but rather become bad examples of terrible behavior that is to be despised and of terrible attitudes that need to be redeemed. Certainly we did not find any godly characteristics in the insensitivity to women found in those specific words and actions of Job, Abraham, Isaac, and Jacob, or in the lustful actions of Samson, David, and Solomon. There was nothing admirable in the murder of "Everywoman" or in the depravity of Xerxes.

Clearly these are all bad examples. In none of these case histories did the men respect the human rights of women. In none of these accounts did the men involved heed God's call to moral purity. In addition, these men also overlooked one salient feature of God's law: the redemptive theme. We may fairly question whether or not Xerxes would have had any knowledge of God's law, but the Israelites had no such excuse for their actions. All through the Old Testament God reminded His people in words to this effect: "You were slaves, and I brought you out of the land of Egypt. You were oppressed, and I freed you. Now *you* act compassionately toward those around you and toward anyone in your power" (*see* Deuteronomy 24:17–22). The Old Testament contains the promise of God as Redeemer, and in recognition of this promise, Israel was to live for Him. His people were not to copy the oppressive and discriminatory practices of the surrounding nations, but to witness to God's redemptive power by acting fairly and compassionately.

It is another measure of the trustworthiness of Scripture that it faithfully records Israel's failure to live as God commanded. We have the true record of Israel's false actions when, in her prosperity, she sought the gods and the value systems of pagan societies. Therefore we do have that sad record of a male-dominated society that failed to act redemptively towards women, although the Bible also records God's repeated commands that His people protect the rights of the widow, the alien, and the orphan.

Recognizing that patriarchalism falls in the category of the true record of the false idea will give us a fresh perspective on our social history. We will see that the misogynist acts set forth in the Bible are only texts of terror if we consider them worthy examples to be copied, or proclaim them as representing innate behavioral patterns and unchangeable character traits. But when we hold up these texts to the light of redemptive truth, as found in our theme passage, 2 Corinthians 5:14–21, we can celebrate the fact that God's ideal is "The old has gone, the new has come!" (v. 17).

The Business We're In

Years ago my minister and I discussed how best to deal with a Sunday-school teacher who refused to take time to prepare the lesson adequately. I can recall saying with a sigh, "Well, I guess you just can't change human nature." My minister smiled and said, "I thought that was the business we're in." I have never forgotten that pointed reminder. Yes, God is indeed in the business of complete change and of total renewal—that conversion experience of the new birth—and we Christians are to be His ambassadors in proclaiming this good news.

We must never forget that God has the power to offer re-creation and that He does not need to offer makeshift solutions to our problems. Therefore as we contemplate the social system of patriarchalism, the real question is not how best to patch up a system that legitimizes discrimination and abuses of human rights, but whether we should patch it up at all.

It has been said that in time of war truth is the first casualty. The Bible tells us a spiritual warfare exists between good and evil, and quite obviously evil will use any trick possible to hide

God's truth. In this warfare the truth of the mutuality and complementarity of men and women has been a tragic casualty.

In one of its tricks evil has gotten people to buy the line "You can't change human nature."

This trick has led some people to believe that because patriarchy is so entrenched, we cannot change it and therefore must patch it up. These persons think that at best we can try to "Christianize" patriarchy by urging men to exercise their power over women in a virtuous and not a tyrannical way (in a kind of loving domination). They fail to see that we Christians are not in the business of making a false philosophy palatable. *Why would we even want to try to patch up a flawed system, when God's Word offers us all re-creation, a fresh start, a new beginning?*

As we saw at the beginning of our discussion of patriarchy, all manner of sinful acts have existed since the beginning of time, but we do not seek to "Christianize" sin! We do not say of someone who tends to lie or cheat or steal, "That's how it is," but we *do* say, "By God's grace that person can become a new creature in Christ Jesus." Remember Paul's words in 2 Corinthians 5:20, 21: ". . . We implore you on Christ's behalf: Be reconciled to God. God made him who had no sin to be sin for us, so that in him we might become the righteousness of God." With that offer, who would ever want to accept a patch-up job? So to those who say, "You can't change the system," I offer the rebuttal, "That is just what Jesus Christ came to do!"

Oswald Chambers made this relevant comment about our human nature: "The Holy Spirit does not patch up our natural virtues, for the simple reason that no natural virtue can come anywhere near Jesus Christ's demands. God does not build up our natural virtues and transfigure them. He totally recreates us on the inside."[7] Yes, nothing less than complete renewal will do to end all those "if onlys" of patriarchalism—and it begins with asking God's forgiveness for our participation in past injustices. David finally began to understand this truth, as we know from his heartfelt cry in Psalm 51.

As we explored in chapter 4, Christ gives those who are His new creatures a new nature with new virtues, and the Christlike virtues of humility and self-sacrifice are inimical to any notion of retaining domination either in theory or in practice.

Therefore the truly "Christianized" person (a new creature in Christ Jesus) will shrink from any philosophy that says, "One person must always be dominant" and will see that to "Christianize" such a philosophy is to end it.

The nameless woman whose murder was recorded in Judges 19 is "Everywoman" because she represents the potential fate of every woman in a society where might makes right, where male domination controls the fate of women. Remember that worst-case scenario for Abraham and Isaac: "They will kill me, but let you live." By the time of Judges 19, the thinking of men in a patriarchal society had degenerated into, "It is all right to kill you, if they let me live."

Contrast that false human reasoning with Jesus' words in John 15:13: "Greater love has no one than this, that one lay down his life for his friends." Listen to Paul's insight in Romans 5:7, 8: "Very rarely will anyone die for a righteous man, though for a good man someone might possibly dare to die. But God demonstrates his own love for us in this: While we were yet sinners, Christ died for us." This was in fulfillment of Jesus' own words in John 10:11: "I am the good shepherd. The good shepherd lays down his life for the sheep." With such an example, is there any question but that we need a Christ-like society instead of a patriarchal society?

Our overview of patriarchy has exposed it as an unjust and sinful system. The scriptural record of a patriarchal society is an example of the paradox of the true record of the false idea. Clearly the Bible itself chronicles male supremacy as a bad example, and the case histories of male domination of women are all variations of that false notion, "This is how men are."

In contrast, the Good News of the Gospel is that men need not remain this way, and women need not suffer such treatment. As God's ambassadors we Christians must proclaim this good news and offer hope to those who think, *You can't change human nature.* The wonder of the Gospel message is: "No, *you* can't change human nature, but *God* can, and that's the business He's in!"

Chapter Six

Equal Opportunity

Again I brought my conclusions to my traditionalist friends, and again I found they wanted to qualify my findings. This time they told me: "Yes, rigid patriarchalism is probably wrong and does have those evils you discovered. However, in this life we still have to conform to certain roles related to our gender. Therefore—as a practical matter—patriarchy *is* still in effect throughout our earthly life. It may not be God's ideal, but like the poor, it is always with us."

Instead of answering my questions, these continual qualifications of Scripture only increased my questions. Second Corinthians 5:17 had clearly taught that when I became a Christian I was a new creation, and certainly I had no desire to be anything else. In addition, I knew Paul had specifically warned in Romans 8:8 that those who act according to the dictates of the flesh cannot please God. This did not mean that there was anything wrong or demeaning about the human body, but simply that Christians have a new focus for their lives. Yet my traditionalist friends told me my flesh somehow qualified my status as a new creation and that in some fashion my human gender restricted my opportunities to serve God.

When I listened more closely, I realized that this notion of gender restriction was also used as a rationale for limiting women's secular career options and volunteer opportunities. Even people who deplored the abuses of patriarchalism told me, "Women should keep to their proper place, because women have a certain role in life." Others declared, "Affirming traditional family values means that women's proper role is to be family oriented." Their conclusion? "Women's place is in the home."

This concentration on a "female" role paid very little attention to the fact that *both* men and women are called first and foremost as ambassadors for Christ. Second Corinthians 5:14–21 teaches that all Christians have the primary task of witnessing. Yes, this spiritual diplomacy can be done in a variety of ways and in many different places. We will not all take part in "full-time Christian service," and we will not all have the same call as to type of service, but we *are* all to be God's ambassadors in spreading His message of reconciliation.

Inescapably sex does not qualify the biblical call to be part of God's diplomatic corps. However, my traditionalist friends gave only lip service to women as God's ambassadors. All too often they thought a woman could only do Christian service when it fitted into her "female" role, rather than considering Christian service her first priority when she contemplated what career opportunity God wanted her to pursue. This was entirely foreign to my own upbringing and contrary to my parents' example of putting the cause of Christ above all else.

Those who taught gender-based role playing chiefly emphasized that all women are called to be homemakers, catering lifelong to the needs of husbands and devoting every energy to child care. Much of what I heard sounded very insensitive to childless women as well as extremely damaging to the self-worth of single women.

The traditional teaching also effectively squashed the aspirations of many women whose circumstances enabled them to contemplate independent careers, including full-time Christian service. Those who taught a rigid role for women usually disregarded factors like marital status, income level, and age of children (which would reflect their need for parental protection and guidance). They also ignored the fact that (as with men) not all women are led to marry, and that even if women do marry, not all women feel drawn to homemaking or child-related occupations. Much more serious, these people denied that any truly Christian woman could ever have a genuine call to a career not related either to homemaking or child rearing.

They concluded that *all* women, married or single, should be limited to a certain role, simply because of their gender.

I discovered at least one very puzzling aspect to this increasing emphasis on role playing. This teaching defined only the female role by a biological function (childbearing), and that definition held whether or not a particular woman performed that function. Strangely enough, despite the fact that no children could exist without fathers, no one gave a parallel definition of a male role. No, only women were considered restricted by the issue of a biological act in which *both* sexes must participate, and those who held this view taught that this restriction carried over to all areas of female life and even affected the status of the celibate single woman. For women only, I was told, biology was destiny.

More Conflicting Signals

People who subscribed to this overall role restriction told me, "You should stick to women's work." Within the context of rigid role playing, women's work was obviously to be in the home, involving things like cooking, serving meals, cleaning, sewing, and child care. But as I pondered this I became aware of another definite double standard.

No one seemed to expect men to do women's work, but women's work was *only* women's work when it was unpaid. Yes, in a home situation women were to do all the cleaning, washing and ironing, cooking, sewing, and child care, but this women's work became magically redefined whenever men wished to engage in it in a salaried situation outside the home. Perfectly legitimately, men could do custodial or janitorial work (cleaning). Men could run a laundry (washing and ironing). Men could be bakers or chefs (cooking). Men could be waiters (serve meals), and men could be tailors or employed in the fashion industry (sew). Men could even pursue careers in interior decorating! Men could certainly become teachers of even the youngest children (child care). What was rigidly considered women's work in the home became fair game for anyone out in the paid job market, because as soon as it became paid work women's work miraculously changed into suitable male work.

I found another discrepancy with regard to the worth of

women's time as against men's time. Because men's work was paid work, their time was considered more valuable. I can recall instances in places like a crowded doctor's office or a supermarket checkout line, where men were taken ahead of women because, as the person in charge put it to the men, "I know your time is money." Although traditionalists told women that their work was honorable and meaningful, such actions demeaned it.

I began to notice other discrepancies between theory and practice. Similar to the manner in which I was being used in my local church situation, in everyday life, when someone needs women's skills, the notion of role playing could be conveniently forgotten. All the church secretaries were women, many being mothers who needed the extra salary, and most of the clerical staff of parachurch organizations were women. Then I realized that many families who subscribed to the teaching that women should not work outside the home themselves encouraged other women to do just that: They hired housekeepers or maids who, like those church secretaries, were usually mothers who needed the extra paycheck.

In addition, most people felt grateful for women schoolteachers and never gave a thought to their family situations. And how many of us have ever asked if nurses are wives and mothers? No, we all just feel terribly grateful that these women are there to help us.

As I considered the issue of role playing, I began to recognize that traditionalists had set up the converse of the straw woman. Just as feminism had become a convenient target upon which to fix blame for social ills, some touted rigid role playing as a convenient solution for those ills.

However, even a casual student of history knows that roles are not rigid. In our own American past we have admired the pioneer woman who helped build and defend her home, and we have valued the strength and courage of the homesteader's wife who struggled with him to tame the prairie. These women were equal partners and not subservient, weak, or sheltered. Someone my age can also put the more recent past into perspective on this issue of rigid roles. I can remember when, with the full blessing of both church and society, during World War

II women were encouraged to leave the home and join the military services or work in defense plants. "Rosie the Riveter" became a familiar figure during those war years.

Yes, in the upheavals of the 1960s and early 1970s, I could understand the temptation to set up the straw woman as the deadly virus carrying our social ills, and I could see that it *was* tempting to set up rigid role playing as the antidote. But in proposing role playing as the panacea for social hurts, again traditionalists sent conflicting signals.

Upon close examination it became evident that role playing was a selective and often a middle- or upper-class phenomenon in families whose economic circumstances permitted their womenfolk the luxury of staying home at any age and stage of life. Obviously acceptance of the game of role playing had a great deal to do with affluence and cultural conditioning and could be conveniently overlooked as it suited the convenience of those willing to play the game.

So my exploration of male-female relationships was becoming a more and more complex task. Clearly my next step must be to return to Scripture, to see if God's Prospectus would give me guidance on this question of roles. How had God used women? What did the Bible teach about role playing?

Old Testament Case Histories

While Scripture records many fascinating accounts of women's lives, within the confines of this chapter we must focus on women who acted in what we can term nontraditional or nonpatriarchal ways. We will look at various Bible women who stepped out of any "female" role and who were commended by the text for their actions.

During the Exodus period, Moses' sister Miriam was his companion in leadership. She was a prophetess (Exodus 15:20) and, along with their brother Aaron, a visible figure at the head of the Hebrew people. Yes, she had a severe moment of failure (shared with Aaron), but we do not write him off for joining her in this or for his abysmal sin in the incident of the golden calf (Exodus 32). Nor do we write off Moses for his murder of an Egyptian (Exodus 2) or his impatient anger (Numbers 20). Therefore we cannot write off Miriam because of the incident in

Numbers 12. We must listen to the words of Micah 6:4, which give God's estimate of the high office He called on Miriam to fill: "I sent Moses to lead you, and also Aaron and Miriam." The plain fact is that God sent Miriam to be a coleader of the children of Israel.[1]

Prominent in Old Testament history was the judge Deborah. Judges 4:4 tells us, "Deborah, a prophetess, the wife of Lappidoth, was leading Israel at that time." Judges 5:7 also tells us that she was a mother. This competent woman was not only a spiritual and governmental leader, but she was the inspiration behind Barak's military expedition against Sisera. She delivered the word of the Lord to Barak and then, at his express request, accompanied him on the campaign. The text of Judges 4 and 5 shows that she was the dominant figure of this era, but more interesting, the account is given in a very straightforward manner. The Scripture includes no disclaimer to the effect that the Lord could not find any man willing to lead Israel, so He was forced to settle for a woman. Clearly not only was Deborah a multitalented individual whose qualities made her readily accepted by the people as their prophet and judge, she also used her gifts of encouragement and exhortation as she helped Barak move out to obey God's command.

Also mentioned in this context is Jael, a courageous woman who killed the enemy leader Sisera, in fulfillment of Deborah's prophecy that Barak's initial timidity would cost him personal renown in the coming victory. Deborah spoke these words in Judges 4:9: ". . . Because of the way you are going about this, the honor will not be yours, for the Lord will hand Sisera over to a woman."

Some people today say that women should not go to war. However, in times of extreme crisis all hands are needed, as they were on the American frontier and in World War II. Women have also participated in underground resistance movements, following the lead of Rahab (Joshua 2, 6), who was commended for her actions (see Hebrews 11:31). Ironically, those today who say women have no place in battle can overlook the tremendous contributions of army nurses, who have courageously risked their lives in combat zones as they have patched up the mess of life that men had made. From Bible times on women have had nontraditional roles in wartime and the courage of women is both commendable and undeniable.

First Samuel 25 records another woman approved by the text for acting in a nontraditional way. The account tells us that David, offended by the insensitivity of a man called Nabal, had decided to mount a murderous attack in retaliation for Nabal's discourtesy and ingratitude. However, God used Nabal's wife, Abigail, to bring David the strength of character to say no to force and to put the matter in proper perspective. In the eyes of the world, Abigail was "just a woman," with no army at her command, but she was a wise woman. She had the inner strength to perceive that David had embarked on a disastrous course of action and to rebuke him for it. Her tactful but force-ful words of wisdom prevented him from a rash act. What David (and most men!) undoubtedly considered strength—the use of physical force—was his weakness (as his story showed later on when he forced Bathsheba to submit to him and then used force to eliminate her husband, Uriah). Although David had many exemplary characteristics, his impetuous use of force was a terrible flaw. But on the particular day recorded in 1 Samuel 25, God used someone whom the world would con-sider weak, the woman Abigail, to bring strength of character to David. That day the greater power lay in Abigail's wise counsel, as David acknowledged when he said to her, "Praise be to the Lord, the God of Israel, who has sent you today to meet me. May you be blessed for your good judgment and for keeping me from bloodshed . . ." (32, 33). Would that there had been many more such wise counselors to help David throughout his stormy life!

The prophetess Huldah figures in the parallel accounts of 2 Kings 22 and 2 Chronicles 34. During the reign of King Josiah, the book of the law was rediscovered and read to the king. His command was: "Go and inquire of the Lord for me and for the people and for all Judah about what is written in this book that had been found . . ." (2 Kings 22:13). Both 2 Kings and 2 Chronicles tell us, again in the most straightforward way, that the king's emissaries went directly to Huldah and that God spoke His message through her. His emissaries relayed that message back to King Josiah, who then acted on Huldah's words and called the nation to return to obedience to God's Word.

Nothing could be plainer than that Huldah gave out the authoritative word of the Lord and that the king and his counselors understood this clearly. Huldah was a contemporary of Jeremiah and Zephaniah. We cannot ignore the fact that in His wisdom God chose the woman Huldah as His spokesperson in presenting His Word to Josiah and that her words helped institute a period of national revival. We also cannot ignore the fact that through Huldah's message Scripture was used in a canonical way, that is, as a measuring rod for religious practice and life views. Again note that the king's agent, Hilkiah, did not say, "I guess we'll have to go to Huldah, because Jeremiah is out of town," or "We know Huldah is a prophetess, but we couldn't possibly go to a woman for an authoritative word from the Lord," or worse yet (but I have personally heard this statement in a congregational meeting), "Going to any man at all would be better than going to a woman." No, five emissaries went openly to the theological college where Huldah lived. They did not sneak off. They went openly, confident of hearing the Lord's word, and they openly took that word back to Josiah.[2]

In addition, note that from the very beginning of human history God intervened to interrupt the operation of patriarchy's offspring, primogeniture. God chose Abel and Seth over their elder brother, Cain. God chose Jacob over Esau, Ephraim over Manasseh, David over his elder brothers, Solomon over Adonijah. Of the twelve tribes, the tribe of Judah was chosen for the human ancestry of the Messiah, not the tribes stemming from the older brothers Reuben, Simeon, or Levi. Then both Numbers 36 and Joshua 17:1–5 tell us that in the absence of direct male heirs, God gave the family inheritance to the daughters of Zelophehad rather than skipping over them in favor of some male relative. Job 42:13–15 records Job's daughters as inheriting their father's fortune equally with their brothers. These incidents show that God chooses whom He will and that women were considered competent to administer the family inheritance.

However, the Old Testament gives an even stronger example of the capability of women. Proverbs 31:10–31 presents the virtues of a wife who is considered to be a paradigm of womanhood. These verses are often read on Mother's Day or to women's groups, and most churchgoers have some familiarity with the passage. However, while in the case of Scripture familiarity does not breed contempt, it *can* lead to blindness. Proverbs 31:10–31 has become so familiar to some of us that we have lost its impact. Here is a woman who was the backbone of the family! The verses do not exactly make clear what her husband did at the city gates (perhaps he was a city councilor) but one thing *is* obvious: While he sat at those gates this woman was a busy, busy person. She supported her family in a variety of ways that many today would consider nontraditional and even unfeminine. She ran the family business, deployed servants, bought and sold real estate, marketed goods, and administered a vast household. She played a number of roles in life: artisan, businesswoman, educator, advisor, devotional leader, and parent. As I studied Proverbs 31:10–31, I discovered that this ideal, strong, and multitalented woman would have been a very hard act to follow. The title of Patricia Gundry's book about her tells it all: *The Complete Woman*!

The variety of even these few Old Testament case histories is very thought provoking. Miriam was a single woman leader. Rahab was a resistance leader, and Jael was a "good soldier." Deborah was a spiritual and judicial leader as well as a wife and mother. Huldah was a prophetess and wife, while the woman in Proverbs 31 was a multicareer wife and mother. Like Abigail, these women were not locked into some sort of artificial role playing nor were they limited by the men in their lives. They lived in a patriarchal society, but they operated in nonpatriarchal ways, and the Bible text commends them for their actions.

The Example of Jesus

Many churchgoers have become so familiar with the four Gospels that the full import of Christ's treatment of women has eluded them. Our Lord overturned patriarchal conventions by encouraging women to listen to His teachings and to ask Him questions. He accepted their help, and He praised their acts of devotion. Although His contemporaries found female physical problems distasteful, He did not withdraw from a hemorrhaging woman, but reached out to heal her. He took time to restore life to a young girl at a time when female life was a throwaway. He associated with women from all walks of life and from countries other than His own. He commended their belief in God, even to the point of lauding a Syro-Phoenician woman for greater faith than He had seen among the Jews. In short, He accepted the full personhood of women and treated them as equal with men.

Women were present in the crowds who followed Jesus and listened to His public teachings. Jesus never said to them, "Go back home—when I have taught the men, they will return and explain what I said." In His illustrations He used both men and women as examples, making it plain that both were account-able for their response to His message.

Jesus' inner circle also included women. Customarily we think of the word *disciples* as meaning the Twelve and overlook the fact that much of the time Jesus' entourage was a larger group—one that included many woman (Luke 8:1–3). In a cul-ture that did not consider women educable, Jesus encouraged women to take part in what some people have called His "trav-eling seminary."[3]

These women remained loyal to Jesus to the very end. Four women (but only one man) stood at the base of the cross during the crucifixion, while many other women watched from a little farther off. At what may have been great personal risk, devoted women helped prepare His body for burial. Then, on what we know as Easter Sunday, women were first at the tomb, and the resurrected Jesus appeared first to Mary Magdalene and other women, entrusting them with the Good News that He was alive! Although we have no way of knowing exactly who was in the Upper Room in John 20, very possibly there were women present when Jesus gave the care of the church into the hands of His disciples. Most probably women were present at the ascension, and women, too, received the Great Commission.

Throughout His earthly ministry, Christ not only encour-aged individual women to speak with Him, but He taught them some of Christianity's central truths. In John 4 Jesus had a most intricate theological conversation with a Samaritan woman. He first taught her that He was the water of life, and in the ensuing discussion He spoke those profound words: "God is spirit, and his worshipers must worship in spirit and in truth." When this outcast woman indicated her awareness of the coming of the Messiah, Jesus announced to her: "I who speak to you am he." This was an amazing conversation to have with a person society considered beneath contempt, and John recorded the surprise of the disciples when they came upon the scene.

Later on Jesus taught another woman truths that are among the most beloved for all Christians. Martha first heard that wonderful message of comfort: "I am the resurrection and the life. . . . Whoever lives and believes in me will never die . . ." (John 11:25, 26). How the Christian community has treasured these words, words first entrusted to a woman.

A study of all the women with whom Jesus spoke reveals much, but for our present discussion the most significant encounter is recorded in Luke 10:38–42:

> As Jesus and his disciples were on their way, he came to a village where a woman named Martha opened her home to him. She had a sister called Mary, who sat at the Lord's feet listening to what he said. But Martha was distracted by all the preparations that had to be made. She came to him and asked, "Lord, don't you care that my sister has left me to do the work by myself? Tell her to help me!"
>
> "Martha, Martha," the Lord answered, "you are worried and upset about many things, but only one thing is needed. Mary has chosen what is better, and it will not be taken away from her."

The message of this familiar story was and is revolutionary, because it taught that women should prefer studying theology over a preoccupation with domestic chores. That is *not* to say that Scripture demeans homemaking! On the contrary, by choosing to be born into a real human family and to grow up in an ordinary human home, Jesus conferred worth and value on the home and on the legitimate pursuits necessary to preserve the home and provide for the family. But in this crucial passage in Luke, Jesus taught that following Him must take first priority and that learning about Him is the most important occupation in life.

115

If Jesus had wished to teach that studying theology is a male prerogative, this would have been the ideal place to do that. If Jesus had wished to teach role restrictions, this would have been the ideal opportunity. He could have said, "Yes, Mary, you must go and help Martha. It is inappropriate for you to be here with the men. I will teach your brother Lazarus, and then he will pass on to you what you need to know." Yet Jesus did exactly the opposite! Therefore many women today find it puzzling that traditionalists say women cannot study theology but must stick to "women's work."

Traditionalists have turned the lesson of Luke 10:38–42 upside down by a perplexing overemphasis on Martha's housework and an incomprehensible underemphasis on Mary's "better" role. Women who want to sit at Jesus' feet today have every right to say: "We want to copy the example of Mary of Bethany." Christians cannot evade the clear lessons of these scriptural case histories. When we put the lesson of Luke 10:38–42 together with the lesson of Proverbs 31:10–31, we find a strong, nontraditional, biblical picture of womanhood.

So as we consider what Scripture itself tells us about the very crucial question of role playing, we see that traditional viewpoints or accepted gender restrictions did not bind Jesus. In His encounters with women He taught that women as well as men have worth and value; both men and women are precious in His sight. Although in His contemporary culture women were believed uneducable and unreliable as witnesses, Jesus took particular care to show that He considered them teachable and trustworthy witnesses. He taught that gender forms no barrier to learning about God and that sex is no barrier to proclaiming His Good News. Christ's interaction with women as equal persons liberates us from confining women to any stereotyped role.

Women in the Early Church

There was no role playing at Pentecost. Both men and women gathered in the Upper Room, again with no thought that women should stay at home, waiting for men to bring them word of what happened next. In fulfillment of Joel 2:28–32, the Holy Spirit was given to both men and women, and both men and women prophesied and spoke in tongues. Acts 2:42–47 describes one new community of believers that emphasized unity and commonality of belief. Those outside this new community also considered men and women equal disciples of Christ; the first persecutions of Christians made no distinction between the sexes (Acts 8:3; 9:2; 22:4).

Although the Apostle Paul is frequently characterized as an "enemy" of women, we need to recognize that the Bible reveals no such thing. In fact, a study of his interaction with women indicates just the opposite, as Don Williams's book, *The Apostle Paul and Women in the Church,* presents convincingly. For example, Acts 16:11–15 tells us that Paul preached his first message in Macedonia to women. Although the text indicates that Paul had probably expected to find a mixed congregation, apparently only women had gathered at the usual place of prayer. Paul did not say, "I must go in search of some men, because my message is too important to waste on females." No, in the most natural way the account shows Paul unashamedly preaching his first European sermon to women and then going to stay with the first European convert, a Philippian businesswoman named Lydia.

Paul's good friend Priscilla, an esteemed teacher in the early church, is particularly interesting for our discussion, because in the Bible text her name usually precedes that of her husband (although some translators arbitrarily reverse the Bible order). This couple had opened their home to Paul (Acts 18:3), and Paul obviously knew of their joint teaching ministry. In Romans 16:3, 4 Paul described them as his fellow workers and expressed his appreciation for their courage in risking their lives for him. Priscilla took an active part in ministry, and Paul commended her actions. She and Aquila must have been among his closest friends, because they were in the group receiving his last farewell (2 Timothy 4:19).

The name of Phoebe, another of his companions in ministry, stands out in connection with Paul (Romans 16:1, 2). Although many translators discriminate in rendering these verses into English, in the original Greek language the words Paul used to describe Phoebe indicate her high position in the early church. The verses tell us that Phoebe was a *diakonos,* using the exact same word translated "deacon" or "minister" elsewhere. The word here is not a feminine one, so even the translation "deaconess" is inaccurate. Paul's words also tell us that Phoebe was a *prostatis*, a strong word indicating some sort of position of overseeing. Dr. Aida Besançon Spencer's book, *Beyond the Curse*, gives convincing evidence that only an English translator's bias will term Phoebe a "servant" and "helper" rather than a "minister" and "leader."[4]

In many other places in Paul's letters we can see that he valued women as strong, capable co-workers.[5] Now, if what these women were doing was in the slightest way questionable, or if they acted in ways never to be copied, surely Paul would have mentioned this. Even a superficial reading of Paul's epistles shows he was not shy about criticizing people, nor was he reticent in pointing out error. But the names of many women appear naturally in the text. Paul's appreciation of their numerous gifts and his enthusiastic endorsement of their positions and their actions is obvious.

A last woman who should be mentioned in connection with leadership is the woman to whom John's second letter was written. This "chosen lady" was a close friend of the Apostle, and she led a church fellowship, which met in her home. (Acts 12:12 shows this was not unusual; the text suggests that "Mary the mother of John, also called Mark" was another such woman.) Although some people have considered this letter allegorical, its warm personal tone makes it much more likely that "the elect lady" was a responsible woman to whom John could entrust his crucial message about the dangers of heresy.[6] (One wonders if commentators would have tried to spiritualize this letter if John had addressed it to "the elect gentleman"!)

"Exceptions" or "Approved by God"?

The many Bible case histories show us that God uses whom He will and that in line with 1 Corinthians 12:4–11, God gives appropriate equipping gifts to whom He will.[7] He simply and creatively uses those who in His eyes are the best people for the task at hand and who yield themselves to be used by Him.

Those of us who wish to base our world view on God's Word must take these case histories seriously. When we do, we see that His creative choosing activity included many women and that He used women in a variety of nontraditional ways. Yes, the Bible shows a remarkable concern for women and an exaltation of women, especially considering the contemporary cultures of the Bible times.

Yet when I took these findings back to my traditionalist friends, they told me: "We agree that those women did do those things and they were approved by the text, but they are exceptions." At first their answer seemed plausible, but when I reflected upon it I realized that once again I faced the problem of people who wanted it "both ways." They wanted to retain their notion that women have a restricted "female" role, but they also wanted to be scriptural. So when confronted with the undeniable fact that the Bible itself tells us God used women in ways that transcend the notion of role playing, they had to answer, "These are exceptions."

Other people pointed out that I could not produce dozens and dozens of Bible case histories showing women used in nontraditional, nonpatriarchal, and nonsubordinate situations, and I had to agree. Although there are many more examples than the few used in this chapter, indeed these "exceptions" are comparatively few in proportion to the whole Bible. However, concentrating on the *number* of these "exceptions" will cause us to miss the basic point: If there is only *one* "exception"—only *one* Deborah or Huldah or Phoebe—that single case undermines the traditionalist position. If there is *only* one woman commended by the text for a nontraditional action, we must draw the conclusion that the Bible does not teach role playing. You see, while we may accept the proverb, "The exception proves the rule," the exception does not prove truth. Truth cannot have exceptions. Truth must be unchangeable.

The Bible had always been my highest authority, but now it became my source of strength as I continued my dialogue with people who tried to tell me that women must always play a "female" role. How could rigid role playing be a timeless truth when Scripture itself not only gave "exceptions" to such a concept, but also commended the women for their actions? I had to keep confronting my friends with the fact that truth cannot have exceptions.

A Hidden Fear

Yet my traditionalist friends still clung to their notion of "exceptions"—and strangely enough added present-day "exceptions." Even in very conservative Christian circles, traditionalists allowed certain women to step out of the rigid "female" role; these women not only spoke and taught publicly, but they did so nationwide.

The traditionalists' rationale was that these modern "exceptions" operated under the "umbrella" of a male presence (such as a minister or a conference convener), but to me this appeared to be specious reasoning, because as a practical matter these women *were* engaged in public speaking and leadership activities. I did not question the sincerity of these women or their supporters, but I did question the logic that permitted them to speak from pulpits and run parachurch organizations. They certainly were not being silent in the churches or anywhere else! Although it contradicted their message, they stepped outside the narrow role inside which they urged other women to remain.

When I confronted my friends with this double standard (one set of rules for the "exceptions" and another set of rules for "ordinary women"), they still refused to abandon their position. I needed to know why, so I pressed them for their reason. I finally discovered this: They recognized that women were gifted both in Bible times and today, but they felt reluctant to acknowledge this fact openly, for fear that allowing *all* women to use their gifts freely would lead to confusion of the sexes. They had an underlying fear that if too many women stepped outside the "female" role, wholesale "role reversal" and social chaos would result.

As the discussion opened up, traditionalists told me that they primarily objected to biblical feminism because they feared gender would become obscured and marriage and the family undermined. They saw maintaining a hierarchical structure in society as the only way to avoid this chaos. Since these people also subscribed to a patriarchal view of relationships, it was important to them that men retain precedence in that hierarchy. Therefore they aimed much of their effort at trying to prove that *all* women are by nature (physically, psychologically, and spiritually) unsuited to positions of leadership—in spite of our everyday experience to the contrary.

A Sad Comparison

As an American, I realized that role playing had obvious parallels to past treatment of minorities in this country. Someone my age remembers when all too many whites gave lip service to the Fourteenth Amendment, but in practice often took a paternalistic approach to the question of racial equality. These people considered blacks incapable of responsible citizenship, in spite of "exceptions" like Booker T. Washington and George Washington Carver. So they promoted racial segregation as a device to maintain what they considered the ideal social order: a hierarchy with whites in the empowered positions. Therefore someone my age also remembers the mockery "separate but equal" made of blacks' opportunities to exercise their civil rights and participate as full citizens.

Although it pains me to write this, when I was young I frequently heard (even from the pulpit) that God had ordained blacks to a subordinate role because of the curse of Noah (Genesis 9:25), a curse ratified by racial separation enforced at Babel. But then I also heard my father agonize over that, saw him open to rethinking, and then saw him move out to uphold racial equality at a time when most conservative religious groups did not generally affirm it.

As I pondered the parallels involved, I concluded that denying women equal civil and spiritual rights was a form of segregation. The same rationale some Americans used to try to support racial segregation was being used to support subordination of women. Now they couched the rationale this way: "Women are full children of God, but in this life women are functionally subordinate to men." I was given intricate explanations of why *equal* meant "subordinate," and *subordinate* meant "equal," but to me the rationale remained a theological version of George Orwell's "Newspeak."

As had been the case with the reasoning behind racial segregation, the traditionalists' explanation of the "female" role made a mockery of women's full humanity, women's full citizenship, and women's full redemption. Under all the clever verbiage, "spiritually equal but functionally subordinate" was still an endorsement of male domination. Yes, just as most racial segregationists had been reluctant to use the term "white supremacy," so traditionalists were loath to use the term "male supremacy." But as I had discovered in my examination of patriarchy, if one group is always subordinate, then the other group *must* always be dominant.

The sugar coating on "spiritually equal but functionally subordinate" was that women would experience full equality in heaven. However, all the fancy language proclaiming "pie in the sky by and by" could not obscure the fact that, as a practical matter, women (as blacks had been) were relegated to second-class citizenship in church and society. People who used this fancy language failed to see the injustice in teaching that men could enjoy the full benefits of their earthly citizenship and their heavenly standing right now, while women would have to wait until the Hereafter.

More Rotten Fruit

However, injustice can breed ugly emotions, and in racism and sexism it has bred pride and envy and frustration. Like patriarchy, rigid role playing had its own rotten fruit that condemned it.

We can follow the parallel tracks of racism and sexism in seeing that the dominant groups became prideful, while the subordinate groups became envious and frustrated. For racism: Behind the irrational fear of miscegenation was white racial pride, a pride in skin color that said: *Whites are so superior to blacks that blacks must want to be white like us. They will try to intermarry to achieve this goal.* For sexism: Behind the irrational fear of women stepping out of their "proper sphere" is a pride in masculinity that thinks: *Males are superior and therefore women must naturally want to be male, like us. If we give them equal opportunity, they will try to defeminize themselves and act in mannish ways.*

In response to the restrictions that false racist and sexist pride have imposed, minorities and women have reacted by envying the empowered group's options and by feeling frustrated that these options are not available to the unempowered. These emotions have sometimes erupted angrily into antisocial actions and even violence.

As we evaluate this rotten fruit of racist and sexist role playing, we must recognize that the societally subordinate groups do not envy skin color or gender attributes but the *opportunities* that the white skin color or the male gender have historically opened up. For example, in the days of racial segregation, what was behind most instances of blacks trying to "pass" as whites? The same motivation as that of Jews who tried to pass as Gentiles during the Holocaust: Not a desire to be white or Aryan, but a desire to survive.

Yet how hard it has been for some whites to think of blacks as equal human beings, and how hard some men still find it to accept the equal personhood of women. A minister in whose church both men and women serve communion hosted a white South African pastor, and after the service the visitor made this condescending comment: "You know, it was interesting to receive communion from a woman. Why, I've even received the elements from a black man."

People seduced, however subtly, by pride in their societal position do not seem able to look beneath the physical "houses" to the common "real me" that is the unifying factor for all humanity. These people do not see that in the "real me" all human beings yearn to enjoy the same human rights and the same spiritual opportunities. But they need not fear that making these rights and opportunities available to all persons, regardless of race or sex, will cause social chaos. Women do not want to be men any more than blacks or other racial minorities want to be white or Gentile. Rather, women and racial minorities *do* want equal opportunity to fulfill their potential as fellow human beings created in the image of God.

Unity, Not Confusion

People who fear that equality of women in ministry, marriage, and society will lead to confusion of the sexes need assurance that biblical feminists do *not* seek to destroy gender distinctions, any more than various races wish to destroy their heritages. Biblical feminists do *not* want human beings to try to act in a unisex fashion. What a dull world that would be! On the contrary, we believe the Bible celebrates the sexes, and we rejoice in sexual diversity as a gift from God. It is sexual discrimination, which comes from fallen humanity, which we wish to reject, just as surely as we reject racial discrimination.

Rather than causing confusion, the principle of equal opportunity complements the New Testament teaching that Christians must live and serve together. In Ephesians 2:19–22 and 1 Peter 2:5, the Apostles use the metaphor of believers as living stones being built into God's temple. These passages explain that we are being built together into one edifice, not kept apart as separate exhibits of salvation operating in separate spheres. In the truest sense, no believer is a single! Therefore, our new cooperation—serving together, being built together—not only ends loneliness but also contradicts any artificial division between "men's work" and "women's work."

Christians are part of a new unity that the Bible describes in a variety of ways: "God's people," "the church," "the Body," "God's family," "God's temple," "a royal priesthood." Whatever the metaphor, it emphasizes oneness and expresses closeness, mutuality, complementarity, helping one another, supporting one another in service. Nowhere does that rich Bible imagery—"ambassadors for Christ," "living stones," parts of the body, family or church members—teach gender restriction. The many word pictures for our new unity all emphasize the inclusiveness of God's call to mission.

Yes, as we explored in chapter 4, all Christians are born again the same way, and all Christians become new creatures in Christ Jesus. We are all equally redeemed and offered equal opportunity to serve in God's diplomatic corps.

However, the fact that in our "real me" we are all now the same spiritual material does not mean that we become the equivalent of clones. Unity of material does not mean uniformity or that individuals or groups have identical function. Unity of material does not imply loss of sexual identity, what some people have termed sexual suicide. I repeat: The Bible celebrates the sexes—just look at the Song of Solomon!

But the Bible does not lock the sexes into rigid vocational roles or into rigid spheres of ministry, any more than it locks races into roles or careers. As Oswald Chambers wrote, "The relation to life ordained by Jesus Christ does not unsex men and women but enables them to be holy men and women."[8] As we have seen, an unbiased look at Bible characters shows a remarkable freedom of those holy men and women to use their gifts creatively in a wide variety of roles.

Our Creative Employer

We must never forget that God is Creator and that His coopting use of us, His creatures, is infinitely creative. We must take to heart the words of Isaiah 45:9–11, words that occur in the middle of a great passage celebrating God as Lord of all creation:

Woe to him who quarrels with his Maker,
to him who is but a potsherd among the potsherds on the ground.
Does the clay say to the potter,
  "What are you making?"
Does your work say,
  "He has no hands?"
Woe to him who says to his father,
  "What have you begotten?"
or to his mother,
  "What have you brought to birth?"
"This is what the Lord says—
  the Holy One of Israel, and its Maker:
Concerning things to come,
  do you question me about my children,
  or give me orders about the work of my hands?"

Those who say it is "against nature" for women to step outside a narrow "female" role must remember that Creator God can call whom He wills and gift whom He wills. If a woman has obvious leadership, administrative, and teaching abilities, then these are gifts from God. How can their use be "against nature"? Was it "unnatural" for Miriam to lead, Deborah to judge, Huldah to prophesy, Phoebe to oversee, and Priscilla to teach? Describing these women's use of their gifts as "unnatural" is really saying their Creator did not know what He was about when He gave them those gifts.

Further, when we observe God's use of women in the various biblical case histories, we see that their Creator never confuses their sexual identity, nor were any of the women confused or frustrated about being women. For example, we do not read that Phoebe could not snare a husband, so she sublimated her sex drive in church work! No, the straightforward accounts simply show God using whoever is most suitable in His eyes, and considering the ancient cultures, the way God used many women was remarkable for going against accepted practice. Certainly God in Christ was radical in relating to women, in respecting their personhood, and in equipping and commissioning them for ministry. We must conclude that fallen humanity, not Creator God, has had the problem with roles for men and women.

Today our Creative Employer still calls believers to be ambassadors in His diplomatic corps. As we move out to serve Him, we need not fear following the biblical examples. We do not need to retreat into restricting the use of women's gifts to a few "exceptions." We can trust the Judge of all the earth to do right and in His perfect judgment to give the right gifts to whom He will. It will never cause confusion when the recipients of those gifts use them as He directs. God is not the author of confusion! Rather, we need to ask the sobering question: *Has the confusion been on our part as we have denied some members of His family the equal opportunity God Himself has offered to us all?*

Equal Opportunity

Scripture's factual case histories show the biblical principle of equal opportunity worked out in actual experiences, and these case histories are exciting evidence that human gender or the ideas of role playing do not limit the activity of God's Spirit. *God* overturned rigid patriarchalism; *He* used men and women in a nontraditional manner.

Therefore, to be faithful to Scripture, we must accept the nontraditional ways in which God used women in the Old Testament. To be faithful to Scripture, we must face the fact that Jesus gave women equal opportunity to interact with Him, to learn from Him, to serve Him, and to proclaim His message. He called both women and men to make things of the Lord their highest priority. Finally in our faithfulness to Scripture, we must acknowledge that Paul followed Jesus in giving women equal opportunity to use their gifts in ministry, and we must acknowledge that women were leaders in the early Christian community.

So to those who keep trying to tell me that there exists a peculiarly "female" role that all women must play, I simply point to God's Word as my authority in the matter. Miriam, Deborah, Abigail, Huldah, the woman in Proverbs 31, Mary of Bethany, Priscilla, Phoebe—the list could go on. These women, approved by God, were indeed the "exceptions" who prove that all believers should have equal opportunity to serve Him as He calls.

An objective look at Scripture shows that the God who created the sexes did not discriminate between them. At creation both men and women were to rule the earth together. Even after the Fall, God gave both men and women equal opportunity to move out into a variety of roles—roles that suited His purposes, rather than conforming to mere human ideas of suitability.

In assigning those roles, God did not confuse the sexes, nor were His servants confused about their gender. Deborah the Judge did not disguise the fact that she was a mother in Israel; Huldah the Prophetess was not ashamed to be a wife; Mary of Bethany was no less feminine because learning from Christ was her first priority.

Today we need to get *our* priorities straight. Our creation in God's image is a truth that transcends gender. Our re-creation as new creatures in Christ Jesus is a truth that transcends gender. God's call to His individual servants transcends gender. When we examine the Bible carefully, putting down our cultural baggage (of which we have a great deal!), we find that the Bible does not teach that biology is destiny.

Men and women are not interchangeable as males and females, but they *are* interchangeable as new creatures in Christ. In both Old and New Testaments, God's Word demonstrates that their Creator appointed His people whenever, wherever, and however He saw fit. Therefore biblical feminists lovingly ask the Christian community to abandon artificial role playing and to be sex blind in assessing each individual's qualifications for ministry and in matching each individual's gifts with service opportunities. We reverently affirm that our great God is an Equal Opportunity Employer. Can His church be less?

Chapter 7

The Forgotten Woman and the Invisible Man

To find God's ideal for humanity, we go to Scripture, but when we do, we must look at *all* Scripture. The many biblical case histories were given to us as examples, either bad examples (1 Corinthians 10:11) or good ones (Romans 15:4). We need to be familiar with the whole Bible to see the difference between these examples and to discern the lessons God wants us to learn.

As my search for a biblical philosophy of male-female relationships continued, it became apparent that many traditionalists supported their notion of role playing by using Scripture selectively. Although these people claimed to have a Bible-centered approach, they were often unbalanced in their use of scriptural role models. They either ignored, attempted to explain away, or even tried somehow to discredit the many women God used in nontraditional ways and commended in the text for their actions.

For example, evil women like Jezebel or Athaliah were singled out to show that women could not be trusted in leadership positions, but people never mentioned godly female leaders like Deborah, Phoebe, or Junia. This manipulative use of case histories would compare to emphasizing only Ahab or Manasseh and ignoring Hezekiah or Josiah. I have heard the friction between Euodia and Syntyche (Philippians 4:2) highlighted as evidence that women cannot stand the strain of ministry, while the place of these two women as Paul's fellow workers was completely ignored. Yet Paul's words in Philippians 4:3 could hardly be stronger when he described them as "women who have contended at my side in the cause of the gospel." Such an unbalanced interpretation is akin to concentrating only on John Mark's failings, rather than his usefulness, or mentioning only the disagreement between Paul and Barnabas and not their ultimate unity.

However, in the same way that the Body of Christ needs all its members in order to function properly, we need to be enriched by *all* the good examples in Scripture, regardless of the person's gender. Women will be the poorer if they cannot profit from studying the life of a Jeremiah or a John the Baptist, but men, too, will be the poorer if they become so preoccupied with role playing that they cannot identify with and emulate what is honoring to God in the lives of women like Huldah or Lydia.

Because this is a relatively new challenge, understandably most men have not given any thought to using Bible women as role models. Until recently there has been little emphasis on these women. But with so many scriptural case histories of women obviously approved by God, continued negligence of these many positive role models can only evidence discrimination.

It is time for the church to end any suggestion of discrimination by celebrating these godly women and holding them up as equal examples, alongside the many godly men portrayed. Hopefully the time will soon come when Christians can not only "dare to be a Daniel" but also "dare to be a Deborah"!

To show how much we all lose by remaining ignorant of the women of the Bible, let us focus on the life of a woman whose characteristics all Christians should copy. As we think about her example, I challenge you—both men and women—to dare to be a Mary.

Protestantism's Forgotten Woman

Curiously, Mary the mother of Christ has been almost entirely passed over by Protestants in general and evangelicals in particular. When we read about women of faith, do we think first of Mary? When we read in Hebrews 11:35, "Women received back their dead, raised to life . . . ," do we think first of Mary and Jesus? How forgotten this woman is!

Though hers has become one of the best-known names in Christendom, all too many churchgoers know little of Mary as a person. Probably because of past tensions with other communions that have overemphasized (or even idolized) Mary, Protestants have tended to downplay her and may even feel uncomfortable discussing her at all. For all too many Christians Mary has been reduced to a plaster figure in a seasonal crèche or to a silhouette on a Christmas card. Yet as a real person, approved and blessed by God, her life must provide an example for us all.

In my childhood, my closest encounter with Mary was being asked to portray her in my third grade's Christmas pageant. I recall being so happy, because as Mary I could wear a nice white bathrobe and put an elegant blue scarf on my head, while Joseph just wore a gunnysack.

I can also recall some years later thinking how daring it was for one pastor to preach an entire sermon on Mary (but perhaps he felt safe because he preached it at the lightly attended evening service). In my strict fundamentalist environment, any serious attention to Mary was considered suspect and linked with possible theological deviations. But was there—and is there today—more to our reluctance to give Mary the study she deserves? Do we subconsciously recognize that if we focus on her example, we all must face the challenge of her life?

The background for Mary's entrance on the historical scene is vital to any understanding of how God used this remarkable woman. The Bible tells us that in order to reach out to restore fallen humanity—this imperfect race with all its "if onlys"—God came into our world and, in the likeness of our imperfect bodies, offered Himself up as the perfect substitution for those imperfections (or sins). That process meant God came into our

131

world to share our human condition from its very conception. He came to experience the restriction of the womb, the struggle for birth, the total dependency of infancy, and then to submit to parental authority and guidance. Only then could the words of Hebrews 2:11–18 be true, that God came to share our humanity and to be made like us in every way so that as perfect sacrifice and perfect priest He could make atonement for our shortcomings and help us in our every temptation. As a result of this incredible process, the Incarnation, God graciously offers those who accept His atonement the miracle of re-creation and the power to become children of God.

For this whole process to start, the prophecy given back in Genesis 3:15 (that the Savior would come from the seed of a woman) had to be fulfilled. God needed a woman, and at what Galatians 4:4 tells us was just the right time, out of all possible women, God chose Mary.

God had trusted a woman, Deborah, with the leadership of His people; He had trusted a woman, Huldah, with upholding the authority of His written Word; now He entrusted a woman, Mary, with providing the earthly home for the Incarnate Word. The necessity for a human womb to be the Savior's entrance into humanity puts the lie to any notion of the worthlessness of women. But Mary's character as a human being transcends gender and makes her life an inspiration to us all.

A Woman Who Listened to God's Word

The Bible gives only sparse facts about Mary's life. She lived in a little town called Nazareth, was a virgin, was betrothed to a man called Joseph, and had a cousin named Elizabeth. What made her special? Why was she approved by God?

We find the beginning of our answer in Luke's account of the miraculous visit of the angel Gabriel to commission Mary as God's servant. The angel said: "Greetings, you who are highly favored! The Lord is with you. . . . Do not be afraid, Mary, you have found favor with God" (Luke 1:28, 30). Then the angel spoke words familiar to us, but surely startling to Mary, telling her that because she was approved by God, she had been chosen to be the means of the Savior's entrance into the world of time and space.

Most of us can recall the sequence. Mary's query: "How can this happen to a virgin?" Gabriel's answer: "This will be the work of the Holy Spirit, and a confirming sign will be the pregnancy of your elderly cousin Elizabeth, because nothing is impossible with God." Mary's reaction: "I am the Lord's servant. May it be to me as you have said."

Why could the angel communicate this amazing message so quickly to Mary? Think of Moses, in Exodus 3, or Gideon, in Judges 6, who dragged out their commissioning processes, even to the point of politely telling God that He probably was not making the right choice! In contrast, Mary's commissioning was simple and direct. Why? Because Mary was already listening to God's Word and was in an attitude of belief and expectancy. She probably could not read or write, but by listening to God's Word in Scripture she had already hidden that Word in her heart. The familiar Psalm reflected Mary's desire: "Thy Word have I hid in mine heart, that I might not sin against thee" (119:11 KJV).

Scripture was part of Mary's life. Her song of praise, the Magnificat of Luke 1:46–55, was primarily Scripture quotations. In her natural and spontaneous use of God's Word, we find that, because she obeyed God as her sovereign, she also trusted in Him alone for her salvation, thus she was ready to be His servant.

Mary knew Scripture. Her example is appropriate for any man or woman who wants God's approval. She found favor with Him because she was grounded in biblical truth. Scripture was the source of her knowledge of His salvation, the source of her acceptance of His sovereignty, and the source of her strength to serve as He called her to do. Therefore our first practical lesson from Mary's life teaches us that to seek approval by God we, too, must listen to His Word. If we listen, that Word can become part of our lives and God can speak to us, too, and tell us what He is commissioning us to do today.

A Woman Who Could Be Interrupted

Because she knew the promises found in God's Word, Mary had an attitude of readiness, expectantly waiting for Him to work. We can learn another lesson from her, one Oswald Chambers expresses this way: "The only way the Christian worker can keep true to God amidst the difficulties of work is to be ready for His surprise visits."[1]

Mary stood ready for God to intervene in her life. She was open to being interrupted, not only having her day interrupted, but her whole life forever changed in this most startling way. Because she had listened to God in His Word, she was prepared for His surprise visit.

However, simply because of our familiarity with the Bible account of what we call the Christmas story, we must not underestimate how startling this surprise visit was to Mary. Yes, she was devout, committed to God her Savior, expectant of the Messiah's coming, but it still must have shocked her to hear, "*You* are the chosen virgin." Surely she felt fear, a fearful awe of the supernatural at work, but also an understandable fear of not being believed or understood.

We know from Matthew 1:18–25 that Joseph did not quite believe her, and he needed divine reassurance. And what about Mary's family? Nowhere does the Bible tell us that Mary's parents supported her during her pregnancy, much less rejoiced with her. But is that so strange? How *would* parents handle being told that their daughter had conceived supernaturally? Mary may have lived in an ultralegalistic home, where love was in short supply and no one willingly gave her the benefit of the doubt. An added concern would be what her little town would make of the situation. Surely she knew her "interesting condition" would become a prime source of speculation and gossip.

The Bible tells us that after the Annunciation Mary left her home and went to stay with her cousin Elizabeth. Mary needed the spiritual fellowship and support of someone who *would* understand, and Elizabeth put God's use of Mary's body into perspective. Elizabeth exclaimed: "Blessed is she who has believed that what the Lord has said to her will be accomplished!" (Luke 1:45). Because Mary believed God's promises, God could interrupt her life and work through her in this miraculous way.

A Living Sacrifice

Usually when we Christians affirm the virgin birth we think of the implications for the Incarnate Christ. We need to remember that for Mary the virgin birth meant voluntarily yielding her body to be commissioned in this most physical way. Mary submitted to God's sovereignty in this total interruption of her physical life because she recognized that she was simply a servant of the Lord, and she knew that all she was or ever would be came from God alone. Mary personified Romans 12:1, 2. She offered her body as a living sacrifice, wholly acceptable and pleasing to God, because her mind had already been renewed by God her Savior.

Again we have a very practical lesson for both men and women. We hear a lot today about women's right to control their own bodies, but for the believing Christian man or woman, God must have control. We Christians know that our bodies are not our own, but that we are bought with a price, the price of Calvary. As we contemplate Mary's yieldedness in giving over physical rights to herself to God, so that she could become His instrument, we see an example of submission and an acknowledgment of divine sovereignty all believers may appropriately follow.

Mary presents a stark contrast to the leaders of the synagogue, who, John tells us, "loved praise from men more than praise from God" (John 12:43). God was always first in Mary's life. Regardless of any misunderstanding or even ostracism she might have to endure, she presented herself as a living sacrifice, and whatever God wanted to do with her and her body was her highest desire.

Watching and Waiting

Again most of us are familiar with how the Bible record continues. After her sojourn with Elizabeth, Mary returned to spend some months in Nazareth; then she and Joseph traveled to Bethlehem, she gave birth in a stable, and the shepherds and the wise men visited them. Mary heard the prophecies of Simeon and Anna, the little family fled to Egypt, and finally she was back home in Nazareth again. What an amazing series of events for a simple peasant girl!

But then what? Years of patient waiting, waiting through the suspense of watching Jesus grow up. She of all people knew who Jesus was, and she must have wondered if Jesus would be different or strange in some way.

During this waiting period, Mary showed another great virtue both women and men can emulate: silence. Mary was not a talker. Luke tells us that after the events of Jesus' birth, "Mary treasured up all these things and pondered them in her heart" (Luke 2:19). Think of the spiritual experiences we cheapen because we talk about them too much! Some things are so precious that we should keep them between us and the Lord.

Certainly during this waiting period Mary had another virtue that we all can copy: She knew better than to try to run ahead of God's timetable. After that trip to Jerusalem, where she found the twelve-year-old Jesus in a dialogue with the temple leaders, she could have felt a temptation to try to push Jesus along as a child prodigy. But again Luke tells us that Mary simply hid this incident in her heart and waited for God to reveal His timing.[2]

Finally, Jesus began His public ministry. We do not know how much Mary knew of the early days of that ministry, but we can speculate that she was part of the excitement Luke 4 records about that fateful Sabbath in their home synagogue in Nazareth. Jesus read a Messianic passage from the Isaiah scroll and claimed to be its fulfillment. We can reverently imagine Mary's anticipation as she must have expected public recognition and acclaim for Jesus at last. But what happened? The people became furious and tried to kill Jesus, and He left His hometown. What a letdown for Mary and what complete confusion must have filled her heart.

A Woman Who Learned God's Lessons

Next we find Mary with Jesus and His little group of disciples at that wedding in Cana (John 2:1–11), and at this celebration she began learning even deeper lessons in sacrifice and submission. Jesus showed Mary that she was now to be in a new relationship to Him. Jesus addressed Mary with the courteous formal title "Woman," and He distanced Himself from her parental oversight.

Jesus has been the perfect human child, and as such He had obeyed Mary as His human parent. But when He went on to consummate His perfect work as Son of God, He had to teach Mary that He was not hers but ours. That Mary intuitively heeded this lesson became evident at Cana, for she rose above any humanly wounded feelings and pointed people to Jesus only. Her words to the servants effectively said, "Whatever Jesus says to you, you do that."

The next time we read of Mary, she and her other children were seeking Jesus out, most possibly to persuade Him to reduce His crushing public schedule. When someone relayed to Jesus the message that His mother and brothers waited outside, He observed: "Who are they? Whoever hears the word of God and does it, those people are my brother, and sister, and mother" (see Mark 3:31–35). Again think of Mary's possible heartache. For a second time she, who in the world's eyes should have had special consideration, had been rebuffed. But consider the importance of the lesson Jesus taught all of us through His interaction with Mary.

Jesus taught a radical lesson about relationships. Yes, He had taught that the last shall be first, and indeed this simple country woman was and is called blessed among all women. But Jesus also said that the first shall be last, so Mary, the earthly mother of the Savior, was now herself no greater than the humblest disciple. Jesus said, "*Whoever* hears the word of God and does it, *that person* is as close to me as my mother." In teaching this lesson to Mary, Jesus gives us all a lesson in mutual submission: The first shall be last and the last shall be first. Jesus also teaches us here (as Paul reinforced in 2 Corinthians 5) that spiritual relationships are the ones that count and that all believers are to be in the closest family relationship with God, their Savior.

Another beautiful lesson for men and women is that Mary did not rebel or question Jesus' teaching. She had already given over her physical rights to God; now she gave over her emotional rights. The key to her yieldedness is that she had first of all given over to God her spiritual rights. Mary knew the truth of John 3:30: "He must become greater; I must become less."

Because she was willing to be commissioned as God's obedient servant, He used Mary to the fullest: for the miracle of the virgin birth, then as a mother so that the Christ-child could experience growth and life in a real human home. But God-in-Christ passed on to a new work. Hard though she may have found it, Mary had to understand that Jesus was no longer tied to her as His earthly parent, but she was now subject to Him as her Lord.

Yet it must have been not only bearable but exciting as she watched or heard of Jesus' teachings, especially His miracles. How incredible was His power over nature, His healing ministry, feeding those thousands, and even raising Lazarus from the dead! How grateful she must have felt for the part God had called her to play in this unfolding ministry, and what a culmination the Triumphal Entry must have seemed to her! But how quickly it all turned to ashes as events rushed headlong down Passion Week to the horror of the cross.

For here we next see Mary's name. She belonged to that sad little group huddled below the crucified Christ. Was it easy for Mary to be there? It must have felt ghastly as she experienced the fulfilling of Simeon's prophecy that ". . . a sword will pierce your own soul too" (Luke 2:35).

But God did not forget that humble woman He had commissioned so many years earlier. Think of that most precious Third Word Jesus spoke from the cross, when He reached out and committed this heartbroken woman to the care of John. Jesus rose above His pain and agony to show Mary His individual care for her in her suffering as He bound her and John together in their hour of need.

As she heard Jesus reach out to help her in the midst of His time of supreme sacrifice, is it not possible that she—before any of the disciples—began to understand the true meaning of the Incarnation? One commentator has these beautiful words: "In that moment the tremendous truth must at last have dawned upon Mary, that He who hung upon the cross was not her son; that before the world was, He was; that so far from being His mother, she was herself His child."[3]

The last Bible reference to Mary is after the Resurrection and Ascension. Acts 1:14 tells us Mary was part of the group in the Upper Room as she stayed close within the fellowship of believers for comfort, support, teaching, and inspiration.

A Type of All Believers

How is Mary a role model for both men and women? What can we learn from her that will help us more fully understand how we, too, can be approved by God?

Mary is more than a good example; she is a type of all believers. Luke's account of the Annunciation parallels Jesus' encounter with Nicodemus in John 3. Jesus said: "You must be born again." Nicodemus queried: "How can that be?" Jesus answered: "This is the work of the Holy Spirit." So also in Luke 1 the angel said to Mary: "The Messiah will be formed in you." Mary asked: "How can that be?" The angel answered: "It will be the work of the Holy Spirit."

Oswald Chambers comments: "What happened to Mary, the mother of the Lord, historically in the conception of the Son of God has its counterpart in what takes place in every born-again soul. Mary represents the natural individual life which must be sacrificed in order that it may be transfigured into an expression of the real life of the Son of God."[4]

So, like Mary, we can give Christ human life when we accept Him as Savior and invite Him to live in our hearts today. Like Mary, we can give Christ a home and food and clothes as we reach out to those in need and hear Him say, "That is exactly as if you had done it for Me." Like Mary, we can give Christ lifelong devotion, and like Mary we can submit to His sovereign will and give Him our absolute allegiance.

In considering Mary as a strong role model for all believers, think again about the characteristics that made her approved by God. Mary was a woman steeped in Scripture, a woman who had committed her life to God her Savior, a woman who wanted only to do God's will, no matter what the cost. She could not know what lay ahead, but when God called, her only possible response was: "I am Your servant. Your will be done in me."

With those words Mary handed God her future—not only her reputation, but her very life itself. If Joseph had rejected her, what then? At best she would have become an outcast and a beggar; at worst, she would have been stoned as an adulteress. Yet her immediate reaction to hearing that God would invade her life in the most intimate way, forever changing it, was to affirm that she was the Lord's servant and wanted only His will for her life. No wonder Elizabeth proclaimed: "Blessed is she who has believed."

What a lesson about service Mary teaches us all, men as well as women. Mary was a living sacrifice, but today most Americans are unused to thinking of Christian service in terms of

sacrifice. Hard work? Oh, yes, we know all about hard work—
special programs, youth groups, Bible classes, church suppers,
planning conferences, attending committee meetings, and on
and on. We are good at hard work! But do we stop to think that
hard work cannot substitute for real honest-to-goodness 100
percent sacrifice of the body, mind, and spirit? We can set the
parameters of hard work, but God sets the parameters of sacrifice. He says: "Only when you give yourself over to Me and
lose your life entirely in My service will you ever truly find life
abundant."

God calls us today to be His servants, His ambassadors. As
He did with Mary, He wants to make His appeal to others
through us. May we each be willing to say with her, "I am the
Lord's servant. May His will be done in me." Then we, too, will
begin to learn what it means to be approved by God. As we
move out to serve as He directs, we will joyfully affirm with
Mary: "My soul praises the Lord and my spirit rejoices in God
my Savior."

Mary's Challenge

Will you dare to be a Mary? Many men and women will find
this crucial question a daunting one, because what first appears
to be a simple invitation to emulate an exemplary Bible character in reality becomes a series of challenges: *Is God your sovereign Savior? Will you give up your rights to yourself and any
entitlement to a certain position, and obey His call? Will you point
others to Christ and not to yourself? Will you put your life in His
hands and serve Him above all else?* Underneath these challenges
lies the most crucial question of all: *Will you accept the authority
of God?*

Our brief study of Mary shows that she was approved by
God because she committed herself to the sovereignty of God
her Savior and therefore to the authority of His Word in whatever form it came to her. Undoubtedly Mary, like all human
beings, wanted peer approval and wanted to be liked and even
respected by other people, but for her—as it must be for all
committed Christians—the bottom line was not what other
people(evenreligiouspeople)approved,butwhatGodapproved.

So possibly the deepest lesson of Mary's life is that it teaches us allegiance to God alone. This is not a popular message to people who live in a culture that constantly urges, "Do your own thing," and seductively suggests, "What feels good is good." But neither will those who have become caught up in role playing like it. The Apostle John concluded his first letter with these sobering words: "Dear children, keep yourselves from idols." Often we Christians can become so busy pointing out the idols in the secular world that we are in danger of forgetting that we, too, can develop our own programs and dogmas that crowd out the message of Christ.

I have gone to seminars where I heard that as a woman I could make no decisions independently of my husband, father, or pastor, because all women must have some sort of male authority figure in their lives, to whom they are accountable. I have also heard Christian speakers say that a husband, father, or pastor can negate a vow a woman has made to the Lord or overrule a decision she has made about Christian service.

But if God had wanted to use a "chain of command," He would have sent Mary's call through Joseph or her father or a synagogue leader. However, inescapably, God's angelic messenger spoke to Mary directly. Therefore the Bible's own record of Mary's life contradicts such teachings.

When the angel appeared to her, Mary did not say: "I'll have to ask my parents if I can obey God."

She did not say: "I'll have to get Joseph's permission. After all, this is going to disrupt his life, too."

Nor did she say: "Let me see if the leaders of the synagogue approve of this plan."

In other words, Mary did not feel she had to get permission or approval for some human authority figure. No, despite her youth, she knew Scripture, and for Mary God her sovereign Savior was her authority. When He called, her immediate and only response was: "I am Your servant. Your will be done in me." So Mary's example takes us beyond artificial role playing and stereotyped gender restrictions and points us all to the Lordship of Christ as the guiding factor in our lives.

It will not do for someone to say, "But Mary's case is different; she is in a class all by herself. She is an exception."

Yes, Mary's call is out of the ordinary for those of us not favored with angelic visitations, but to exclude her as a role model on that account must also mean excluding people like Abraham, Moses, Gideon, Paul, and any other Bible figures to whom God or His angels spoke audibly. And yes, Mary was unique in that her specific work for God can never be repeated, but to exclude her on that account is to forget that each of us is an individual and will have an individual call and ministry.

Much as some might wish to, we cannot get away from the fact that Mary is a type of all believers and that we need to learn significant lessons from her life. Her direct submission to God brings to mind Peter's words in Acts 5:29: "We must obey God rather than men!" Her experience foreshadows Paul, when he recounts in Galatians 1:15–17 that after his conversion and call to ministry, ". . . I did not consult any man."

Scripture is united in teaching that when God has called an individual, nothing—and certainly no artificial notion of role playing—must stand between the individual's call and obedience to that call. In demonstrating this truth Mary is one of the greatest human examples of sacrifice for all Christian men and women down through the ages. Will *you* dare to be a Mary?

The Forgotten Man

There is another important role model in this story: Joseph. Because we know so few hard facts about this man, it has commonly been assumed that he died before Jesus reached adulthood, but such an assumption is gratuitous. We do not know how old Joseph was or how long he lived after that trip to Jerusalem, when Jesus was twelve. But while we do not know much about him, we do know this: Joseph was not afraid or ashamed to take second place.

Undeniably, in this couple, the woman was the more prominent figure. Very possibly this is one reason many have relegated Joseph to obscurity. Those taught to think of male-female relationships in terms of rigidly dominant/subordinate roles will not only find it hard to think of Mary as a role model, but they will also feel most uncomfortable facing the tremendous challenge in the life of Joseph.

Those preoccupied with sex roles and the bogeyman of "role

reversal" need to see that we are to concentrate on the inner characteristics of a person, not his or her gender. Second Corinthians 5:16, 17 gives us the message that we must no longer think of ourselves in terms of our human nature, our physical "houses." People preoccupied with role playing also need to remember that God calls us as He wills, and His creative use of His servants transcends any human barriers.

As we look at Joseph's inner characteristics, his less prominent role need not make us uncomfortable. Just as God chose Mary for her special work, so God called Joseph to his unique place.

Matthew 1:18–25 records Joseph's commissioning process, and the text says, ". . . He did what the angel . . . commanded him and took Mary home as his wife." Think of the strength of character Joseph displayed in this obedient act. Most likely his reputation became tarnished, and he also must have endured the hurt of gossip, which can sting more severely than the lash. But he put aside his personal confusion and his personal desire for a normal marriage relationship. He helped Mary give birth in that stable far from home, a difficult and intimate time for a man who had not had conjugal relations with her. Then, along with Mary, he must have felt astounded at the visit of the shepherds and the wise men and amazed at the words of Simeon and Anna. Luke 2:33 tells us, "The child's father and mother marveled at what was said about him."

Next came the hurried and terror-filled flight into Egypt, the burden of providing for the family in a foreign land, and then absorbing the impact of another angelic message, telling them all to return to Nazareth. Once back home, is it not possible that gossip continued as people whispered: "They fled, hoping we'd have forgotten the circumstances of the little boy's birth when they returned"? Yet regardless of inner turmoil, loss of outward reputation, or risk to his personal safety, Joseph had the strength of character to go on serving as God had called him to.

In our quest to discover how God views roles, the sequence of events in this story is most significant. Mary's call came first; she obeyed that call. Joseph was in a quandary about how to respond to her call, until God called him, too; then Joseph obeyed the angel's directive and supported Mary's call. Joseph had the supporting role: A man was called to be less prominent than a woman.

In obediently taking second place to Mary, Joseph did indeed exhibit great inner strength. We need to be reminded that strength does not always mean being vocal or being visible. Although he might not have put it in these terms, Joseph was an example of the person who knows that all parts of the body are necessary and that the more prominent parts cannot exist without the secondary parts. Nor can the central roles in a drama be properly played out without the full participation of the supporting cast. Joseph felt content to be in that supporting cast and secure in his role, because he knew he was where God wanted him to be.

Beyond Role Playing

Years ago I knew a couple connected with a particular mission, where the wife held the more prominent position. At various conferences I heard some men say: "I wouldn't want to be *her* husband." Those men really meant: "I wouldn't want to be a Joseph."

Joseph's case history challenges men like those. They need to ask themselves these tough questions: *Should Christian men find it hard to identify with a man who was a supporting member of the Bible cast? Should a Christian man find it hard to come out and say, "God has called me to be in a secondary role to the woman in my life?" (or indeed to any woman?).*

Secular society urges us to be "out for Number One," and emphasizes getting to the top of any field or profession, but Christ calls all His ambassadors to be servants. Our examination of the lives of Mary and Joseph takes us beyond any artificial sense of competition and beyond any false notion of role playing. Instead it focuses our thoughts on the inner strength God gives His servants so that they can serve where He wants them to.

Yes, these two were weak and simple in the eyes of the world around them. When they came to Bethlehem that Christmas Eve so long ago, who would have given them a second glance? Later on, if a Roman soldier had traveled through Nazareth, why would he have paid any attention to the humble carpenter and his wife? But think of the strength of their dedication to the call of their Lord.

Think of Joseph's courage in identifying himself with Mary's mission, risking misunderstanding, guilt by association, and even physical harm from Herod's wrath. Think how Mary's courage shone forth as she followed her mission through to the end, risking religious censure and even physical peril by continuing to identify herself with Jesus, even at the base of the cross. Compare the heroic selflessness of these two "common people" with that selfishness of Abraham—"They will kill me but let you live"—or that awful cowardice in Judges 19, where the overriding motivation was self-preservation at whatever cost to the human life of another.

Both Mary and Joseph presented themselves to God as living sacrifices, and both exemplified the highest ideals of servant-hood. It did not matter to them which was to be the more prominent or which was to have the subordinate place. The only important factor was: "We are the Lord's servants. Be it unto us as He wills." What a magnificent inspiration these two are! How tragic that the lessons of their lives have been warped or ignored.

So in the final analysis, who can say which of them did have the greater role? This man and woman are an example of the unity of believers; they typify the Bible truth that in human relationships it is not one without the other; and they challenge us today to recognize that obedience to God's call is what counts in life.

Both men and women need the freedom to emulate this remarkable couple. Both men and women need to ask: *Will we dare to be like Mary? Will we dare to be like Joseph? Will we dare to abandon role playing and move out to be the individuals God calls us to be?*

Chapter Eight

Crucial Choices

Choices! From the moment we awake until the moment we fall asleep, our days are filled with them. Beginning with deciding what to wear and ending with choosing when to put out the light at bedtime, our lives involve one choice after another. Young and old alike constantly make choices, and choices made when young affect choices made when older. The child who always procrastinates may turn into the adult who cannot follow through on business projects.

The fact that not all choices are equally important complicates this question. Choosing what to wear is not as important as deciding how to prepare a lesson or present a professional report. One of the signs of maturity is knowing how to prioritize the day's events so you can make the important choices.

The crucial questions we have examined together in this book also involve a series of choices: Choosing to accept the offer of new life found in God's divine Prospectus; choosing to make that Living Word our guide through life; accepting our finiteness and therefore humbly choosing to be open to more truth about Scripture; choosing to avoid legalistic stereotypes and to open ourselves to the leading of the Holy Spirit; choosing to use our gifts as members of God's diplomatic corps; choosing to emulate the godly women and men we find on the pages of His written Word.

The "Female" Choice

From childhood on, most women have faced a question that requires the expenditure of vast amounts of psychic energy, a question that can dominate the economic and social status of some women, a question that can become emotionally paralyzing, a question whose answer is usually controlled by men. Society asks women the peculiar question: "Will you choose marriage or a career?"

In the conservative Christian circles in which I grew up, a woman could get married or have a career of some sort, but doing both was not considered appropriate. In addition, because marriage was obviously seen as the preferred choice, few women were adequately prepared to think of their possible vocational options. From an early age parents urged their sons to think about future jobs or professions, but for daughters there was no equal emphasis on the need to make an occupational choice, because in the back of everyone's mind was *she will probably get married*. Translation: "Then she will not need paid work."

This did not mean wives led lives of sybaritic ease, but that they would perform their unpaid work within the confines of the home. Thus for the brief time they might be in the paid job market, it was considered wrong of them to invade "male territory." I have heard people decry the entrance of women into certain fields, because "they're taking away men's jobs." The underlying thinking reasoned that men need paid jobs lifelong and, as sole providers for their families, should be entitled to the more highly paid jobs. The secondary jobs were considered more suitable for women because they would probably leave the paid work force early. Not only did this thinking limit women's opportunities for meaningful paid work, but it took no account of the increasing numbers of single women—including those who were heads of households—who desperately needed such work because they, too, were of necessity lifelong members of the paid work force.

Often some very superficial and even cruel factors came into play in determining what answer a particular woman gave to that query, "Marriage or career?" An heiress might be able to pick and choose her future options, but a girl in a low income bracket could be forced to rely on her physical characteristics. Thus a family might designate the "pretty" daughter for marriage, while marking the "plain" sister for domestic service or a religious vocation.

But pretty or plain, if a young woman decided that she would try to seek marriage as her life's occupation, then (although no potential husband might yet be on the scene) she would usually bypass higher education and simply "mark time" until a husband did appear. For this woman, if a husband never materialized, she might well find herself in a dead-end vocational situation, one she did not like and possibly was not suited for, but one she was now too old to change. All too often she would withdraw into herself and become what people callously termed a "dried up old maid."

Other women were selected as "sacrificial lambs" in difficult family situations. Usually large families would make every effort to help sons concentrate on their job opportunities, and every effort would be made to help married daughters concentrate on their new homes. But the single daughter or the unmarried female cousin could often find herself drafted into being companion and nursemaid to the sick or elderly, because, even though she might have no aptitude for such work, it was "respectable" and also neatly took the burden off the other family members. Lines from Thomas Hardy's poem "The Orphaned Old Maid" reveal the thoughts of such a woman:

> I wanted to marry, but father said, "No—
> 'tis weakness in women to give themselves so". . . .
> But now father's gone, and I feel growing old,
> And I'm lonely and poor in this house on the wold,
> And my sweetheart that was found a partner elsewhere,
> And nobody flings me a thought or a care.[1]

If a woman opted for a career path, she would usually go on to further education of some sort—such as secretarial school, nursing school, or teachers' college. If she really enjoyed what she was doing, she often had to contend with family or friends who kept warning her, "Don't be too intense—you'll never catch a husband that way." If she persisted in pursuing a fulfilling career track, she, too, might find herself labeled *spinster* and put on the social shelf. If she ever questioned the hurtful practice that made spinsters unwanted but bachelors in demand, she kept this to herself.

Obviously some women crossed over from one track to another. Some women, openly in the marriage market, but who did not marry, eventually found meaningful careers, and some on career paths got married after all. The two separate tracks could even merge. However, in conservative religious circles, when the career-path woman married, the pressure was on her to conform to that original set of choices—marriage or career—by abandoning her career and making her marriage her primary occupation in life.

In my study of male-female relationships, I became aware that—although decades had passed and a much greater percentage of women enjoyed higher education and many more women had places in the paid work force—a new generation of women still faces the same choice I faced thirty-five years earlier. The question is still being asked: "Will you choose marriage or a career?"

Most single women today must decide on a career path simply to put bread on the table, but some still hear, "Be careful you don't scare off potential husband material." Wives and mothers who hold down paid jobs out of economic necessity or personal preference are still being forced to agonize over working outside the home.

The source of this tension appears to lie in the traditional assumption that marriage is the highest possible goal for women. This assumption may indeed have been understandable in centuries past, when women were uneducated, economically unempowered, and disenfranchised. Until fairly recently marriage was the chief means of conferring social status on women and of providing them with a measure of economic security. A married woman assumed her husband's name and even his title. Others could speak of a woman as "Mrs. Doctor Jones" or "Mrs. Attorney Brown," and most married women were defined in terms of their husbands: "That's So-and-so's wife." Thus the nineteenth-century researcher Krafft-Ebing wrote: "The ultimate aim, the ideal, of woman, even when she is dragged in the mire of vice, ever is and will be marriage."[2]

Now, in the latter part of the twentieth century, in America, conditions are far different. Women have the right to vote. They have equal educational opportunities with men. Their varied job options have not only helped them achieve economic independence, but also have given them a sense of personal worth, rather than vicarious worth. Yet how puzzling that many people persist in clinging to the notion that a woman (unlike a man) is "improved" or "completed" by marriage and that the wife and mother has some sort of superior position, compared to single or childless women.

Adherents of this notion do not seem to understand that those single or childless women find it an exceedingly painful concept to accept. It becomes even more painful when others tell these women that God has ordained the role of wife and mother as their highest goal. A just God would not set up an ideal role and then close it to so many aspirants. These women need reassurance that, as we saw in chapter 4, the one common role and the highest role that God has set up for *all* believers— men and women alike—is that they be ambassadors for Christ.

As we have also explored, the Bible makes it clear that God has not ordained any one specific "female" role or any one specific "male" role. Remember that Judge Deborah was also "a mother in Israel." God did not ask the women we studied in the biblical case histories of chapter 6 to choose between marriage and career, any more than he asked it of men. These Bible characters *did* choose to use their gifts and talents in the service of God. Therefore we must ask: *If God does not force women to make a choice between marriage and career, does the choice itself (like patriarchy) represent another flawed concept?*

A False Question

Let us put this matter in the reverse. Think how ridiculous it would be to say to a male high school or college student: "What are you going to choose—marriage or a career?" After his initial look of disbelief, that young man would instinctively answer: "I don't understand your question. Marriage is not a career." Although no one has ever asked men to articulate this, they instinctively realize that their marriage is one thing, and their vocation is another. Thus the young man in our illustration might go on to say, "If I choose to marry, unless I marry 'money,' I *must* have a career of some sort to support my wife and family." If our conversation continued, he might add that even if he did marry an heiress, he would want to find some sort of meaningful work, because he wouldn't want to sit around "doing nothing."

No, common sense tells us marriage is not a full-time occupation for men. But if not, why not? Marriage cannot exist without a man and a woman, and in Genesis 2:24 the man was told to leave his parents and be united to his wife. If marriage is considered "women's work" because of the children, we must remember that it takes both a man and a woman to produce children and that in Genesis 1:28 the command to multiply was given to both sexes jointly.

Why then is marriage thought of as an occupation for the wife but not for the husband? Does this whole problem stem from a basic misunderstanding of what marriage is, which in turn leads to a basic misunderstanding of the function of a marriage partner?

As I concentrated on the problem of marriage and career, it became apparent that the institution of marriage and whatever occupation defined a person's career are two vastly different things. Thus to ask a woman to choose between marriage and career means asking her to try to choose between two concepts that are not even in the same conceptual "family." Marriage is not a career for either a man or a woman, for this very simple but crucial reason: Marriage is a relationship, not an occupation.

Marriage is a commitment of two persons to become united into one flesh, to use the biblical imagery for the intimacy and closeness of that relationship. As long as they live, both parties must work to nurture and sustain this relationship, but as they do that they work at a relationship, not an occupation.[3]

A relationship means a connection between people, a state of being interrelated with another person or persons. Marriage is a relationship (between two persons). So are the connection of parent with child and the family connection between relatives. The very word *relative* indicates a tie or a bond.

In contrast, an *occupation* means pursuing a trade or vocation, using a skill to earn one's livelihood or occupy one's time. The word *career* indicates the pursuit of a certain occupational direction, chosen (sometimes out of necessity) as a means of providing for a person's physical sustenance.

A career may also provide mental, emotional, and psychological satisfaction. People who do not need an income-producing occupation may still opt for a career path to occupy their time with what they consider to be meaningful work, because, like the young man in our illustration, they do not want to sit around "doing nothing." This is why, once the most demanding years of child care are over, many homemakers use their increased discretionary time in some sort of community service. You will recall that unrecognized career—volunteerism.

An objective appraisal of the two diverse terms used in society's false equation of marriage with career shows us that *marriage* describes a connective process, a joining of two individuals into one relationship of lifelong interdependence. *Career* describes the type of activity a person chooses as his or her paid or unpaid vocation.

In the Beginning . . .

An examination of the biblical account of our human origins will help us understand the distinction between and purpose of marriage and career. We can learn crucial lessons from the first two chapters of Genesis.

In Genesis 1 the Bible uses the simplest possible language to record the creation of the immensely diverse plant and animal kingdoms, but does so with no particular emphasis on gender. Yes, a study of the natural world indeed shows a fascinating sexual variety: differing methods of reproduction and a variety of methods for caring for the products of reproduction.

While most life forms have two sexes, some are hermaphroditic (possess both sexual attributes in one organism) and some reproduce by parthenogenesis (without need for fertilization). Though in most animal forms the female actively nurtures the offspring, in many instances the male assumes those responsibilities, and in other cases nurturing is a group function.

Further, while the wealth of lower life forms fulfill a multiplicity of purposes, Genesis does not delineate those purposes (or "occupations"). The Genesis account gives no details of plant and animal life forms, beyond the simple statements that God created each kind in a separate creative act and placed them in their various environments and that they multiplied. Genesis does not emphasize the plant and animal worlds, rich as they are. Instead, the account zeroes in on details of the creation of a unique life form, humankind, because only that life form was created in the image of God.

We find the initial record of this final creative act in Genesis 1:26–28, which reads:

> Then God said, "Let us make man in our image, in our likeness, and let them rule over the fish of the sea and the birds of the air, over the livestock, over all the earth, and over all the creatures that move along the ground." So God created man in his own image, in the image of God created he him; male and female he created them. God blessed them and said to them, "Be fruitful and increase in number; fill the earth and subdue it. Rule over the fish of the sea and the birds of the air and over every living creature that moves on the ground."

This passage has been called the cultural mandate, but we can break it down into two parts, an occupational mandate and a relational mandate, because the words describe two different activities: Ruling and multiplying. These two diverse activities represent two distinct concepts. *Ruling* refers to occupation, and *multiplying* refers to marriage.

The text indicates that both sexes receive equal opportunity for an occupation, and both sexes are given equal opportunity to enter into the marriage relationship. These words tell us that God delegated authority to rule the earth to *both* man and woman, thus giving them the same vocational opportunity. This text also tells us that God created men and women as interdependent sexual beings, thus giving them both equal opportunity for interpersonal relationships.

The fact that God said, "Let *them* rule," and told *both*, "Be fruitful and increase in number," clearly implies mutuality, both in service and in procreation. Paul's words in 1 Corinthians 11:11 help us put the biblical male-female ideal in proper perspective: "In the Lord, however, woman is not independent of man, nor is man independent of woman."

The First Relationship

As God had done with various lower life forms, He could have created the human being as one self-propagating entity. Instead, God chose to create humankind as a heterosexual life form, and then He chose to create the two sexes sequentially rather than simultaneously.

One initial lesson from the creation of man and woman is that (as in the case of lower life forms) our sexual diversity enriches us, making the world a more interesting and pleasurable place. But we may learn deeper lessons from Genesis 1 and 2 about relationship and occupation.

The distinctive account of the creation of man and woman as found in Genesis 2 emphasizes the complementarity and mutuality of human beings by contrasting the man's condition before and after the creation of woman. The text tells us (2:8) that God placed the first male human being in the perfect environment—perfect except for one thing. The man was alone, and God's own comment on man's solitary situation was "It is not good for the man to be alone. I will make a helper suitable for him" (2:18).

These words tell us that the lone man was inadequate; he was vocationally and emotionally incomplete. Then, by using the parade of animals, God went on to demonstrate to the man that no lower life form would adequately complete him. The dog may be man's best friend, but even the dog is not a "suitable helper"! By means of this object lesson, God took great care to show the man that only the woman would be his equal.

The very manner in which the woman was created confirms this equality. God did not say to the man, "Look how overworked and lonely you are. I will go over to that obscure heap of dust and fashion another person." Woman was not some sort of subservient afterthought! Rather, the words of Genesis 2:21, 22 contain a very special message about likeness.

A simple illustration will help us grasp the wonder of this account. Think of a sculptor molding and fashioning a very special kind of clay into a design and then saying: "The location for which this sculpture is intended requires a companion piece.

One alone is unbalanced; two will be perfect. So because I want these sculptures to be true companion pieces, I will take some of that very special clay from the first sculpture and fashion the second sculpture from that. As I make one from the other, these two pieces will truly be a matching pair."

By taking part of the man's own flesh and using that "one flesh" for the creation of the two persons, God placed woman far above the role of mere animal sexual partner. By this intricate act, God ascribed the highest worth and value to the woman. Having shown that her creation was necessary to reverse man's condition from "not good" to "very good," the actual manner of her creation proved that because of her equality of substance, she was eminently "suitable" to be man's co-worker and social partner.

In this very beautiful and profound way God said: "People are in God's image. Neither the woman nor the man is an animal. Both are created in My image, and therefore their relationship is to be on a far higher plane than merely that of a sexual union to keep propagating the species. Men and women are to be close, to have fellowship. They need each other to complete each other socially and to help each other vocationally in overseeing the world in which I have placed them."

It cannot be emphasized enough that only after the creation of *both* sexes do we read in Genesis 1:31: "God saw all that he had made, and it was very good. . . ." Man alone was not good. Man and woman together were very good.[4]

In the marriage relationship, man and woman can give the fullest expression to this concept of the unity of humanity, the need of one sex for fellowship with the other, the need to end "aloneness." Human beings are made up of body, mind, and spirit, and in marriage man and woman can affirm physically, intellectually, and spiritually that "we are one flesh." The first male's understanding of this becomes evident in his cry of recognition in Genesis 2:23: "This is now bone of my bones and flesh of my flesh." Genesis 2:24 underscores the oneness of the two, with words indicating that the married couple becomes a separate social entity.

Again Paul helps us understand the divine ideal of equality and mutuality in the marriage relationship. In 1 Corinthians

7:2–5 he writes that each partner has power over the other and that each partner should yield to the wishes of the other. Thus *both* partners are initiators, but within a context of mutual consideration. Enjoying equal power over each other's bodies incorporates equal responsibility to preserve and enhance the relationship.

The First Occupation

The God-ordained task for humankind is to rule over all the earth and to subdue it. The inclusive language of Genesis 1:26–30 indicates that both men and women are to be involved in this overseeing activity. In Hebrew, the word for "man" in these verses (as in Genesis 5:1, 2) is the word for all mankind (or humankind) and is distinct from the word for "male."

The more detailed account in Genesis 2 also supports the mutuality of our overall occupational mandate. Adam was first placed in the garden ". . . to work it and take care of it" (Genesis 2:15), but alone he was not adequate for the task. After the creation of woman, together they carried out the occupational function God intended for human beings. Again we must remember that only after woman's creation, God saw that it was very good. Only when the two had been created could humanity successfully begin to fulfill its occupational mandate.

As we think about the lessons in Genesis 1, 2, we human beings must recognize that only the tremendous fact of our creation "in the image of God" makes us suitable to act as His representatives in overseeing this world He has made. We realize, of course, that humanity's imaging function reflects but in no way defines or limits the immeasurable richness and complexity of our Creator. However, as man and woman perform their ruling activity, the Genesis ideal is that they enjoy an interdependent relationship that mirrors (as far as the finite can mirror the Infinite) the unity and fellowship of the Persons of the Godhead. God said, "Let us make mankind in our image, in our likeness, and let them rule . . ." (*see* v. 26). Thus the man and the woman created in His image reflect that divine "us" and in their reflection reinforce the truth that each sex has equal worth and value and equal capability to carry out the occupational mandate.

A further aspect of our creation "in the image of God" is important for our discussion: An image is not the reality it reflects. Therefore not only is humanity's prominence in the creation order a mere reflective or derivative prominence, but so also humanity's power over that creation is only reflective or derivative power. Creator God authorized men and women to rule the earth and subdue it. He delegated His power to them, and they were humbly to exercise this power within the framework of obedience to Him (Genesis 2:16, 17).

So as recorded in Genesis 3, a desire to cease using delegated authority and to try to become the authority source themselves lay at the heart of Adam and Eve's joint disobedience. Although many people have tried to place the greater blame on Eve and her "tendency to be deceived," Adam was also culpable, as Romans 5:12 clearly states. Adam, too, had the choice of saying no, but openly disobeyed. The tragic results of this disobedience, which we call the Fall, were the marred relationships and the occupational toil and trouble that have plagued humanity ever since.

However, as we saw in chapter 4, in the miracle of redemption God has reached out in love and has offered re-creation to all who put their trust in Him. Those of us who have accepted the plan of renewal in God's Prospectus have now become new creatures in Christ Jesus. Therefore we no longer aim to image fallen humanity, but to return to the ideal for which God created us. By His grace, we must seek to fulfill our original purpose of imaging God as we interact in our relationships and as we work at our occupations.

Family Values

In my dialogue with my friends, I sensed that much of their reluctance to rethink the false equation of marriage with career has stemmed from their uncertainty about how to apply the results of that rethinking. Increasingly, some voice fears that any serious practical application of equality and mutuality in marriage or career will erode traditional family values.

In some contemporary circles it has been popular to describe the ideal family as one with a "working" father and a "nonworking" mother, who live with their children in a single-family home in a safe rural or suburban environment. Yes, for many people this may indeed be the great American dream, but does not accurately describe biblical family values. To discover those values, we must first consider the word *family*.

From Bible times on, in a predominantly patriarchal society, families have been identified with the name of the "founding father." We read of "the families of the sons of Noah" or "the tribe of Judah." The wording indicates descendants of that founding father. Occasionally genealogies feature a female name, but the names listed in family groups are predominantly blood relations of a male.

A character in one of Louis Auchincloss's novels says: "Well, what is family? Is it anything more . . . than the predominance of male issue over female? We speak of families 'dying' simply because the direct male line from father to son has been snapped."[5] Men might think how mothers and daughters feel about such a definition! Just because many women feel a woman's identity "dies out" when she assumes her husband's name, more and more women choose to retain their maiden names or to use them as middle names. Yes, use of the male name has been a convenient device for tracing ancestry, but surely there is more to "family" than identification with a man's name.

We must begin any discussion of family with Genesis 2:24, which tells us that the man and the woman were to be joined together in a new social unit that would be separate from that of their parents. Thus one dictionary defines *family* as "the basic unit in society having as its nucleus two or more adults living together and cooperating in the care and rearing of their own or adopted children."[6] The fact that our Incarnate Lord was born and raised in a family situation emphasizes the importance of the family relationship for all human beings.

No dictionaries mention occupations in connection with family members. In describing family, dictionaries do not focus on "working" or "nonworking" parents, because—like marriage— the family is a relationship, not an occupation. The family is a connection of relatives.

Nor does Scripture prescribe occupations for the family

members. Rather, the Bible gives guidelines for the relationships between the family members.

We have already seen that the marriage partners are to be monogamous (only two are to become one flesh), that those partners are to be in the most intimate relationship, and that they are to be faithful to each other (Malachi 2:13–16; Matthew 19:1–11; 1 Corinthians 7:10, 11). Other passages tell us that when these partners become parents, they are to care for their children responsibly, lovingly, and to bring them up "in the nurture and admonition of the Lord" (Deuteronomy 4:9; Proverbs 22:6; Ephesians 6:4; Colossians 3:21). In return, the children are to honor and respect both parents equally (Exodus 20:12; Leviticus 19:3; Deuteronomy 5:16; Proverbs 1:8, 6:20; Ephesians 6:1; Colossians 3:20).

In its most basic form the phrase "traditional family values" describes a faithful husband and wife who provide a stable home with mutual love and respect between the family members. The phrase will be inaccurately used if it attempts to describe family values in terms of occupations or economic circumstances. Rather, biblical family values are concepts that explain how people should interact within the family relationship.

Children: Occupation or Relationship?

Genesis 1, 2 make it clear that in marriage two persons commit themselves to become as one, but while this is a very serious choice, the resulting relationship will not completely occupy the couple's time. Therefore God commanded man and woman to rule as well as to multiply, to work at an occupation as well as to be in a relationship.

This general occupational mandate includes no indication of any delegation *by gender* to specific spheres of oversight. Adam was not the animal trainer, and Eve was not the florist! Yes, the curse resulting from the Fall predicted pain and toil in both relationship and occupation, but it did not lock female or male into any particular "suboccupation." From Genesis 3:15–19 one cannot effectively argue that all women must engage only in child-related occupations, anymore than one could argue that the only suitable occupation for all men is farming.[7]

Yet the traditional position has advocated that women should assume all the child-related duties. This position is based on the notion that "form defines function," and thus, because the female one is the childbearing form, women are limited to child-care activities. To me this begs the question: *What function does the male form then define for men?*

We need to examine the "form defines function" argument as we ask: Why are women limited by their form and men not limited by theirs? Both parents (of biological necessity) have an equal part in conceiving a child. All children (even in cases of artificial insemination and surrogate mothers) result from a mutual act. Why then does not the male form mandate a narrow male function? Only because the male does not actually bear the child?

But women cannot reproduce by parthenogenesis (without need for fertilization). The female form cannot fulfill the childbearing function unless the male form has also fulfilled its function. Yet there is never any thought of limiting a man's sphere to begetting offspring or describing the man's primary role as siring children (although, to be consistent, people who support a patriarchal system, with its emphasis on sons, *should* consider begetting heirs the most important act a man could do!).

Today we hear people say: "Women are now free to have a career and have children, too." Let us put this in the reverse. Have people ever said of men: "They have the freedom to have a career and have children, too"? No, because again (as with marriage and career) men unconsciously realize that careers and children are two different things.

Men do not think of having children as a career, because having children is a biological act and not an occupation. But it is a unique act that creates a new life and, with that new life, a new relationship. So when a man *does* question whether he can have both children and career, the question will not be phrased, "Can I take on another occupation?" but rather, "Can I take on responsibility for a new life?"

We need to see that the same is true for women. For them, too, conception of a child is not an occupation, but a biological act that eventually brings into being a new life, a new responsibility. A woman, too, must not ask, "Can I take on an occupation?" but, "Can I assume responsibility for a new life?" For her, that responsibility begins with her pregnancy, as she protects the new life growing within her body.

Once we recognize that for both man and woman, conceiving a child is not a career but—after the child's birth—is the establishment of a new relationship, we see that simply because women bear children, it does not follow that only they should engage in child-related activities. There is no corporate womb function for women, anymore than there is a corporate begetting function for men. A woman does not have an occupation in life to bear children, anymore than a man has an occupation in begetting children.

Conceiving a child is not deciding to enter a new occupational field. Instead it means that by a mutual act a new life comes into existence and a new relationship is established— that of parent and child. Both father and mother must assume equal responsibility for that new life and that new relationship.

I knew a missionary whose board vigorously objected to the missionary's wife attending college classes in the evening. The ground of the objection? That when she was away her husband was changing their baby's diapers and this was "role reversal." These critics failed to see that changing diapers is not women's role or men's role, but an act of simple compassion for a helpless child. I don't know any woman who enjoys changing diapers, but I do know that women do this because they are responsible for the well-being of the little life in their care. For a man to refuse to assume the same responsibility when necessary or appropriate is to show callous insensitivity. After all, what would a widower do if left with a baby to care for? We need to see that participating in the nitty-gritty of child rearing is not "feminizing," but "humanizing."

For parents, biology is destiny for *both*. Form defines function for *both*. Their forms have united to create a new life, and their mutual "one flesh" relationship now expands to include parenting. They have *both* assumed responsiblity for a new relationship with a new human being—an utterly helpless human being. Both parents are equally and mutually accountable for providing suitable care for the safety and well-being of this new life that *together* they have brought into the world.[8]

Here we must recognize that not all children have the privilege of growing up in a two-parent family, and not all parents are a child's natural parents. Death, illness, disability, divorce, or some other tragic circumstances may shift responsibility for the child to adoptive, foster, or stepparents, to a guardian, to relatives, or to other interested persons. However, the distinction between parenting and child care remains. These people, too, must understand that they assume responsibility for a relationship and that fulfilling that responsibility will mean more than simply providing care in the form of food, clothes, shelter, medical help, education, and daily supervision. Any person who acts in loco parentis must have a greater degree of concern and involvement with the growth and development of the child than merely providing for the bare necessities that insure the child's continuing existence.

Parenting: A Mutual Responsibility

Understanding the difference between parenting and child care will help couples see their parenting function in a new light. Their joint parenting function will include providing child care, but it is not synonymous with child care.

Parenting describes the responsibilities involved in the new family relationship of parent and child and encompasses the entire process of supporting and guiding a child from infancy to maturity. *Child care* describes the occupation of someone who works at supervising the child on a full- or part-time basis and who may or may not be paid for that occupation.

We can sharpen the distinction between parenting and child care when we reflect on the fact that child care is limited to a certain time frame (except in cases of chronic illness or some sort of handicap), whereas the parent-child relationship lasts throughout life. Child care normally stops when the child reaches maturity (which will vary in different societies), but while the parenting function will take on different nuances, the parent-child relationship never ceases.

Now, nothing in Scripture indicates parenting should be done *only* by mothers or women, or that it should remain the sole province of mothers or women until the child reaches a certain age. There is nothing particular to be drawn from accounts like 1 Samuel 1, where Hannah dedicated her son to the Lord, but kept him at home until she had weaned him, because Samuel could not enter the Lord's service until he was old enough to help Eli the priest.

While Scripture speaks of mothers nurturing children and contains many mother-child metaphors, the strongest parent-child imagery tells of our loving heavenly Father caring for us, His children. There is no scriptural justification for a distant, uninvolved father. In Christian homes, *both* parents are actively to provide parental guidance, including spiritual guidance.

We are becoming increasingly aware that making child rearing strictly "women's work" can have some very deleterious effects. We recognize that the visible presence of a loving father in even the earliest nurturing situations is vitally important to balanced child development. Yet the traditionalists' emphasis on women's so-called role has centered more and more on proclaiming motherhood as women's highest goal, *without* proclaiming fatherhood as men's highest goal.

I have heard many people say that there is no higher calling on earth than that of being a mother, but I have never heard anyone proclaim that there is no higher calling on earth than being a father and that men should devote all their energies to that. However, unless they uphold fatherhood equally with motherhood, these people really mean that fathering is not as important as mothering.

What has caused this imbalance? Not a lack of concern for the needs of children, but another confusion in terminology. Just as marriage and career confused two different concepts—relationship and occupation—so also parenting and child care have become confused and thought of as one function. So the presupposition that the mother should provide all supervision of the children has all too easily led to a slide into considering her responsible for all the parenting as well.

We need to get away from stereotyped slogans like, "Men are providers, and women are nurturers." That sort of thinking leads fathers to believe they can fulfill their parenting responsibilities by providing material support, and it leaves mothers with the entire burden of child rearing.

In chapter 3 we exposed the false idea that only women have responsibility as caretakers of society's morals. Now we must expose the false idea that a woman's career is marriage and that she has a chief occupation of performing the primary parenting function. *The vice is that when marriage is thought of as the wife's career (read job) then she will be expected to work harder and in a different way at the marriage than will her husband, and the same will hold true for parenting.*

No matter what lip service we give to the importance of fathering, if *in practice* we make the mother primarily responsible for both child care *and* parenting, we place on her a burden that—as any single parent knows—cannot easily be borne alone. We place her in yet another no-win situation: solely responsible for relationships Scripture tell us God designed to be mutual. Understanding and accepting the scriptural ideal that both partners have a responsibility for their marriage relationship (not "one without the other") and both parents have responsibility for the physical and spiritual welfare of their children will correct this unbiblical imbalance.

A Contemporary Challenge

People who pronounce that it is only woman whose place is in the home forget that in the beginning home and workplace were one for both man and woman. Many occupational distinctions we now make simply did not apply in the most ancient times. Our twentieth century money-dependent society is vastly different from the dawn of human history!

The earliest people produced their own food, manufactured their own clothing, and built their own shelter. Both men and women helped grow food, tend livestock, make clothes, and build tents or houses. All able-bodied family members were needed, and all but the very rich or powerful engaged in work activities.[9] Sometimes families would use the barter system to procure necessary goods, but meeting basic human needs was still a cooperative venture in which—even for nomadic peoples—home and workplace merged.

In dramatic contrast to earlier centuries, the late twentieth century West has an intricate economy where jobs are highly compartmentalized and goods and services are primarily procured by cash. Most families are no longer even remotely self-sufficient, but depend on some form of wage earning for survival.

Current usage of the term *bread winner* reveals the monetary basis of our urbanized, industrialized Western society. When we say of a job, "It puts bread on the table," we unconsciously acknowledge the drastic shift from the days when that bread was a homegrown staple produced by the collective family labor pool. For most families—and certainly most singles—survival depends on someone being out "bringing home the bacon" (as against producing it in the home-workplace) and earning the wherewithal to "put bread on the table" (as against baking it from homegrown ingredients). Thus in America today, when the majority of people marry, both members of the couple are in the paid work force, and most are there out of economic necessity.

One of the positive results of the women's liberation movement is that many working couples now see the fairness of sharing the household tasks. It has become obvious that when both husband and wife work full-time, it is inequitable for *only* the wife to cook, clean, market, and do the laundry. Most couples will figure out a shared arrangement that suits their particular circumstances.

When these same couples decide to have a child, they must reevaluate their whole situation, because it involves a new life. Now they face the crucial question "How can we best provide for child care?" In the ideal two-parent home, both share responsibility for determining the most suitable arrangement.

If their economic circumstances allow one parent to stay home, in most instances it will be the mother. A practical reason for this is that (especially if they plan more children) she may find it hard to reenter the work force after pregnancy leave. But a more compelling reason is that many, many women feel drawn to child care as a worthwhile and meaningful occupation. Many women desire the privilege and challenge of supervising the daily care of their own children.

However, a couple in which the mother provides the child

care must understand that she is still in the work force. (I personally abhor the term *nonworking mother*.) Therefore as part of their reevaluation of responsibilities, the couple will need to factor in the husband's continued help with various chores. Just because the mother stays home with their child will not mean that she, too, has not put in a full workday.[10]

In a family where the mother provides the child care, the couple must also be sure that the father fulfills his parenting function and brings to the child or children the balance of a male role model. Parents must discuss issues like discipline, so that when she parents alone, the mother's actions will reflect a mutual policy.

One challenge of parenting is to provide safe and reliable supervisory care in which the best interests of the child are paramount. Mainly for this reason we consider it ideal when one parent can provide that care, because we assume a parent will put the needs of this helpless new life first.

But honesty compels us to recognize that designating a parent (or even a close relative) as primary care provider is not necessarily foolproof. Parents or relatives who—for whatever reason—cannot handle the very real demands of child care can become inefficient, neglectful, or even abusive. We have all known or read of instances where, in the best interests of the child, parents or others have found a foster home or some other alternative method of care. So it is dangerous to make sweeping generalizations about who must or must not *always* supervise children.

In this context of generalizations, we should also recognize that not all women feel drawn to child-care occupations, and we must respond sensitively to those who are not. Again let us apply our questioning process. We do not censure a man who says, "I am very fond of children, but I just don't want to take care of them on a daily basis." Why do we censure a woman who makes the same comment? Only because we have bought into that false idea that only for women "form defines function." But as with fathers, mothers, too, can function effectively as parents, even though they do not provide the primary child care. The parent-child relationship does not stand or fall on who does the child care.

Thus many couples starting families today explore non-traditional options for their child-care needs. Some mothers provide most of the care but feel happier and more fulfilled if they also continue working part-time at an occupation outside the home or if they continue with their education. Other couples have deliberately sought job situations that allow both father and mother to help equally with the child care.[11] Most nontraditional of all, the father can be the primary child-care provider, although this has most often happened in families where the father is disabled or has been laid off from his paid work.

However, the challenge of providing safe and reliable child care in which the best interests of the child are paramount still remains. In the ideal situation, as they meet that challenge, both parents will accept their responsibility for the new life entrusted to them and make the best arrangements they can for the daily supervision of that life. Yes, the ideal is that one parent is the primary child-care provider or that both parents share this care, even if this means a lesser income or a simpler life-style. To achieve this ideal we need a renewed emphasis on the importance of child care as a challenging and meaningful career option, rather than just unpaid "baby-sitting."

But again honesty compels us to acknowledge that not all families are in this ideal situation. As with single parents and parents who *must* rely on two paychecks for economic survival, some families *must* make outside arrangements for child care. Their only alternative to some sort of day care is leaving the child improperly attended or unattended. To say to them, "A parent should be home with the child," is like saying to a hungry person, "Be fed." Words alone will not help, but actions will.

Therefore Christians should express concern that all day-care centers be as well run and well staffed as possible, and Christian women *and* men should consider careers in the field of child care. Christians should also become involved with programs (like extended parental leave) that will help these families return to the ideal. Churches could make day-care centers a part of their community outreach. Surely we who affirm the sanctity of life must be intimately involved in providing Christian answers to these contemporary problems.

A Crucial Occupation

Nowhere does Scripture specifically address the matter of child care as an occupation. Obviously the multiplying activity of human beings resulted in children, and the Bible contains commands and admonitions to both parents and children. For example, the Fifth Commandment enjoins children to honor their parents; Deuteronomy 6:6–9 commands parents to teach their children God's Word; parts of the law deal with family problems; the Book of Proverbs contains advice to both parents and children; and the New Testament writers also address family relationships. But nowhere does Scripture set forth the actual details of who should supervise children on a day-to-day basis.

Yes, after the mutual act necessary for conception, the child gestates within the mother and comes forth from her. However, if the mother dies, the child can be nursed by another woman or can be sustained in some other way. Once a child is born, that child does not solely depend on the natural mother for survival. Throughout human history extended families and interested friends have cooperated in providing for child care. The account in Luke 2:43–46, where Mary and Joseph assumed for an entire day's journey that the boy Jesus was in the care of relatives and friends, illustrates this. Baby-sitters are nothing new!

But although the Bible gives no set formula for child care, the importance of this occupation is based on a principle we discussed in chapter 5: the sanctity of human life. Each human being, from conception, has infinite worth and value, and must never be carelessly treated. We are to protect the human rights of children. Simply because they are helpless, we must never consider children expendable objects to be manipulated. Children should never be thoughtlessly conceived. Once they are born, we need to see supervising their care as a most valuable occupation, because it involves the safety and well-being of human life. By healing children and encouraging them to come to Him, Jesus taught us to give the highest priority to the needs of "the least of these."

A job description for a child-care position might list these requirements: stamina, patience, creativity, flexibility, and love! As with other "people-oriented" occupations, the working day will be varied and the duties involved will rarely conform to a set schedule. Each day will combine repetitive tasks, hard problems, some surprises, and new joys. People (especially mothers) who choose this occupation will work very hard indeed, but if they see child care as a true career calling, they will find a tremendous satisfaction in knowing that they have had a share in the growth and development of a new life—a satisfaction money cannot buy.

The Gift Nobody Wants

Most discussions of human relationships center on questions about marriage and the family, but to be inclusive we must examine another area: the needs of singles. It in no way undermines the God-ordained institution of the family for Christians to recognize that we are in danger of developing an almost cultic emphasis on family that discriminates against singles. Many singles today get the message that their concerns will always come last on the church's agenda. Pious affirmation of "welcome to our fellowship" has a hollow ring to singles.

I have participated in innumerable church planning sessions where, only at the end of those long discussions, someone has said, "Oh, we probably should do something for singles." Because of the late hour, those in charge have deferred the problem by asking someone to "look into it." No, we never exactly forgot those singles—but we never did get any significant programs going, either.

Why not? Why do the needs of singles seem to come last on the programmatic totem pole? I suggest that part of the problem has been unquestioning acceptance of that false equation of marriage with career. As long as we Christians think or teach that marriage is the accepted goal for all women (which by implication means it is for all men, too) we will find it hard to think of singleness as an option, and it will be practically impossible to think of singleness as a gift.

Yet Paul's words in 1 Corinthians 7:7 strongly suggest that singleness is just that—a gift. He wrote, "I wish that all men were as I am. But each man has his own gift from God; one has this gift, another that." This entire chapter deals with human relationships and puts a premium on singleness. Have we distorted Scripture so that singleness has become the gift nobody wants?

In recent years there has been a tremendous resurgence of interest in spiritual gifts. The women's movement within the church has expressed one very valid concern that traditional practices make it difficult or impossible for women to use their spiritual gifts. Now we must ask: Has our preoccupation with marriage and the family made it difficult or impossible for single men and women to accept their singleness as a gift and use it for the glory of God?

Single men need support and friendship, being included and feeling wanted. The myth of the single man as always in demand and thus choosing from among a wealth of social invitations is usually just that—a myth. In reality he often spends a succession of solitary evenings on make-work projects to help him pass the time.

Yet since custom still dictates that men control the question of marriage, single women can resent single men (and even men in general) for leaving them in their "unfinished" state. The patronizing term *God's unclaimed blessing* leads to feelings of rejection as single women ask themselves: *Why didn't anyone claim me?*

A variation of that false notion "form defines function for women" is the saying: "A man is what he does; a woman is what she is." I suggest that some conservative circles have expanded that to: "A woman is whom she marries, and if she does not marry, she is in danger of becoming a nonperson."

In her book, *Leaving Home,* Evelyn Bence recounts a poignant conversation with her father. She wanted to explain her career goals, but her father could not accept her as the person she was. He insisted on discussing her singleness. His comment on her "failure" to find a husband: "It doesn't seem to me that you've been trying very hard."[12] As I read this deeply moving book I thought: *With devastating remarks like that, is it any wonder that singleness is a gift nobody wants?*

We must understand that whenever we imply or state outright that marriage is the highest Christian life-style, it forces singles to conclude that they are "losers." The easy criticism of singles, "You're just too picky," quickly translates into, "You're such a loser, you should be grateful if *anyone* wants you."

So possibly one of the most damaging areas of fallout from the unquestioning acceptance of marriage as a woman's career is this devaluation of single women. Single men are not devalued per se, because marriage has never been considered the ultimate male goal; marriage does not particularly "enhance" men (unless they marry "money" or their professions require a wife who fills the role of a full-time hostess). But as long as society, or segments of society, consider marriage the ultimate female career goal, single women will *always* be considered "losers." What a tragic underestimate of precious human resources!

Yes, teaching marriage as the universal goal for all women denies their full personhood, because it indicates that women will only become fulfilled when they marry. Yet neither women nor men gain personal identity through marriage. Women as well as men are complete individuals, whether or not they marry. How hard even Christians have found it to accept this truth.

We need reminding that in the Genesis 1, 2 account of our human origins God did not pronounce the marriage of the man and woman or their sexual activity "very good." It was the initial creation of the individual man and the individual woman in God's image that He describes with these words.

Note that the man spoke the words in Genesis 2:23 ("This is now bone of my bones and flesh of my flesh . . .") *before* any rejoining of the two in sexual union. The single man recognized the single woman as a person equal with himself, a person of the same substance and created in the same divine image. Only her creation ended his aloneness and changed his state from "not good" to "very good," *and that turnaround occurred when they were both "singles."*

So our common status as human beings forms the basis for human social interaction. Whether man with man, woman with woman, or man with woman, all human friendships have one common denominator: We are the same life form, and God created us both in His image. As we interact together, we do so on that basis, and that is why human relationships can be on a plane far above even the closest attachments to pets.

Yet it is becoming increasingly difficult to relate to other people in terms of pure friendship. Our American society has an obsession with sex. The entertainment industry concentrates on exciting human sexuality, and pop philosophers proclaim, "What feels good is good." Secular society's acceptance of all varieties of "meaningful relationships" leads many people to think they have a right to achieve sexual gratification and can exercise it whenever they desire.

Unfortunately, this preoccupation with sex makes it harder than ever for singles to form close friendships. Regardless of whether singles become good friends with a person of the same sex or of the opposite sex, society will tend to put the worst possible construction on it. It is not too farfetched to say that it would be difficult for Paul and Timothy to travel about today without tongues wagging, or for Paul to commend Phoebe so warmly without someone wondering if there were not more to their friendship than mutual admiration.

Concentrating on the fact that in the Incarnation Jesus remained single will help singles realize that He does indeed understand their every temptation and know their every need. Pondering passages like Matthew 19:10–12 and 1 Corinthians 7 will help singles dedicate their relationships to the Lord's service. Certainly if Jesus appeared today and said to a man or a woman, "I give you the gift of singleness," that would put this whole matter in proper perspective!

Neither secular society nor the Christian community may value the gift of singleness, but God values it, and that is what counts.

So the Christian community must hear the anguish of singles as they struggle with celibacy in a sexually saturated society, and must not add to the tensions of singles by an excessive emphasis on marriage and the family that effectively excludes singles, and must always respond sensitively to the natural human desire of singles for balanced social interaction and for genuine friendships. Any Christian philosophy of human relationships needs to include full acceptance of singleness.

Crucial Choices

Remember my airport encounter with the man who said: "Equality of women? That's an issue that doesn't touch me at all. I never think about it"? He was not unique. All too many of us never think about issues of human relationships unless we find ourselves personally affected. But once we do become aware of these issues, we instinctively try to find a scapegoat to blame for all our problems. So you may also remember the catalog of ills that has been so quickly blamed on feminism: divorce, abortion, promiscuity, and latchkey children.

Now it is time to face these issues and to stop trying to find scapegoats. Christians need to be honest. We need to ask ourselves: *Have we been part of those problems?*

Have we accepted false traditions, false views of life and work? Have we drifted into relationships simply because our peer groups expected us to? Have we been insensitive to the social needs of others, simply because our own needs have been satisfied? Have we been blind to the tragic consequences of confusing the two dissimilar concepts of relationship and occupation?

Equating marriage with career warps and commercializes that relationship. It leads a woman to marry for the wrong reason: to benefit from the social and financial status of a vicarious career, that of her husband. The confusion also leads a man to marry for the wrong reason: to have an available, respectable combination of sexual partner and housekeeper. When the veneer of romance wears off such a couple, the husband becomes a "meal ticket," and the wife turns into a "ball and chain." Is it any wonder that we see unhappiness, abuse, infidelity, and divorce?

Yet how often parents say to a girl in need of vocational guidance: "Well, you can always get married." Translation: "Then you'll have that meal ticket." How often parents say to a young man having trouble finding a career path: "Well, when you get married, you'll settle down." Translation: "That ball and chain will teach you what adult responsibility is all about." What terrible reasons for entering into a lifelong commitment. The girl thinks: *He'll solve my problem of what to do with my life.*

The young man thinks: *Maybe she'll make something of me. Can* such a couple live happily ever after?

What about their children? How many couples pray about this matter long before a new life is conceived? How many couples thoughtfully and prayerfully consider how many children they can care for responsibly? How many Christian homes are open to foster children? How many couples consider the alternative of adoption? I am impressed by one Christian couple I know, who have chosen to remain childless and to use their talents and resources to help families in need.

Unfortunately, all too many couples never think through the relevant relational and occupational issues involved in their individual circumstances. So often couples have a child for the poorest reasons: It is the "expected" thing to do; it perpetuates the male family name; "It'll bring us back together"; or, "It just happened." When the novelty of the baby wears off, such couples can discover that they are not prepared for parenting and that they cannot provide adequate child care. Is it any wonder that we see abortion, child abuse, and latchkey children?

These crucial issues involve crucial choices, choices that should never be made by default. If decisions about careers and relationships "just happen," then opportunities will be lost and lives will be hurt.

A New Perspective

When we see marriage as a relationship, not a career, the whole question of career choices opens up for women, and we can explore it as the separate issue it is. Here we can bring to mind the diverse occupations of those godly women we studied in chapter 6. Certainly that paradigm of womanhood, the lady in Proverbs 31, worked at a variety of occupations that some narrow twentieth century definitions of women's role would prohibit.

The married woman will have many choices to make. If her husband's career is a potential two-person career, she might choose to join in that. Examples of such careers would be the family farm, the owner-operated business, high-level government posts, and the clergy. Most spouses of farmers, presidents, and pastors may not be salaried, but they are certainly fully employed!

The mother who understands the difference between parenting and child care will see that she will probably make a minimum of two or three career choices. She might have a vocation prior to making child care her career during the years her young children are at home. Then she will look forward to further career opportunities when the children no longer need her full supervision, because, while she will always be their parent, they will no longer need her full-time care.

Mothers who have made child care their career should prepare for the equivalent of "early retirement" from that job. As women's longevity increases, homemakers who wish to be good stewards of their time must then ask: "What does God want me to do at this new stage in my life?"

Some women will return for further schooling, to prepare them for their next career choice, while others, whose economic circumstances permit, will choose volunteerism. However, women who have been full-time homemakers must realize that their discretionary time will increase markedly as their children grow up. Christian homemakers are accountable to God for responsible use of their expanding "free time."

As we face these issues, we must always challenge *both* partners. It is unbalanced to ask, "Can *she* have it all [children and a career]?" The only accurate question is, "Can *they* have it all?"

If a couple is adequately to fulfill their parenting function, is it so revolutionary to suggest that *both* parents may temporarily (or even permanently) have to leave "the fast track" in order to put their family needs first? Here we can think of the successful businessman who has proved anything but a success at home or the pastor who has become estranged from his wife and a stranger to his children. Yes, the husband, too, must factor in his fair share of the child-rearing responsibilities, *plus* (in line with 1 Peter 3:7) sensitivity to the often-ignored intellectual and emotional requirements of his wife as she seeks her own particular career paths during the various stages of her life. Men, too, are accountable to God for how they prioritize their time.

All time is a precious gift from God. How men and women use their time will involve these crucial choices about the two general areas delineated in Genesis 1:26–28: relationship and occupation. The Christian must make these choices within scriptural guidelines. We who want to be approved by God know that only His Word will have the answers to our needs for security, and the "something more" to enhance our life. We do not believe that security will lie in paychecks or "meal tickets," and we know that if we depend only on our fellow human beings to provide the "something more," we will doom ourselves to eventual disappointment.

When we have studied God's Prospectus and accepted His plan of renewal, we recognize that not only have we entered a new spiritual relationship—membership in God's family—but we are also engaged in a new mission as ambassadors for Christ. In the light of these central truths, we must evaluate all our earthly activities. Will our relationships and our occupations help or hinder our new spiritual relationship and our new spiritual calling? How can we use our time and our resources to God's glory?

As we ask all these questions, we will have a new perspective on what may have at first appeared to be private decisions. Now we will see that if we sincerely want to serve Christ above all else, we can no longer compartmentalize our lives into "our time" and "His time." We must weigh whether we can serve our Lord better single or married. We must ask if we are ready for the awesome responsibility of parenting. We must decide which occupation will allow maximum use of the gifts He has given us.

These crucial questions will involve commitments: commitments to career paths, commitments to relationships, commitments about how we will spend our time and for whom we will spend it. For Christians, choosing to enter into these commitments should never "just happen."

Once more Paul gives us further insight. In 1 Corinthians 7:32–35 he warns both husband and wife about becoming so concerned with each other that they forget their primary purpose: serving God. Paul's words clearly imply that the great danger in excessive concentration on each other is that the couple will no longer concentrate on "the Lord's affairs." Paul concludes: "I am saying this for your own good, not to restrict you, but that you may live in a right way in undivided devotion to the Lord." Within this context Paul lauds singles as the persons freest to follow God's call.

That many Christians will feel embarrassed at being asked to consider their choices of careers and relationships as spiritual matters is a telling commentary on how far the church has departed from the urgent sense of mission that pervades the New Testament. Some may even feel that this challenge is fanatical in its intensity. But for those who make the primary commitment to enter God's diplomatic corps, the bottom line must always be: "Not our will, but Yours."

Jesus said, "If you love me, you will keep my commandments." He commanded His own to follow Him, to be His witnesses, to love others as He loved them, to bear one another's burdens, to take His Gospel into all the world. These are the orders we find in our diplomatic pouch. Only when we make the crucial choices about our relationships and our occupations in harmony with these orders, will we hear Him say, "Well done, good and faithful servants."

Chapter Nine

Who's in Charge Here?

When human beings interact together in both relationships and careers, there can be a certain jockeying for position and a certain defining of turf. A sense of competition seems to pervade every aspect of contemporary life as people watch out for Number One.

In chapter 1 we saw that our competitive nature is reinforced by the advertising industry as it plays on our insecurity (our fear of never measuring up) in order to entice us to buy products that will help us compete—whether it be for shinier hair or floors, a marriage partner, or a business contract. We are constantly urged to ask ourselves: *What can I do to be more attractive and more in demand than my peers? What can I do to insure that I get ahead?*

Part of this competitiveness, of course, results from accepting the world's definition of success. Overly influenced by the catchy saying, "You can never be too thin or too rich," we diet and jog to become "beautiful people" so that others will want to establish relationships with us. We work overtime in the hope that our increasing net worth will make us people to be reckoned with. However, the competitive ladder most of us climb is not always as attractive as that advertising industry would like us to believe. All too often, pursuit of worldly success becomes a "rat race," and we must divide people into "winners" and "losers" simply because we can only afford time to cultivate "winners."

So we practice one-upsmanship as we strive to be alert to what will advance us yet another rung up the ladder. Is our potential marriage partner a "catch"? Do we have the best house on the block? Is our new job a "plum"? Will that committee chair go to someone else? Who has the most honorary degrees?

Part and parcel of the sense of competition pervading modern life is the desire to control. If we are thin and athletic, we are in control of our bodies. If we are on the "fast track," we control our careers.

Often we feel sure that our circumstances would improve or our job prospects would be enhanced if only others would "see things our way," so we connive and manipulate and (if we are able) order other people around in our efforts to make these things happen. Yes, beginning with that tragic desire of Adam and Eve to become the ultimate authority source themselves, human beings have been obsessed with gaining control both of their own lives and the lives of others.

Now, many people do indeed have the willpower to control their own bodies, and many people do indeed have the willpower to focus their every energy on "getting ahead." But when it comes to controlling other people, we enter an uncontrollable area. Unless a person is a direct subordinate or someone over whom we have some sort of "hold," as we interact we find that it can become difficult to make another "dance to our tune." When it comes to personal friendships, family relationships, and interacting within the church, it can seem much harder to control the actions of others.

When we find that our competitive modus operandi does not always guarantee control in the area of human relationships, we can feel a sense of frustration. It may surprise us to find that some people are not impressed by our thinness or our athletic prowess, do not care if we won a beauty contest or played on an All-American team. We discover persons who are not automatically in awe of a Ph.D. We find that many could care less if we are executives in a Fortune 500 company, or if we ski the Alps or snorkel in the Caribbean. We meet others who have little interest in our "house beautiful," because they are not interested in "pride of place" but only in the people who inhabit the place.

Yes, it can feel frustrating to meet people whom we cannot control, and it is more frustrating if these people are not even interested in the concept of controlling relationships and careers. But they should force us to stand back and ask some basic questions: *Is the desire to control biblical? Have we bought into another false idea? Has our desire to be in control of our lives, our affairs, and the lives and affairs of others been the result of another trick of the enemy?*

Yet in any discussion of male-female relationships, one question always gets raised: *Who's in charge here?* In the church, who makes final decisions about policy and programs? When an impasse occurs between husband and wife, who breaks the deadlock? Within conservative Christian circles the traditional answer has been: "The man has the deciding vote. Men are in charge here."

My traditionalist friends told me that the order of creation determined that male-female relationships were to be hierarchical, with women subordinate to men, and that certain New Testament passages reinforced this two-tiered structure of society. Although they told me this hierarchy primarily facilitated the decision-making process, it was apparent that I was again being confronted with male supremacy. Equality and mutuality could not exist in male-female relationships if only the male made all the final decisions. So once more I went back to Scripture to ask: "Who's in charge here?"

Back to the Beginning

Returning to Genesis 1, 2, we see that the creation account presents two series of progressions. In Genesis 1 the creative process begins with the lowest life form and progresses to humanity. Genesis 2 presents the creation of humanity as a sequence from man to woman.

An objective look at these two progressions can be enlightening. I use the word *objective* deliberately, because people can be so used to hearing a presupposition that they unconsciously impose that presupposition upon Scripture. Then the presupposition becomes a self-fulfilling prophecy. Thus some groups have become so accustomed to hearing "order of creation" that when they read Genesis 2, they impose this notion upon the text by assuming that because God first formed man, he must take precedence over the second-formed being, one created to be his "helper."

However, once we recognize that there are two sequential progressions in the creation account, this presupposition becomes open to question. If someone says that the first-formed creature should take priority, then animals (and the most primitive animals at that!) should take precedence over human beings—a position no one would ever take seriously. Only man and woman were uniquely created "in the image of God." But if someone says the last-formed creature has priority (thus acknowledging that human beings, made "in the image of God," are the capstone of creation), that person cannot ignore the sequential details of the creation of humankind, but is forced to say woman should take precedence over man, because she was God's final creative act. Only after *her* creation did God pronounce His world "very good."

Clearly the traditionalists' position involved special pleading. Those who wanted to teach that the last-formed life form (humankind) was the culmination of creation, while teaching that within that life form the first-formed would take precedence, wanted it "both ways." They could only have it "both ways" by imposing the presupposition of male supremacy upon the text, because—if anything—the supposed order of creation would indicate female supremacy. Christian scholar Alvera Mickelsen alerts us to the pitfalls in imposing presuppositions on the text in her humorous yet provocative essay, "Does Order of Creation, Redemption, and Climax Demand Female Supremacy?" (*see* Appendix I).

When I questioned my traditionalist friends about this very evident problem, they answered that the matter hinged on the description of woman in Genesis 2:18.[1] Clearly, they said, woman had been created to be Adam's helper and therefore his subordinate. But *was* that so clear?

A Misunderstood Word

Much has been made of woman as "merely" a helper, but any suggestion that the word for "helper" indicates a secondary function is not in keeping with the meaning of the original

Bible language. The Hebrew word for "helper," *'ēzer*, does not indicate a weak or subordinate person, but someone who is strong. Of all the times the Old Testament uses this word, most of the uses refer to God. For example, Psalm 121 describes the Psalmist's helper (*'ēzer*) as being ". . . the Lord, the Maker of heaven and earth" (v. 2). If in the many instances where *'ēzer* is used of God we gave it the subordinate meaning that has traditionally been used in the case of woman, what heresy we would perpetrate about the nature of God! No, *'ēzer* does not indicate subordination or subservience.[2]

You will remember that Genesis 2:18 described man as emotionally and vocationally incomplete, unable to function properly alone, and needing woman's strong help. Nothing in the text even *hints* that only man has some sort of authoritative role. (Genesis 1:26–28 had already declared that both men and women were to rule the earth together.) Yet think of the tension and competition between men and women, single or married, that has arisen because of the tragic misconception that the word *'ēzer* means a subordinate.[3]

As we saw in chapter 8, man and woman emerge from a distinctive creative act, in their case alone designed to portray their fellowship and unity, their partnership and mutuality of mission. There was no independence of the one or dependence of the other. In Eden there was no portrayal of dominance or subordination. Of exactly the same substance as man, woman was an equal human being, suitable to be a strong helper. When God took woman from man's side, she was to be his "completer," not his competitor.

Yes, men and women are individuals, and yes, they are different sexes. But they are equal human beings, designed to complement and complete each other, as the marriage union demonstrates. Scripture says that when they unite, the two "become one flesh," not "the two become a hierarchy." The two now side by side should carry out God's order to multiply and to oversee the world together.

As shown in chapter 6, Scripture itself tells us that God overturned any rigid notion of male hierarchical role in either family or society. God bypassed the "first-formed" male, choosing Abel and Seth over Cain, Jacob over Esau, David over his brothers. God accepted the inheritance claim of the daughters of Zelophehad. God chose Miriam and Deborah as leaders. God used Abigail and Huldah to speak for Him. The New Testament presents women in positions of strength and leadership. So to the question "who's in charge here?" the Bible clearly answers, "the individual person God chooses."

The "Hard Passages"

Once more I reported my findings to my traditionalist friends, and they now answered: "You can't put it off any longer. Regardless of what you discovered about 'ēzer, you must study the New Testament texts that we know will prove to you the subordination of women."

So at last I returned to these passages: 1 Corinthians 11:2–16; 14:33b–36; 1 Timothy 2:8–15. Within the confines of this book, I have condensed my journey, but in reality over a decade had passed since my experiences in chapter 4, when I first was asked to think about these passages. Despite the time interval, I found that scholars, commentators, and writers for learned journals *still* disagreed over the meaning of these passages. Over ten years had passed, and there was no consensus on the meaning of these three passages, although books and articles about them proliferated, often bringing more heat than light.

This fact sent me an immediate message. Since scholars still could not agree on the verses' meaning, they could not agree on their interpretation, either. It would therefore be most unwise to try to use these particular passages as definitive guides to male-female relationships.

The many difficulties found in these three scriptural portions have been something of a well-kept secret from the average churchgoer, but on the other hand the average churchgoer has not usually had much interest in exegetical and hermeneutical problems (problems of meaning and interpretation). However, the layperson needs to be aware of these problems, because even the laity can appreciate the fact that if these passages are filled with difficulties, we must proceed very cautiously before proclaiming them theological "yardsticks."[4]

With the increased interest in Bible study, many "ordinary" Christians have become aware that in the New Testament letters we have only half the correspondence. So when we study these letters, we look for clues as to what topics the writer was addressing. Often these clues are obvious, such as in 1 Corinthians 1:11, where Paul writes, ". . . Some from Chloe's household have informed me that there are quarrels among you." In 1 Corinthians 7:1 Paul begins, "Now for the matters you wrote about. . . ."

However, in our three "hard passages," the precise practical questions Paul addressed are not that obvious, making it hard to answer the underlying question: *What is the exact purpose of each of these passages?*

In addition, we face many translation difficulties, some of which are compounded by our inadequate information about the cultural background of these passages. A further severe difficulty is that the parts of these passages that seem to restrict women's role do not reconcile with each other, nor do they reconcile with the actual practice of Jesus and Paul or with those Old and New Testament case histories we examined in chapter 6. Again, what do we do with Bible women who were "exceptions"?

In view of these various difficulties, we can see that it will be most unwise to pull individual verses out of these "hard passages," for use as proof texts. Until we have a better grasp of the exact meaning and context of these three passages, as well as better understanding of their relationship to all of Scripture, we must avoid the pitfalls of selective exegesis.

Some Specific Difficulties

Anyone interested in serious study of these passages will find immediate challenges. The following is only a small sampling of questions we need to answer about them.

1 Corinthians 11:2–16

1. What is the meaning of *head* in verse 3? The most frequent suggestions are "authority over" and "source."
2. What exactly is the head covering Paul had in mind? Is it hair or a veil? (The word *veil* does *not* appear in the Greek text.) Does this head covering reflect Jewish or pagan customs? By requiring head coverings, is Paul making a theological point, a plea for common decency, or both?

3. What does Paul mean by the word *authority* in verse 10? (The word translated "sign of authority" in the New International Version and the New English Bible and as "veil" in the Revised Standard Version is simply *authority* in the Greek text.) Suggestions range from considering the veil as a sign of the husband's authority over his wife to considering the veil as a sign of the woman's own authority in Christ to pray and prophesy.
4. What is the connection between angels and women's head coverings in verse 10?
5. How can verse 5 be reconciled with 1 Corinthians 14:33–36, which seems to forbid women from speaking in the assembly of believers?

1 Corinthians 14:33b–36

1. What is the meaning of *speak* in verse 34? Suggestions range from speaking in tongues to pagan wailing in worship.
2. In verse 34, to whom or to what must women be "in submission"? Their husbands? The elders of the church? The law? If the last, what exact law is referred to?
3. Is the prohibition of women speaking in the church Paul's own quotation or a Corinthian slogan? Often in 1 Corinthians Paul quotes a Corinthian maxim, which he then discredits. Is this the case here, with verse 36 being Paul's contradiction of a slogan he has quoted in verses 33b–35?
4. If verses 33b–35 are not a Corinthian slogan, how can this passage be reconciled with 1 Corinthians 11:5, which indicates women pray and prophesy in public?

1 Timothy 2:8–15

1. In verse 11, to whom or to what should women be in "full submission"?
2. In verse 12, what is the force of "I do not permit"? Is this a timeless command, a temporary injunction, or a personal preference?
3. Also in verse 12, what is the precise meaning of "to have authority over"? The Greek word translated this way is exceedingly rare.
4. Is verse 14 merely an illustration, or is it an indication that all women are easily deceived?
5. Does "be kept safe" (or "be saved") in verse 15 refer to a woman's physical safety in childbirth or to her salvation?

6. Does the word *childbirth* in verse 15 refer to labor and delivery, to motherhood as exemplary of women's ideal role, or to *the* childbirth (the birth of the Messiah)?

7. If verse 15 refers to salvation and not physical safety, and if *childbirth* does not refer to the birth of the Messiah, how can we reconcile this verse with Paul's teaching of salvation by grace through faith alone?

8. Again, how can we reconcile "she must be silent" in verse 12 with the praying and prophesying of women in 1 Corinthians 11:5?

These questions are only a small indication of the complexities in these texts. In order to resolve these difficulties one way or another, literally *dozens* of choices must be made about the *dozens* of exegetical problems yet to be solved. Appendix II is not an exhaustive list of these problems, yet it presents over fifty difficulties, giving a graphic picture of the amount of research still needed before interpretation of these passages can be resolved. This appendix will be of particular interest to scholars and the professional clergy. However, it will also be educational for laypeople to glance through Appendix II, so that they, too, can appreciate the magnitude of the task involved in arriving at clearer understanding of these "hard passages." Even the shortest look will make it readily apparent that the precise meaning of these three passages *cannot* be determined at this time.

Although traditionalists who would teach subordination of women draw heavily from these three Pauline passages, we must be aware that (although our English translations do not indicate it) the passages contain these many difficulties. New Testament scholars openly admit that exegesis of the relevant verses in 1 Corinthians 11, 14 and 1 Timothy 2 is arduous, regardless of whether the approach is hierarchical or egalitarian. I have even heard the word "tortuous" used! One severe logical difficulty with 1 Timothy 2:13, 14 is why a deliberate sinner (Adam) would be better qualified to teach than a deceived person (Eve).[5] Certainly the differences of opinion about 1 Timothy 2:15 are very revealing of the difficulties inherent in that one verse alone.

Putting Problem Passages in Perspective

Recognizing problem areas in the Bible need not shake our affirmation of the trustworthiness of Scripture. There are indeed difficult passages in the Bible and with very good reason.

First, the Bible is the Word of the Infinite God, and we are only finite. Some sections, such as the apocalyptic passages, have details that are simply beyond us. We may never understand these Scriptures, in this life or the next!

Second, we must recognize that our understanding of Bible times is as yet incomplete. We must avoid imposing a presupposition on any text, simply because we have inadequate background knowledge. Yes, it is dangerous to take the easy way out of an unclear passage by labeling it entirely "culturally oriented," but it is equally unwise to close our minds to the possibility that a deeper appreciation of the culture of Bible times will open up new meaning for us.

For example, laypeople especially find it perplexing to be told that knowledge of Bible times will enhance their Bible knowledge, but on the other hand to hear that the culture of Corinth or Ephesus (where Timothy was when Paul wrote him that first letter) does not affect the meaning of the "hard passages." The usual reason given is that Paul's references to Genesis in 1 Corinthians 11:2–16 and 1 Timothy 2:8–15 make any contemporary cultural material irrelevant. Yet since his arguments are not completely clear to us (again *see* Appendix II), surely we may legitimately bring all possible light to bear upon these verses.[6]

Third, we need to be aware of another area of textual difficulty—one that has particular bearing on our discussion, namely, places where one text seems to contradict another. In his book *Biblical Revelation*, theologian Clark Pinnock has a very helpful chapter on this subject, entitled "The Phenomena of Scripture."[7] Pinnock gives as an example the puzzling "moral blemishes" we appear to find in God's Word. These result from the seeming contradictions between verses that tell us that God is love and other passages, particularly in the Old Testament, that indicate a warlike or even vindictive aspect to Deity. It is incontrovertible that these passages are in God's Word. So we study these phenomena as best we can, but if we cannot resolve them, we must put them aside and concentrate on the larger truths that are clear to us.

To continue with this illustration, everything I know about God indicates that He is indeed love, so loving that He came Himself to die for me. Therefore I put to one side passages like the Imprecatory Psalms or the Canaanite Wars that I do not understand. But I do *not* throw out the known truth "God is love," simply because some passages about the nature of God puzzle me.

So we should also treat the three "hard passages" about women, which we find in the New Testament and which appear to place specific restrictions on women only. To these we could add Colossians 3:18; Ephesians 5:22–24; and 1 Peter 3:1–6, and the dogmatist might even say that the ultimate rationale for women's subordination is Genesis 3:16. For some these passages do appear to teach a secondary place for women.

But over and against those texts are the passages we have explored together in this book, passages that show that women are fully redeemed, women are equal ambassadors for Christ, and women do serve God equally and are commended by the text for doing so. Paul assures us in Galatians 3:28 that in Christ there is no male or female and tells us in 2 Corinthians 5:17 that in Christ all believers are now new, in complete harmony with John 1:12, which proclaims that all who believe are given the power to become God's children. Finally, Romans 8:17 adds that His children are now His heirs. *All these clear teachings add up to the larger truth of the equality of all believers, and we do not ever throw that out.*

As with all Bible difficulties, the sooner we can come to a better understanding of the three "hard passages" about women, the better. However, until we have that understanding, we cannot allow these passages to cancel out truth that *is* clear.

A Further Caution

Problem passages in Scripture are no reflection on the clarity of God's Word, but rather reflect our human inadequacy. As we saw in chapter 1, we ask questions about the Bible because some passages (like 1 Peter 3:18–20) are at present beyond our full comprehension.

Remember, too, the discussion at the end of chapter 3: We are only finite beings, and it should not surprise us if we do not understand everything the inspired writers set down in the Bible! We can all agree with Peter, who said that while Paul wrote ". . . with the wisdom that God gave him," nevertheless ". . . his letters contain some things that are hard to understand . . ." (2 Peter 3:15, 16).

Yet today, as in the past, one source of error is yielding to the temptation to give answers when we do not know them. In considering the "hard passages," we can apply this adage: "Be willing to await further light, rather than make a bad choice at the moment." Accepting Scripture as God's inspired Word does *not* mean we have to resolve every difficult question right now, or our faith is in jeopardy. We may never know the answer.

So we who respect God's Word cannot become like the person who says, "Don't confuse me with the facts; my mind is made up." Since these "hard passages" are so difficult that their meaning remains unclear and their interpretation problematical, until we have that further light, we dare not use them as "the last word" in making up our minds about who's in charge here.

We must conclude that any definitive interpretation of the "hard passages" is at present impossible. Only by imposing presuppositions upon them can we use them as theological "yardsticks."[8] However, those of us who respect God's Word cannot force meaning where meaning is unclear. Therefore we may legitimately put these Scripture portions aside for the very reason that they *remain* "hard passages"—hard exegetically, hard hermeneutically, and hard theologically.

Then What *Do* We Do About Relationships?

The male-female relationships we have considered can take the form of friendship, marriage, and membership in Christ's church. Let us think first about friendship as we pursue the question *Who's in charge here?*

In a true friendship, although one friend might be older or better educated or more talented than the other, that person does not say, "I must always be the chief decision maker." Hardly! Within true friendship, both want the best for the other, and neither has any desire to dominate the relationship.

We can think specifically about David and Jonathan. We do not know their exact birth dates, but one was probably older than the other. How unthinkable that the elder would have said, "I was formed first; therefore I will set up the rules of the relationship. If we can't agree on what day to go hunting, I'll always be the one to break the deadlock." Such an imaginary scenario jars us. Why? Because true friends do not argue over what to do and when to do it. A true friendship is not fraught with deadlocks.

Friendship is not like a business arrangement, where one person is "in charge." It is a relationship of persons attracted by mutual affection and mutual esteem, who want to share their life experiences. Therefore true friendship involves a process of "give and take" that the Bible calls mutual submission.

Next think of the tragic nonrelationships David had with the women in his life: the failed multiple marriages, the callous use of concubines, the inability to sympathize with his daughter's hurt. Why did David dominate and oppress women? Because to David women were subordinates and even objects. He had no appreciation of the one-flesh relationship of marriage and no thought of women having worth and value equal to his.

As we did in chapter 5, again contrast David's use of women with his deep friendship with Jonathan. Precisely because David saw Jonathan as a person equal to himself, he would *never* have said, "I must run the show." Rather, both David and Jonathan would have said, "I want what is best for *you*." We know Jonathan risked his very life to save David.

Yet as I pursued the question of *Who's in charge here?* I discovered that in what can be the deepest friendship of all, marriage, many persons still found it hard to think of marriage as a relationship. For so long marriage had been confused with career that many people thought of the married couple in terms of a business connection, instead of an interpersonal relationship. Therefore these persons described marriage as they would a business hierarchy, and they subscribed to hierarchical concepts about marriage, which they would never have accepted about friendship.

Yes, keeping the married couple supported with the necessities of life will involve business decisions and have business-like aspects. However, this does not mean that the marriage is a business. Similarly, supporting the family will involve business matters, but as we explored in chapter 8, neither is the family a business. It, too, is a relationship.

If we think of both marriage and the family in business terms, we will perceive who "runs the show" as important. In contrast, if (as with friendship) we consider marriage and the family loving relationships, we will see the whole question of *Who's in charge here?* in an entirely different light. Just as a friend does not try to "run the show," neither will one marriage partner or family member always want to have "the last word." Instead, as with true friendship (and in harmony with Philippians 2:4–8), each partner and each family member will want only what is best for the others.

A Jarring Concept

Although I grew up in a very conservative Christian environment, there was no emphasis on what is currently called "male headship." Possibly people had no reason to define *head*, because pre–World War II societal mores dictated certain attitudes and behavior. Women, like blacks, usually knew their "place." But it still bears mention that in my youth, missionary couples like John and Betty Stam were thought of as a team, and during the war years women were encouraged to abandon any rigid "female" role and to enter the work force or join the armed services.

Not until the early 1970s did I begin to become aware of an increasing emphasis on rigid male-female roles and a hierarchical "chain of command." It appeared that these concepts were part of the desire to impose order on a disintegrating social scene, but they jarred me personally because the example of my parents and the practice in my own marriage and family life was that of mutual submission.

In my early homelife, Dad very much wanted to please my mother, and she him. They made their decisions jointly. I never heard him "put his foot down" in relation to her. I respected both my parents equally and would have felt shocked to hear that one was ordained to be "over" the other.

In our married life, if Phil and I heard someone refer to the husband as "head," we did not pay much attention, because in our actual practice we saw no need for a "head" who had final say. Of course at times I got carried away with some project, and Phil had to say, "No, that's not going to work." But there were also times when he wanted to do something, and I said, "No, that's not appropriate." Neither of us, in putting on the brakes, did so to try to exercise some sort of authority over the other, but because the project did not reflect the best interests of our marital or our family unit. Like all husbands and wives who love and respect each other, we did not want to make decisions unilaterally. Although we did not "bat a thousand" (because nobody's perfect!), we did try to put the interests and the welfare of the other above our own.

But during those 1970s, as an adult-Bible-class teacher I received literature about male headship to critique, because my students felt uncertain about this concept. In addition, a series of seminars on life problems began to gain popularity in our part of the country, and I attended those. In both the books and the seminars, I came up against the notion of rigid roles for men and women, with the man always in the dominant role.

Because my parents' example and my own experience was that of marriage as a relationship between equal persons, it not only felt jarring to be asked to think of marriage in decision-making terms, but the use of "chain of command" introduced overtones of power and even oppression that disturbed me. I found that this interpretation of male headship incorporated a type of male political control over the wife and family that appeared to be in severe tension with the Bible's teaching about servanthood and mutual submission.

I also found it startling that some persons expanded *headship* to mean that all men should be "over" all women everywhere, so that even adult single women were to be under some sort of male authority figure such as a male relative or a male priest or minister. Again this raised the question *Is this what the Bible says?*

More Translation Questions

Where had this notion of power-oriented headship come from? The two relevant verses quoted to me were 1 Corinthians 11:3 and Ephesians 5:23, which (in our English Bibles) state that the man is head of the woman or the wife. The meaning would seem to indicate that men have authority over women, because although English dictionaries give a number of synonyms for *head* (including "headwaters" or "source"), usually the word *head* is understood in English today as "chief" or "leader."

But can the word used for *head* be so readily defined in these Bible texts? In New Testament Greek was it a politicized word? In the context of these two passages, does it mean a person who has authoritative power over another?

Again, as with the Hebrew word *'ēzer*, we must go to the original Bible language. The actual Greek word Paul used was *kephalē*. This word had a variety of meanings in the ancient world; the two most frequently suggested by Bible translators are "authority over" and "source." Obviously the meaning selected will color a person's interpretation of headship.

Careful scholarly research shows that it is more than wishful thinking that *kephalē* can sometimes mean "source" as well as "authority over."[9] A comprehensive (as against selective) examination of ancient literature gives evidence for considering the use of "source"—including evidence from the early Church Fathers. For example, within the space of a single paragraph, Archbishop Cyril of Alexandria defined *kephalē* four times as "source." In Appendix III, research by Christian classicist Catherine Clark Kroeger presents this material. Scholars and the professional clergy will find this particularly interesting, but it will also be important for laypersons to check the evidence for themselves.

There are some very good reasons for researching this question as thoroughly as possible. If *kephalē* is interpreted as a head that has "authority over," then we have to contend with at least two severe difficulties. The first is with our understanding of the doctrine of the Trinity, and the second is with our understanding of servanthood and mutual submission.

For the first difficulty: If we define *head* as "authority over," then 1 Corinthians 11:3 can mean that there is a dominant to subordinate hierarchy within the Trinity, a position that does violence to the equality of the Persons of the Godhead. Early in its history, orthodox Christianity took a firm stand against any teaching that would make Christ a subordinate figure. To say that God is somehow authoritative over Christ erodes the Savior's full divinity and puts a Christian on dangerous theological ground.

In this verse the word translated "God" is not *pater* ("Father"), but *theos* (the general Greek word for "deity"). If *kephalē* means "source," then—although many difficulties remain—at least the question of the subordination of Christ is eased.[10] Certainly all orthodox Christians affirm that in coming from the Godhead Jesus Christ is Very God of Very God.

For the second difficulty in translating head as "authority over": If a person says that the man always has authority over the woman then, although that person may give lip service to obeying the scriptural injunction in Ephesians 5:21 that believers be mutually submissive one to another, in reality the practice will be unilateral submission (submission of the woman only). If women must always submit, but men need never submit, how can we reconcile this with *mutual* submission?[11]

Again, as in chapter 5, I am *not* suggesting that all men are organized into a global sexist conspiracy! I am simply pointing out that if men are thought to be forever dominant (*always* having "authority over" women), then women must be forever subordinate, regardless of whether we call the teaching patriarchalism or male headship. To urge that men exercise their "authority over" in a Christian manner does not change this fact, nor does the plea that women voluntarily subordinate themselves change the situation.

If the man is always entitled to be over the woman, whenever he serves her, he will do this as a "favor." He will be unable to avoid thinking: *I don't really have to do this, if I don't want to.*

If the woman is always under the authority of the man, when she serves him, she will do this out of compulsion. Deep down, she will be unable to avoid thinking: *I am forced to do this. I have no choice.*

Change only comes when both sexes are seen as equally human and equally redeemed (Genesis 1:26–28; 2 Corinthians 5:14–21; Hebrews 7:25) and therefore equally free to practice the mutual submission commanded for all believers by Ephesians 5:21. They are all simply fellow sinners for whom

Christ died and, out of reverence for their Savior, put the interests of the other person above their own.

Keeping in mind the tension between mutual submission and female subordination, we turn to the use of *head* in Ephesians 5:23. When we examine this verse in its immediate context, we find that in addition to *kephalē* there is another Greek word whose translation is open to question. This word *hupotassō* has been translated "submit," but some evidence suggests that in the ancient world it could also mean "identify with." In common parlance today, submitting is thought of as "giving in" or "knuckling under" whereas "identify with" will express unity. As with *kephalē*, obviously the meaning used for *hupotassō* will color a person's interpretation of headship. Appendix III also presents research that helps us understand the possible alternative meaning of submit as "identify with" or "become one with."

Again it is evident that these translation possibilities give an entirely different flavor to this familiar passage. If they are used, the passage then emphasizes the couple's oneness as they identify with each other's interests. Wives would identify with their husbands as they would with Christ, surely a beautiful metaphor for the unity of Christian marriage. (Significantly, Scripture does not tell the wife to *obey* her husband, but to *submit* to him. This should encourage us to dig more deeply into exactly what Christian submission is all about.)

For the wife to think of her husband as source would not mean that he has power over her, but that in symbolically coming from him (as woman came from Adam) she is of him and one with him. Again, while not neatly answering every question about Ephesians 5:22–24, these possible alternate meanings of *kephalē* and *hupotassō* would ease tension between seeming female unilateral submission and the clear command in 5:21 to mutual submission. They would also harmonize with Paul's words in 1 Corinthians 11:11, 12, where he emphasizes unity and oneness in the Lord.

The Larger Picture

We will miss the overall teaching in this entire passage, however, if we stop here. The general admonition in verse 21 is that all believers be mutually submissive (or as one) with each other.[12] Then Paul goes on with words of wisdom for the Christian husband. He writes: "Love your wives, just as Christ loved the church and gave himself for her. . . . In this same way, husbands ought to love their wives as their own bodies. . . ." Paul concludes his call to unity within marriage by reiterating in verse 31 that the couple is "one flesh."

Some people may find it hard to appreciate how revolutionary this teaching was in the ancient world. The norm was a marriage of convenience, with the wife considered useful for her dowry or her production of heirs. How most wives must have resented, despised, or even feared their husbands! Those husbands had been taught to consider women inferior beings, and most men looked to find companionship, intellectual stimulation, and emotional satisfaction from men, not women.

So it would not have been new if Paul had echoed secular society by commanding wives to knuckle under to male authority. Paul's asking wives to adopt a new attitude toward their marriage relationship *was* new. But much more radical were Paul's words to husbands. Now men were not only to love their wives (something contemporary secular society considered unnatural and even impossible), but they were to love their wives as completely as Christ loved His church.

Some traditionalists have said that the mutual submission enjoined in verse 21 does not apply to husbands because the words to husbands do not use *submit* (or *identify with*). But saying that just because the husband is not told to submit to the wife, he is then exempt from mutual submission within marriage evades the command of verse 21. Without submitting to or identifying with the best interests of the beloved, no one can practice sacrificial Christ-like love—the love described in 1 Corinthians 13. For Paul to command this kind of love was a stronger constraint on husbands than "mere" submission. Only truly Christ-like love could break the shackles of the male domination that produced the awful degradation and depersonalization of women in the ancient world.

Strangely enough, our contemporary notion of marriage as career has not much differed from the ancient world's business-like perception of marriage, although we modern Americans usually do give marriage a veneer of romance. But Christian marriage is something far different, and Paul's words remain as relevant in twentieth-century America as they were in ancient Ephesus.

Now let us make these two new concepts about wives and husbands more contemporary by comparing them to the two slang terms we used in chapter 8, "meal ticket" and "ball and chain." In Ephesians 5:21–33 Paul teaches that the wife is to be as united with her husband as she is to her Savior, a far cry from thinking of him as only a material convenience who puts bread on the table. The husband must not think of the wife as a dead weight he attached himself to in a weak moment because of her dowry, her sexual attraction, or his desire for heirs. He should love her with lasting, sacrificial love. She should be as one with him, just like his own body. Both engage in this mutually submissive process, this becoming one flesh, out of reverence for Christ their Lord and Savior.[13]

Getting Off Track: Three Wrong Turns

Oswald Chambers wrote, "The majority of us are blind on certain lines; we see only in the light of our prejudices. A searchlight lights up only what it does and no more, but the daylight reveals a hundred and one facts that the searchlight had not taken into account. An idea acts like a searchlight and becomes tyrannous."[14] When people are guided only by a narrow searchlight, they can indeed get off the track.

For example, some groups have developed an expanded version of headship that would make all men "authoritative over" all women. This position depends on that presuppositional approach to the order of creation, misunderstands 'ēzer as meaning "subordinate," and arbitrarily imposes its preconceptions on the dozens of difficulties in the "hard passages." Then as the tyrannous searchlight focuses on the Ephesians 5:21–33 analogy of the husband to Christ and the wife to the church, the person holding that searchlight concludes all too quickly that because these verses liken the husband to Christ, *all* men must have a dominant role over *all* women.

This argument completely overlooks the fact that the biblical imagery used here does not lock people into male-female roles.

197

Note that the Christian husband, too, is part of the church (or Bride) of Christ and therefore is included in the "feminine imagery" used for the wife, as Paul teaches in Romans 7:1–6 and 2 Corinthians 11:2.[15]

Further, concentrating only on the analogy of Ephesians 5:21–33 will overlook the parallel teaching of Peter. In 1 Peter 3:1 the Apostle refers to Christ's sacrificial death in urging wives "in the same way" or "in like manner" to image Christ to their husbands. In so acting the wives are now included in the "male imagery" that refers to the Incarnate Lord.

So not only must the wife think of the husband as imaging Christ to her, but also the husband must think of the wife as herself imaging Christ to him. Scripture commands *all* believers to imitate their Lord (Ephesians 5:1, 2; 1 Thessalonians 1:6). Husband *and* wife can represent Christ to each other, because both sexes were created in God's image; and because Jesus is God, they can image Him. Any teaching that focuses solely on the analogy in Ephesians 5, in order to place the husband (much less all men) in an exalted position over women, will be another dangerous road to go down: It verges on male idolatry.

A second example of getting off the track is the teaching that says the husband is "head of the home" (sometimes even further expanded to mean high priest in the home). Because some Christians have so often repeated this notion, it, too, has become a self-fulfilling prophecy. However, no passage in the Bible states this concept. Not only is "the husband is head of the home" found nowhere in the Bible, but the slogan also contradicts the many Scripture passages where God's Word teaches that *both* parents share responsibility for the family.

Based on the biological fact that both father and mother produce the child, and continuing with the Fifth Commandment, in Exodus 20:12, Scripture enjoins children to honor and obey both parents equally (Leviticus 19:3; Deuteronomy 27:16; Proverbs 1:8; 6:20; Ephesians 6:1–3; Colossians 3:20). Luke 2:51 raises mutual parenting to the highest level by stating that the child Jesus was under the authority of *both* father *and* mother. The biblical ideal is that both parents are "homemakers," because when the two individuals become one in procreation and in

198

parenting, they have joined together to make an even stronger unit, the Christian family.

Yes, the particular passage we have examined in Ephesians does go on to give a specific command to fathers only: "Fathers, do not exasperate your children; instead, bring them up in the training and instruction of the Lord" (6:4). A similar command occurs in Colossians 3:21. However, in the light of *all* Scripture and not just the searchlight of male headship, it is evident that these injunctions are given in this context to the father, because he was the person society empowered to be "over" the children. In most first-century marriages the mother was not considered a responsible individual. But it would be wrong to be so literal minded as to say that, because it does not specifically mention her, Scripture exempts the mother from the intent of Ephesians 6:4 and Colossians 3:21. Certainly I as a Christian mother did not have carte blanche to exasperate or embitter my children.

Just as serious, we would be wrong to become so literal minded as to say that because the word *mother* is omitted from the command of Ephesians 6:4 to provide for the children's spiritual training, mothers are not equally responsible for that training. Deuteronomy 21:18–21 declared a son liable for disobeying *both* parents. Proverbs 1:8 tells the child to listen "to your father's instruction and do not forsake your mother's teaching." We know from Paul's own words of praise in 2 Timothy 1:5 how well taught Timothy was was due to the godly instruction he received from his grandmother, Lois, and his mother, Eunice.

So in the very broadest sense, Christian leadership in the home includes both husband *and* wife. Both parents can and should follow Christ's sacrificial example by giving themselves up to the best interests of each other and of their children. Under the Lordship of Christ, both will be head and source of the home. When both parents submit to and identify with Christ, they will both image Christ. When the children respond to that imaging process, then both parents will be the leaders and thus the source of their children's spiritual development.

A third example of getting off the track is the constant preoccupation with authoritative decision making within the family structure. Only as we bring the light of mutual submission to bear can all the relationships become balanced.

Even the most well-meaning families can be sadly off center on this issue. We can think of homes where children act like little tyrants, and the spoiled child who "runs the show" disgusts most of us. Instinctively we feel put off by a child who has "power over" the parents.

But what about those adults? Although current fashions make the metaphor outdated, we also react adversely to a wife and mother who "wears the pants of the family." However, *if we are honest*, we feel uneasy with and even repelled by the husband or father who "throws his weight around." In one of the most uncomfortable moments of my life I heard a domineering Christian husband squelch a perfectly logical suggestion from his mild-mannered wife with: "Shut up. You don't know what you're talking about."

How desperately we need to see that mutual submission in marriage and the family is not subtraction of wifely submission, but the addition of husbandly submission. Only that is the perfect biblical equation. *In decision making within marriage, the "one" who makes the decisions should be the "two become one."*

Yet people always ask, "If we actually try to practice mutual submission, who will make the decision when the couple is absolutely divided over an issue? Then who's in charge here?" Both Gilbert Bilezikian and William Spencer have made the very creative suggestion that the decision should be made by the partner who is most affected by the outcome of that decision.[16] Others have suggested that the couple take turns in breaking such impasses.

However, if deadlocks occur with any frequency we must ask: "How 'Christian' is the marriage? If the marriage partners are constantly polarized, how can they act as 'one flesh'? Can two walk together, except they be agreed?" The answer to the last question, of course, is that they cannot. Any marriage characterized by persistent division and and not mutuality of both operation and goals is in trouble. Christian partners are not competitors or adversaries! In truly Christian marriage, each partner *must* want only the best for the other. No partner would ever want to domineer or manipulate to try to get "my way."

If the partners frequently find themselves at odds, they must prayerfully ask God to help them establish a true "one flesh" relationship. Instead of arguing over male headship, they must both focus on Christ's Lordship.

A First-Century Challenge

In John 13:34, 35 Jesus gave His disciples that new commandment to love one another as He loved them. Paul's words in Ephesians 5:1, 2 amplify this commandment: "Be imitators of God, therefore, as dearly loved children and live a life of love, just as Christ loved us and gave himself up for us as a fragrant offering and sacrifice to God."

Within this context Paul went on to give those practical words about human relationships in Ephesians 5:21–6:9. His parallel teaching in Colossians 3:15–4:1 is also given within the framework of mutual submission. The words of 1 Peter 2:13–3:8 harmonize with Paul by continuing to counsel obedience and submissive "identification with" in terms of emulating Christ's sacrificial death.

To Paul's categories of husband-wife, parent-child, and master-slave, Peter adds the ruler-citizen relationship. The parent-child relationship has always been involuntary for the child, but in the first century all those other relationships were involuntary for the unempowered person. The woman had little or no say about whom she would marry. Slaves were trapped in involuntary servitude. The average citizen could not influence a totalitarian government.

So we can imagine the Christian woman locked into a difficult marriage saying: "I am now a new creature in Christ Jesus, and I will leave this distasteful union, to start my new life."

The Christian slave might feel tempted to think: *I am now a new creature in Christ Jesus, and I don't have to remain in this dehumanizing bondage.*

The Christian citizen might say: "I, too, am a new creature in Christ Jesus, so I don't have to obey this hateful regime."

They all might think: *Surely the God of justice does not expect us to remain in these unjust situations.*

But what do Peter and Paul say? They point every believer to that most unjust situation of all, the cross, and say: "As Christ gave Himself, so you give yourselves to act as Christ would act."

However, we must not forget that these passages also call the empowered person to account. The Apostles give the advice to *both* parties in the relationships.[17] How revolutionary for masters or slave owners (again women would not be exempt) to be told that they should act as Christ would toward the slaves or servants in their power! How radical for husbands to be told that they were to love, cherish, and honor their wives as Christ loved the church! How unique for the all-powerful fathers to be told to be sensitive to their children! When we read these passages with first-century eyes, we suddenly understand how novel they were to *all* parties involved.

The various New Testament passages about male-female relationships all occur within the larger context of the Christian's new walk and the Christian's new attitude. Inescapably, we must conclude that as Christ, our ultimate role model, abandoned claims to power and position, so also must any empowered person who seeks to follow Him. The overall thought in these passages is always to put the other person's interests over that of our own, which brings us back to mutual submission. What a radical conclusion for first-century society! Sadly enough, what a radical conclusion it still is today.

"Not My Century"

We need to read the Bible with sensitivity for the way in which it was written. We need to read Bible books or sections of these books for their unified thought. Scripture is not a smorgasbord of proof texts!

Since they are so short, we should read Ephesians, Colossians, 1 Timothy, and 1 Peter as the complete letters they are. Surely their writers intended that the people to whom they wrote would read them all at once. Don't you think Paul and Peter would have felt bemused if their readers had isolated only a few sentences from each epistle, latching on to only those?

It is most enlightening to read these books as "wholes." The person who does this finds that references to women assume their proper perspective. In Ephesians, Colossians, and 1 Peter, references to male-female relationships occur in sequences urging general submission of all believers to societal order, so that others will perceive Christianity positively and not write it off as a disruptive social or political movement. While 1 Timothy has a slightly different thrust, even there in chapter 2 the context is one of order, beginning with the believer's submission to governmental authority.

When we read these letters as units, it seems clear that (as in Philemon) the Apostles do not aim to lock people into roles, because then the Apostles would be lumping the evil institution of slavery with the God-ordained institution of the family. Rather, they emphasize the believer's attitude, not his or her place in society. (*See also* Titus 2:5, where Paul urges women to act harmoniously with societal expectations "so that no one will malign the word of God.")

In the sequential passages about relationships occurring in Ephesians, Colossians, and 1 Peter, both the empowered person (master, husband, parent) and the unempowered person (slave, wife, child) are urged to maintain a Christ-like attitude, as is the citizen. This is especially clear in 1 Peter, where Peter extols Christ as the highest example of submission, because He went to the cross for our sakes; then Peter exhorts people in various societal positions to act "in the same way. . . . in the same way. . . ." Peter urges both wives and husbands to act in the way Christ did. When we read these letters as "wholes," we can get the proper perspective on human relationships, because we see the biblical injunctions in context—and that goes for 1 Corinthians 11 and 14 as well.

Here I am reminded of an incident that happened when my husband and I were at Cambridge University, taking an extra-mural course in the social institutions of medieval England. One day we heard a guest lecturer discuss the English legal system in the thirteenth century. During the question period, I asked him how some of his concepts related to developments in the fourteenth century. He refused even to attempt an answer. His reason? "That's not my century." Our Cambridge professor was amused, but also faulted him for so isolating his scholarship that he had no feel for its relation to the sweep of English history.

So also we cannot isolate passages about women and refuse to consider how they relate both to their immediate context and to all Scripture. For example, when I hear some intricate exposition of 1 Timothy 2:11, 12, proclaiming those verses "the" definitive word on the role of women in the church, and when I ask, "How does that fit with 2 Corinthians 5:17 or Galatians 3:26–28 (or even with the preceding two verses in Timothy!)?" so often the person who can see *only* 1 Timothy 2:11, 12 comes back to me with the equivalent of "that's not my century."

Here again we must be alert to the danger of selective exegesis. Many who would cling to 1 Timothy 2:11, 12 as restricting women's role have felt free to ignore 1 Timothy 2:8, 9. Some have even severely disapproved of men (or women!) who raise hands during worship (v. 8) as well as ignoring the admonition against gold jewelry and pearls (v. 9). We can fairly ask these groups: *Why do you feel free to ignore 1 Timothy 2:8, 9 but retain 1 Timothy 2:11, 12?*

Christians are called to be "doers of the truth." If our scholarship is to have integrity, it cannot serve special interests. Our teachings must be compatible with larger known truth and in harmony with scriptural principles that are accepted as clear. We cannot isolate any Scripture portions as final, transcultural truth without studying them in their immediate context and subjecting them to the broader truth of each believer's full redemption and equal spiritual standing as a new creature in Christ Jesus.

The *Real* Hard Passages

So often a traditionalist will say to a biblical feminist like myself: "Let's see you try to explain away the 'hard passages.' " I answer: "There's no need to explain away anything. The difficulties in the 'hard passages' caution us from overestimating them as being 'the last word' about 'who's in charge here.' " When that person says, "Let's see you try to get around male headship," here, too, I respond that there is no need to try to get around anything. As with my call to abandon role playing, I can claim the Word of God as my authority for urging mutual submission.

If people will put out that tyrannous searchlight of male

headship and subject their presuppositions to the light of *all* Scripture, they will see that the Apostles themselves describe the role of head in such a way that *in practice* it makes no difference whether head represents an empowered figure or a source figure.

In Ephesians 5:21–33 Paul's own words present *head* as a sacrificial figure, by referring to Christ as "Savior" and telling husbands to "love your wives, just as Christ loved the church and gave himself up for her. . . ." In 1 Peter 3:7, Peter reiterates this description of the husband's role, when he, too, commands men to treat their wives "in the same way"—with that phrase clearly referring to the great passage about Christ the Suffering Servant in 1 Peter 2:21–25.

In our consideration of the "hard passages," we face the problem of reconciling the seeming restrictions on women with the actual practice of Jesus and Paul and with the many instances of women whom Scripture commends for leading God's people and proclaiming God's Word. Now we must recognize that interpreting male headship as "power over" conflicts with Scripture's own description of *head* as "sacrificial servant."

Yes, many traditionalists do say, "Of course men must be servants." But if they persist in clinging to a dominant/subordinate hierarchy in human relationships and if they desire to retain "power over" women (even under the guise of its being "appointed" power), then these men will miss one of the deepest lessons of the Incarnation—a lesson Jesus taught in passages like Mark 10:45 and John 12:23–26.

In 2 Corinthians 10:5 God's Word urges us to ". . . take captive every thought to make it obedient to Christ," and that includes all thoughts about *Who's in charge here?* When we subject those very human thoughts to His Lordship, we can hear His words in Mark 8:34: "If anyone would come after me, he must deny himself and take up his cross and follow me." Jesus makes His challenge to servanthood clear in John 13:1–17, and He still asks His followers that searching question of Luke 6:46: "Why do you call me, 'Lord, Lord,' and do not do what I say?" These are the *real* hard passages.

Only as the Christian man—or woman—willingly gives up all rights to power and position can this believer be freed from self-interest and move out to submit to and identify with Christ's interests. Here we need to remember that lesson from the life of Mary. Only when we tell our Lord, "Not my will, but Yours," will we, too, image Him to brother, sister, husband, wife, child, fellow believer, and unbeliever alike.

Hard passages indeed—passages that tell us we must give up all thought of power and place—and hard lessons to learn— lessons about sacrifice.

Yes, humanly speaking, we do like challenges we can control, and we do not mind being asked to be Christ-like as long as we control what Christ-like-ness involves. Therefore people today still try to control the parameters of sacrifice by clinging to strategies that insure they will remain "in charge here." How hard it has been even for some Christian men to say, "I am my wife's servant; I am my sister's servant."

What if Christ had said, "I must have My proper place"? What if He had said, "I do not have to identify with a woman"? No, thank God that Christ did not merely condescend to inter- act with us: He came to *be* one with us—to identify with us so completely that He could take our place at God's bar of justice. That is what Christ-like sacrifice is all about, and that is the final outworking of His teaching that "whoever will be greatest must be servant of all."

Christ's Deciding Vote

One of the most subtle tricks of the enemy has been to get human beings to concentrate on the wrong agenda. By fooling us into concentrating on the question *Who's in charge here?* and into looking for the answer on the human level, ever since the Fall evil has fostered competition and strife between the sexes. We have been tricked into trying to protect imaginary roles, and our prideful strategies have resulted in power struggles and manipulative behavior. The inevitable deadlocks have re- sulted, because neither side has wanted to "lose face" by "giv- ing in."

It is sobering to ask: *In the light of Scripture's clear call to mutual submission, is the current notion of a power-oriented male headship another false idea—an artificial concept some have developed in their attempts to remain "in charge here"?* Note that the term itself—

male headship—does not occur in the Bible and that any dominant/subordinate interpretation of human relationships is very difficult to defend, once we recognize patriarchy as a false human philosophy and role playing as an unscriptural idea. Remember, too, that if God had wished to teach a "chain of command," He would not have called Mary directly, but would have sent her call through Joseph.

In this matter of male headship, have even dedicated Christians been tricked into concentrating on how to break deadlocks, instead of concentrating on a strategy of mutual submission that will keep those deadlocks from happening in the first place? Have all too many Christians had tunnel vision about protecting rigid male-female roles and so lost the larger vision of our primary role as ambassadors for Christ?

Yet people continue to be preoccupied with the thought that someone must have "the last word." My traditionalist friends continue to say, "Men must retain power over women, because when the chips are down, *someone* has to have the last word."

We need to ask: *What did Christ do when the chips were down?* In that greatest relational impasse of all time—God and fallen humanity confronting each other—how did God in Christ choose to cast the deciding vote?

If ever there was a claim to position and power, Christ had it, but He did not decide to claim that position or to use that power. Instead He humbled Himself and became as a servant. Although Jesus had every right, He did not say to fallen humanity: "I am the one who is highest on the ladder, I am first and foremost, so I will force the issue by using my power and authority to cast the deciding vote." No, instead of calling for legions of angels, He went like a lamb to the slaughter.

In the standoff between Christ and sinful men and women— the ultimate relational confrontation that represents the ultimate test of *Who's in charge here?*—our Lord's concept of the deciding vote was to become total sacrifice. Can His servants do less?

Chapter Ten

Liberty and Justice for All

"Ladies and gentlemen, those of you who are on the right-hand side of our aircraft will see the lights of Sydney. Please fasten your seat belts and extinguish all smoking materials in preparation for landing." My time of introspection ended. Over twenty-one hours of flying time were over, and now I began my experience in a new country.

As I had discovered on other travels, geography may vary, but "the tie that binds" remains the same. I felt an immediate oneness with my Australian hosts as we celebrated our common bond as ambassadors for Christ. I also found the same concerns. Although I was 15,000 miles from New York City, here, too, sincere Christians wrestled with issues of human relationships.

The conference convened in Sydney particularly focused on equality of men and women in ministry, with specific emphasis on the question of ordination of women. There, as at similar gatherings in the United States, I found women eager to study theology and earnestly desiring to use their gifts in the pastoral ministry. Like many of their American sisters, whose communions were also closed to full participation of women, these Australians experienced severe tension between their individual calls to serve God and the traditionalists' denial of the validity of their calls.

A Sense of Call

Again I thought back over my own inner journey. During my years of searching for biblical answers to these crucial questions, I had experimented with suppressing my own call. I had entered a field completely opposite to church work.

I had two very practical reasons for trying an alternate to volunteerism. First, my husband—a trusts and estates lawyer—was familiar with the fact that statistically wives outlive their husbands. Now that our children were older, he and I felt that it would be good for me to see what I could do about a paying job. If I were widowed, I might have a real need to support myself.

The second reason for my reentrance into the paid job market was that our three closely spaced children had all reached senior high school. Contemplating the upcoming years of university costs was staggering! Thinking that a job allowing some flexibility would be ideal, I approached a good friend who was a real-estate broker. She and her partner invited me to join their sales force, and I worked with them for three years. I enjoyed the challenge and variety of this profession.

During these years I was also offered expanded opportunities to teach the Bible, and I soon realized that this was my "first love." It was not fair to give my real-estate colleagues less than 100 percent on the job, so I eased out of the marketplace and back into serving my church full-time. My experience illustrates the undeniable fact that persons who have a sense of call do not feel happy and fulfilled unless they answer that call.

I am well aware that today some persons teach that women who aspire to certain areas of ministry are not obedient to biblical authority. These people have described a woman who feels called to those areas as misguided, deluded, or sinful. They deny that a woman can have a genuine call to enter the field of theological education or the ordained ministry. However, the validity of a woman's call will not be established by what *people* say, but by what *Scripture* says. We cannot decide this matter on feelings or custom. We must return to the Bible to review the entrance requirements for God's diplomatic corps.

Reviewing the Evidence

The finished work of Jesus Christ (Hebrews 7:25) guarantees the Christian's spiritual rights and therefore a woman's spiritual rights. First Timothy 2:5 and Hebrews 10:19–22 tell us that all persons are free to come directly to Him, and His own words in John 6:37 assure us, ". . . whoever comes to me I will never drive away." The wonder of the substitutionary atonement is that He gives *all* who believe in Him the power to become children of God. Both men and women are included in the spiritual principle of "sonship" as set forth in Romans 8:15–17, and the words of 1 Peter 2:4–10 affirm the priesthood of all believers.

Our theme passage, 2 Corinthians 5:14–21, has further told us that we new creatures in Christ Jesus all have a new mission, the ministry of reconciliation. We are all to proclaim the Good News. The inclusive message tells us women as well as men are fully redeemed; women as well as men are called ambassadors for Christ.

The many biblical case histories illustrate our mutual call to serve God. Scripture presents women who were used in leadership and administrative capacities and women who were called to proclaim and teach God's Word. Scripture also tells us that women can study and discuss theology: Some of the greatest truths Jesus taught were originally given to women and passed on to the Christian community by them. Jesus described Mary of Bethany's desire to hear His teaching as "choosing the better part." Yes, scriptural evidence shows that all Christians have equal inheritance rights and equal opportunity to serve God.

But further evidence needs to be introduced here: spiritual gifts. The biblical case histories revealed that the women God called were individuals with individual gifts. For example, Miriam and Deborah had leadership abilities; Abigail had a gift for peacemaking; Huldah received the gift of prophecy; Phoebe had pastoral gifts; Priscilla had the gift of teaching. As He did with gifted men, God called these women to their various "ambassadorial posts" because of the unique gifts He had given them, and the inspired text commends them for their use of these gifts.

Further evidence for equality of women in ministry that *must* be objectively evaluated is that nowhere does Scripture limit the gifts by gender. The three New Testament passages that tell us the most about spiritual gifts (Romans 12:3–8; 1 Corinthians 12; Ephesians 4:11–13) make no mention of gender restriction. We can properly ask: *If women were not to be given certain gifts or were not to exercise certain gifts, would it not have been important for Scripture to have made this plain?*

The Question of Authority

Once again my traditionalist friends told me: "It is unnatural for women to be in positions of leadership and for them to have such a call. It simply goes against nature for women to be in authority."

Yet no matter what translation I looked at, Miriam was a coleader; Deborah was chief of state; Huldah proclaimed the authoritative word of the Lord to God's people; Paul clearly commended his co-worker and fellow minister Phoebe; and Priscilla taught the man Apollos. So when people persisted in saying, "It goes against nature," I began to wonder: *Whose nature?* After much thought I began to conclude that it was fallen man's nature, a sinful nature that can deceive any of us into wanting to be Number One. Yes, it does go against the nature of those who have accepted the false philosophy of patriarchalism and who have bought the notion "That's how men are." Such people will find it impossible even to consider giving up a sense of entitlement to being "over" women and taking a secondary role.

Was it possible that unconsciously my friends had fallen into the trap of being guided by the flesh? Surely any man who was a new creation would want to follow Christ's teaching that servanthood is the highest role. Only the person who copied the world's way of looking at things would always want to retain all authority.

However, it also seemed to me that my friends had not thoroughly investigated this matter of authority. Just as I had to ask, "Whose nature does women in leadership go against?" I also had to ask, "Whose authority is really at stake here?"

As we established in chapter 1, for the Christian, God is the ultimate authority, and God's Word presents that authority to us. Our great Creator God has the authority to call whom He wills, to give equipping gifts to whom He wills, and to place whomever He wills in the ambassadorial post of His choosing. So as we examine the question of ministry we must avoid the false notion that individuals or denominations in any way control God's authority.

As we saw in chapter 5, because God is truth, all truth is God's truth. That truth is validly proclaimed, whether by a woman or a man. The ultimate authority with which any human being speaks does not reside in the human agent, but comes from God.

Ambassadors for Christ are like their secular diplomatic counterparts who are called to transmit the message of the government that sends them out. The individual diplomat's authority comes not from himself or herself, but from the sending agency. So Christ is the Christian's "sending agency," and His Word—the Bible—is our source of authority. *His message* is what is authoritative, not the representative proclaiming it or some office that representative may hold.

The person—man or woman—who faithfully proclaims the Word of God exercises true authority. The power to exercise that authority is delegated by God alone, to whom He calls. Jesus Christ is our universal Head of Staff! We are all under His authority as His deputies, and we should all open ourselves to being deployed where He wills.

In this connection we must recognize the contribution of all the women who teach in the younger Sunday-school grades and in daily vacation Bible schools. Many have thought of these areas as "women's work," but just as in grammar school, teaching very young children is a tremendous responsibility. We affirm the message of Proverbs 22:6 that proper childhood training is vital for adult spiritual well-being. Yet do we honestly face up to the fact that most childhood training, including spiritual training, lies in the hands of women? Whether or not traditionalists admit it, women *are* entrusted with leadership and teaching in the most crucial years of children's development. Women have indeed proclaimed the authoritative Word of God to these little ones.

Here, too, is an appropriate place to comment on present-day "case histories." More and more evangelical women have been and are today using their gifts in new areas. Many lead parachurch organizations, write books, teach at conferences, and even preach from pulpits. Why is this happening in even the more conservative circles? Because these women's gifts are evident, their constituencies recognize their gifts, and the women themselves feel called to present their message. This illustrates the fact that we should celebrate spiritual gifts and use, not bury, them. God-given gifts will out! When these women faithfully expound God's Word, they lead, write, speak, and teach with authority.[1]

From personal experience I can testify to the way congregations have moved forward when they saw authority in the church as God's authority and when the church freely allowed women to use the gifts He gave them. Rigid role playing had forced people to try to fill kingdom jobs for which they were not suited. For example, when church leaders assigned service openings according to a supposed male-female role restriction, men who had no gift for teaching tried to teach Sunday school, and single professional women were placed in charge of child-care programs any young father could have set up more efficiently! But once jobs were matched with gifts, freedom existed. People trying to use gifts they did not have were liberated from being square pegs in round holes. Women were free from the anxiety and guilt they felt when their gifts were denied and the Spirit's prompting in their hearts was quenched.

So traditionalists must think very carefully about the question of authority before they deny women freedom to use their spiritual gifts. James 1:17 assures us that God is the author of our gifts, and 1 Corinthians 12:4–11 tells us that God the Holy Spirit gives gifts to whom He will. Certainly God can delegate authority to whom He will! Therefore it contradicts Scripture to say women cannot proclaim the authoritative Word of God. Saying a woman may not use her leadership in God's service dishonors the divine Giver of the gifts. When such a woman is forced to use her gifts in the world, because she has no liberty to use them in the church, the Christian community is diminished.[2]

But What About Ordination?

Ordination is a word that traditionally has set some men apart from their fellows, a word with an aura of mystery. But when we turn to the Bible to examine it, we find a perplexing fact. Although it may come as a surprise to the average church-goer—as it certainly did to me!—even the scholarly experts do not know what ordination meant in New Testament times.

Ordination is mentioned in the New Testament as something that apparently was done to set a person apart for ministry, but *exactly* what it involved is unknown to us. Unlike the elaborately detailed rituals set down in connection with the Old Testament priesthood, the New Testament says very little about Christian ordination. Paul's advice in 1 Timothy 5:22 ("Do not be hasty in the laying on of hands . . .") indicates that ordination should not be administered casually.

Over the centuries "laying on of hands" has accompanied ordination, primarily because this was done in the case of Barnabas and Saul (Acts 13:3) and Timothy (1 Timothy 4:14; 2 Timothy 1:6). The phrase "laying on of hands" also occurs in Hebrews 6:2, but it is not entirely certain whether that refers to ordination, healing, or some other practice. ("Laying on of hands" was common in supernatural healing, as in Acts 9:10–19; 28:8, beginning, of course, with the many instances where Jesus touched those He healed.)

The tremendous variety we see in ordination requirements and ceremonies today reflects the scarcity of hard information in the New Testament. It bears noting that while most church leaders pray before ordaining someone, not too many fast prior to the ceremony, although that was the scriptural example in Acts 13:3.

Yet when confronted with legitimate questions about current ordination practices, many groups fall back on custom and say: "We've always done it this way. We've never ordained women. After all these centuries, it's just not possible that we could be wrong." But as we saw in chapters 3 and 5, tradition is not always a reliable guide. Certainly many Christians erred for centuries in turning a blind eye toward racism in the church. Now in the matter of ordination of women, we need to ask: *Is our tradition in harmony with Scripture?* Remember Jesus' strong words about human tradition in Mark 7:6–13 and His terrible indictment of the legalists in Matthew 23.[3]

Here we need to be aware of the pressures of our culture on our exegesis. Some people (myself included) suspect that it is not the Bible text, but our later-twentieth-century trends in evangelicalism that promote a philosophy of role playing that effectively excludes women from the ordained ministry today. In this context Janette Hassey's book *No Time for Silence: Evangelical Women in Public Ministry Around the Turn of the Century* gives much food for thought.[4]

Of course, no one can ever approach Scripture with a completely open mind. Our backgrounds, current social trends, and peer pressure will affect us. Nevertheless, those who want to be guided by God's Word begin their search for truth by studying the Bible text with as much objectivity as possible. When we do that, we find that while ordination undoubtedly figured in church order in some way, no New Testament text mandates ordination before a person can go out to preach the Gospel. In the New Testament, ordination is not set forth as a prerequisite to proclamation or to the exercise of certain spiritual gifts like those of pastoring, teaching, or administration.

One popular rationale for limiting ordination to men comes from appealing to those "hard passages" we discussed in chapter 9: 1 Corinthians 11:2–16; 14:33–36; and 1 Timothy 2:8–15. Yet, as Appendix II shows, these passages are filled with difficulties of meaning and interpretation. We must face this fact, along with the flaw in the traditional rationale. Traditionalists have said women should not be ordained because Scripture has a "clear command" that women be silent and not teach or hold authoritative posts. However, the difficulties in these passages make any "clear command" problematic. We must be very cautious about trying to use these "hard passages" as the basis for normative, transcultural truth. We *all* need further light on their precise meaning.

Until we have that light, we are left with these many questions: *Does the Bible tell us exactly what ordination is? If believers in apostolic times were not preoccupied with ordination, why are we today?*[5] Why do some groups use ordination as a device to restrict women's full use of their spiritual gifts and their practical opportunities to serve God? If the Bible does not mandate ordination as a qualification for the pastorate, why should we today? Should not those of us who respect Scripture as God's Word be very cautious about narrowing a concept the Bible does not spell out in detail? Certainly Paul warned in 1 Corinthians 4:6 not to go beyond what is written.

How tragic that women's ordination has become a major point of division among Christians, when no one today can say for sure exactly what ordination meant in New Testament times. Here we need to remember the emphasis of the apostolic writers. They called all believers to use their gifts to serve God and not to get sidetracked into criticizing other servants or judging another servant's calling. We cannot ignore the sobering message of Romans 14:4: God's servants are accountable to Him and not to us. We can think of Jesus' words to inquisitive Peter, effectively saying, "What is your concern with John's role? Your job is to feed My sheep."

As our Lord taught in the parable in Matthew 20:1–16, He has the right to do what He wishes with His servants. So if He picks a Deborah as head of state, a Huldah to present His authoritative message, a Phoebe to oversee, or a Priscilla to teach, who are we to question His use of His own? Remember that message to Peter in Acts 10:15: "Do not call anything impure that God has made clean."

I am an ordained elder in the Presbyterian Church U.S.A.; therefore obviously I believe women's ordination is fully biblical. However, I would call all readers to go beyond conscience or personal preference and address the underlying issue: Any believer who has a specific call from God should be free to answer that call.

If we are faithful to Scripture, we must affirm the priesthood of *all* believers. Within that overall context there will be specific vocations, either "full-time," such as pastor or missionary, or "part-time," such as elder or deacon. Since Scripture includes women in the priesthood of all believers, why should we feel surprised if women feel led to one of these specific areas of "priestly" service? As with men, women, too, can heed God's call to a particular "ambassadorial post."

Onward Christian Soldiers

As long as churches require ordination for the pastoral ministry and for certain offices within church structure, women called to these posts will continue to seek ordination. However, the groundless fear that if ordination is freely "opened up" to them, all women will want to be ordained has no more validity than the idea that all men might want to be ordained.

Again matters of calling and gifts come into play. As with men, only the women who sincerely feel called to the pastorate or other ordained posts and whose gifts are commensurate with that calling will desire ordination.

Here we must put to rest the fear that women who affirm equality of ministry really demand to take over ministry, and we must expose the false allegation that the entrance of women into full participation in the church will result in the loss of male participation.

Yes, I am aware that there are bossy women, squabbling women, aggressive and fractious women, and emotional women. However, as a longtime church worker, I have seen my share of bossy, squabbling, aggressive, fractious, and even emotional men. So the claim that admitting women into full participation in ministry sometimes causes men to fall away cannot rely on the premise that only women are "difficult types" who make it impossible for men to continue to serve.

We must think more carefully about this allegation that the entrance of women into full participation in ministry discourages male participation. If indeed men do fall away after women begin serving, whose fault *is* that? It is not as if there weren't enough jobs to go around, as if the fields aren't white with the harvest, as if our diplomatic corps had finished its work. If men become inactive when women become active, could the problem be not with the women's arrival on the scene, but with the shallowness of the men's commitment?

We are engaged in spiritual warfare, not spiritual détente. We need all the Christian soldiers we can get! Can you imagine a resistance group in World War II saying, "Women are now joining us, so we men will no longer fight"? That would have

217

been ridiculous. Rather, the men said, "Now we have twice the help."

So also truly committed Christian men should welcome their sisters and see equality of ministry as an opportunity to double the ranks of the salvation army. Truly committed Christian men will not take a "dog in the manger" attitude that selfishly refuses to share the work load, nor will they stop working themselves.

In that spiritual warfare, the Bible warns us to be alert against attacks of the enemy. In all warfare an effective strategy is to divide and conquer, and Satan will use any method possible to divide believers and trick them into competing with one another for kingdom posts. Men will lose if they are tricked into thinking that equality of service will blur their sexual identity, and—just as bad—women will lose if they are tricked into thinking equality of service is a chance to gain power to push someone else out. We all win if we think of partnership in ministry as freeing us to maximize our individual opportunities to serve in God's salvation army.

The Burden of Proof

Scripture assures us that our new standing in Christ must destroy all division between believers (1 Corinthians 12:12, 13; Galatians 3:26–28; 6:13–15; Ephesians 2:11–22; Colossians 3:9–11). In Him we are members of one Body, one spiritual family, one temple of God, one diplomatic corps. Concentrating on our unity in Christ will help us guard against the divisiveness of discriminatory or competitive tactics. Yet how sad when the enemy does trick fellow believers into artificial divisions. We cannot ignore the fact that many members of the Body are hurt by practices that restrict or even deny their spiritual rights to full personhood and full ministry as God's children.

Nowhere does Christ teach that gender, race, age, physical condition, social or economic circumstances, political affiliation, or any other factor hinders our salvation or bars us from serving Him. In Luke 9:49, 50 Jesus Himself warned against discrimination when He rebuked the disciples for wanting to exclude from ministry those who did not do things exactly as the disciples did.

In Acts 9 we are told that Ananias did not want to have anything to do with Saul (later Paul), because of Saul's past. The Lord's answer: ". . . This man is my chosen instrument. . . ." In other words, no matter how unlikely it seemed to Ananias, God had called Saul, and it was not up to Ananias to question that call. The continuing record of the early church in the Book of Acts shows an inclusiveness reinforced by Paul's call to unity in Galatians 3:26–28.

Thus many sincere Christian women and men feel puzzled that some groups still would bar women from full participation in ministry. As women seek to answer God's call to them, their question is: "Since 2 Corinthians 5:21 assures us that we, too, have become the righteousness of God, how can we not 'measure up' to your human requirements for ministry? Is this verse for us, or not? If it is, then we, too, are full ambassadors for Christ, and to us, too, is committed the privilege of proclaiming the message of reconciliation."

In the light of the full humanity of women and the full redemption of women, the burden is not on women to prove that others should allow them to use their gifts as God calls. The burden lies on those who would restrict the spiritual gifts of women to prove that they are not discriminating against their sisters in Christ.

Another Hidden Fear

As I interacted with people opposed to equality in ministry, it became apparent that they feared such equality would result in two basic problems: Social confusion and theological confusion. In chapter 6 we examined the first hidden fear. Now we must examine the second.

Many of my traditionalist friends informed me that the basic reason for preserving rigid male-female roles in the church is that only men can effectively represent God. I was told that the presence of ordained women representing God would cause theological confusion. Where did this idea come from?

Their position linked the Old Testament male priesthood with the masculine language and imagery used for God in the Bible. Their thinking was that, as the ordained clergy presented God's message of salvation through Christ, the congregation would more readily identify with the person proclaiming that Good News if the person were male.

They told me the function of the clergy is not only representing the people to God (as did the priest in the Old Testament sacrificial system) but also representing God to the people. Therefore, while either a woman or a man could perform that first function, a woman could not perform the second function, because the predominantly masculine language and imagery for God determines that only men can make a harmonious representation of God to the people. I was told that the masculine language and imagery for Father and Son would prevent women from accurately imaging God to the congregation, and if women tried to do so, it would cause theological confusion.

I saw a number of problems with my friends' position. First, carrying over the Old Testament priesthood into the New Testament era by considering Christian ministers as an extension of the Old Testament priests violated the Book of Hebrews, which clearly teaches that the Old Testament priesthood is superseded by Christ the Perfect Priest, who made His sacrifice "once for all." Matthew 27:51 tells us that there is now no more physical temple barrier between humanity and God, and 1 Timothy 2:5 assures us that post-Calvary there is no mediator needed between God and humanity, except Jesus Christ. First Peter 2:4, 5 proclaims the new priesthood of all believers. As such, ministers are no longer types of Old Testament priests who performed blood sacrifices, but servant-proclaimers of the Gospel.

Second, while the Old Testament priest did indeed represent the people before God, the prophet represented God to the people. Our authority, the Bible, tells us that women like Huldah and Phillip's daughters prophesied, and Paul's words in 1 Corinthians 11:5 indicate that women were free to prophesy.

In addition, the awesome responsibility of representing God to the people means representing His Word, not His Self. No one can or should ever dare to say, "My male body is somehow a representation of God." For the very reason of *avoiding* theological confusion, God commanded us in Exodus 20:4, 5 not to make any graven image. We finite creatures simply cannot imagine or ever adequately portray what infinite Deity is truly like. As Isaiah 40:18 (NEB) puts it, "What likeness will you find for God, or what form to resemble his?" The Old Testament is full of constant warnings against idolatry, because it is impossible to reduce God to an image.

So teaching that an ordained clergy must be male, because only males can harmoniously and effectively represent God the Father and God the Son proves too much. In spite of any protestations to the contrary, people who affirm this position do indeed end up with a male God—a larger-than-life masculine deity. They have fallen into the trap of confining God to their image.[6]

A proponent of this view was C. S. Lewis, who wrote: "But the masculine none of us can escape. What is above and beyond all things is so masculine that we are all feminine in relation to it."[7] This statement creates severe problems with Genesis 1:26–28 and 5:1, 2, and also with the clear teaching in 2 Corinthians 3:16–18 that *all* believers (not just men) are being transformed into God's likeness.

These problems are compounded when Lewis further writes: "Only one wearing the masculine uniform can . . . represent the Lord to the church: for we are all, corporately and individually, feminine to Him. We men may often make very bad priests. That is because we are insufficiently masculine. [But] it is no cure to call in those who are not masculine at all."[8]

Should we not rather say that people make bad priests (or pastors) because they are insufficiently *Christ-like?* Reducing imaging to gender means that simply because women do not have the "right uniform," they cannot represent Christ *anywhere,* not just behind the altar rail or within the ordained ministry. This position causes unspeakable pain to the woman who seeks to be conformed to Christ. It also compounds theological confusion, instead of avoiding it. The argument for the "male uniform" necessitates a masculine deity, as Lewis's own words demonstrate.[9]

But what does Scripture say about God? Numbers 23:19 tells us, "God is not a man . . . ," and in Hosea 11:9 God distinctly says: ". . . I am God, and not man. . . ." Passages like Job 38–41 should humble any who try to liken humanity to Deity or vice versa, as should God's words in Isaiah 55:9: "As the heavens are higher than the earth, so are my ways higher than your ways and my thoughts than your thoughts." Jesus taught in John 4:24 that God is not as we are. It is we who are in His image, not He who is in ours.

Nor can the male vehicle for the Incarnation be used to imprison God in human sexuality. The Bible's language for God is a communication device, not a gender preference. Surely this becomes evident in the simple fact that nowhere in Scripture does God say, "I like men better," or "Men are more like Me than women are." Yes, Christ did come in the form of a man, but maleness or masculinity cannot be the essence of God, or woman's creation in the image of God is not true. The male language used for God and God's use of a male body in the Incarnation must remain a mysterious method of communication between Infinite and finite, but we cannot seize upon it as a reason to exclude women from ministry, without sliding into male idolatry.

Such appropriation of male language as an exclusionary device completely overlooks Scripture's own use of feminine imagery for God. In Isaiah 42:14 God likens Himself to a woman in labor; in Luke 13:21 the kingdom of God is likened to a woman using yeast; in Luke 15:8–10 Christ's parable likens God to a woman with a lost coin; in Matthew 23:37 Jesus likens Himself to a mother hen gathering her chicks. How can we forget the feminine imagery of the new birth process that is the work of God the Holy Spirit? How can we ignore God's beautiful assurance in Isaiah 66:13: "As a mother comforts her child, so will I comfort you . . ."?

Beloved devotional writer Hannah Whitall Smith helps us put this matter in perspective. She writes: "But God is not only father. He is mother as well, and we have all of us known mothers whose love and tenderness has been without bound or limit. And it is very certain that the God who created them both, and who is Himself father and mother in one, could never have created earthly fathers and mothers who were more tender and more loving then He is Himself. Therefore if we want to know what sort of a Father He is, we must heap together all the best of all the fathers and mothers we have ever known or can imagine, and we must tell ourselves that this is only a faint image of God, our Father in Heaven."[10]

G. Campbell Morgan sums up the inclusiveness of God this way: "In God there is Father—'Like as a Father pitieth His children'; and there is Mother—'as one whom his mother comforteth.' And even then God is not complete in revelation. There is childhood. The likeness of God is completed in the Son."[11]

Masculine, Feminine, or Christian?

Theology is the study of God and His relation to our world. More simply put, theology is talking about God. For God's children this will mean talking about their heavenly Father. Excluding women from this study says: "You can't talk about your Father." So when brothers in Christ have not only said, "Imaging God is my province," but have added, "Studying about God is my province, too," they have inflicted double pain on their sisters.

I know, because I have felt that pain. I have sat in congregational meetings where men have said, "Using any unqualified man at all is better than choosing a qualified woman to serve." I have heard a man say, "Any woman in church office has copied Eve by grasping at the apple of power." I was told that an ordained woman had committed the grossest sin.

Denying women ordination is really saying to women: "You can't fully serve your heavenly Father." Denying women's ability to "do" theology is really saying: "Daughters of God can't talk about their heavenly Father." No wonder there is frustration and even alienation among women. Many feel like Mary Magdalene at the tomb: "They have taken my Lord away, . . . and I don't know where they have put him" (John 20:13).[12]

In their pain, many women have reacted by developing their own "territory." Women excluded from theological study (and thus from the ordained clergy as well under today's restrictions) have concluded that Christian theology is masculine theology. To them Christian theology is really a theological perspective controlled by men and expounded in the interests of men. So in their reaction against what appears to them to be male theology, many women have decided to develop a femi-

223

nist theology. In its most extreme form their reaction declares that God is feminine. This results not only in a strange theological dualism, but also in a severe breakdown of communication between the sexes on the one common ground to us all, knowledge of our Maker.[13]

However, both masculinized theology and feminized theology ultimately end up with a God in a human image. Neither a male-controlled theology nor a female-controlled theology is biblical: God is not masculine or feminine. Jesus taught us in John 4:24, "God is Spirit, and his worshipers must worship in spirit and in truth." How sad that people seem to reduce worship to worshiping in the flesh, not the reborn spirit.

We must not forget that at the Fall Satan's basic trick was to get humankind to desire to be as God. We *do* want to think of ourselves more highly than we ought to. But since they could not be as God, fallen men and women have competed with one another ever since. Once more (as we did with that false question *Who's in charge here?*) we come up against the desire for power. As some men concentrate on male language and imagery, they may feel closer to God as Power Source. Some women will react by trying to prove God is feminine. Both seek to bolster the desire for power by saying, "I am more like God than you are."

The antidote for this confusion will be to focus on our mutual creation in the image of God. Both men and women have equal worth and value; both sexes can know God and learn about Him; both can image Him to a hurting world. So we need to work to create a climate where both sexes are affirmed as equal children of God, where both sexes can freely study about God, and where both sexes are free to use their gifts in ministry to image God. Men and women alike need to take the focus off gender and therefore off any petty struggle to control who images God and who appropriates language about God.

Truly Christian theology and ministry are neither masculine nor feminine. A truly Christian theologian or minister can be either a man or a woman. Christ is made wisdom to the woman as well as to the man (1 Corinthians 1:30), and the woman as well as the man can aspire to develop "the mind of Christ" (1 Corinthians 2:16). Both can claim the promise of James 1:5:

"If any of you lacks wisdom, he should ask God, who gives generously to all without finding fault, and it will be given to him."

Both sons and daughters can discuss the things of God their heavenly Father. Both sisters and brothers can minister under the Lordship of Christ their Brother.

Again, as I said in the conclusion of chapter 6, equality in theological study and in ministry will not mean a unisex approach, but will bring balance. The church will not be harmed, but will be enriched by the insights and participation of all members of the Body. The presence of both men and women in theological education and the clergy will be a visible symbol that all God's children—brothers and sisters alike—can image Him in whose image we both are.

But What About Our Human Sexuality?

Some have further expressed fear that if women enter what has previously been a "man's world," they will become "mannish" in some way, and that if women enter into all phases of ministry, they will lose their femininity. In part this fear has been justified by the actions of some women who, as secular career opportunities have opened up, have tried to enhance their prospects by copying their male counterparts in as much detail as possible. But these women did this because they thought that acting like men was the only way they could enter that "man's world."

The Bible, however, tells us this is a human world. Scripture informs us that both sexes were to rule the earth, and it presents case histories showing equal opportunity for both men and women in ministry. We need liberation from buying into the false idea that the sexes are compartmentalized into "man's world" and "woman's place." Men must be freed from trying to copy some artificial macho stereotype, and women must be free to develop as full persons, with full use of their gifts.

So when people glibly justify using only males as leaders by saying, "God called men to be fathers and women to be mothers," we must ask: "Just what does that have to do with women serving the church?" Our question becomes more pointed if the women involved are single, childless, or if their children are grown.[14]

In their preoccupation with gender-based roles, some persons still say women in leadership will destroy the home. This is another easy allegation that needs further thought. If a mother cares for their children as a full-time homemaker, she is as fully occupied as her husband whose full-time job is outside the home. But do we say, "It destroys the family when he goes off to church committee meetings"? No, we do not, although if we were really honest, we might say just that, because all too many men are absentee fathers!

We need to recognize that if a mother has leadership gifts, it is not only healthy for her to get a change of pace, but her gifts are needed to enrich the Body of Christ. It is also time we recognize that it will be very healthy for the father to have a change of pace by staying home and becoming better acquainted with his children, when she is out.

We can make a useful parallel with our discussion of parenting in chapter 8. The biblical ideal is that both father and mother fulfill the role of parent. Yes, they will do so in their individual ways: Fathers bring masculine traits and instincts, and mothers bring feminine traits and instincts, but balanced parenting requires *both*. The two who have become one will still bring their individual traits and talents to their one-flesh decision-making process.

Similarly, both men and women can fulfill roles of leaders, administrators, and teachers in the one Christian Body, and again they will do so in their individual ways. There is no reason to think God intended our mutual ruling or occupational function to be done in a unisex fashion. Men will bring a male perspective and women a female perspective. When both minister together—in line with their mutual creation in the image of God and in fulfillment of Jesus' prayer in John 17:20–23—they will begin to mirror the unity, equality, harmony, and cooperation of the Godhead.

Yes, we do accept the ideal of two parents as bringing proper balance to the family. So if a one-parent family operates under a handicap, why is the Christian community different? Why do we accept the imbalance of one-sex leadership in the church?

Inclusive or Exclusive?

Not surprisingly, issues of male-female relationships have involved reevaluating our ideas about gender. As we have explored the many questions asked in this book, it has become apparent that we must take each problem area on its merit. Each question must be fairly examined and—to the best of our ability—fairly answered.

The question of the scriptural language used for human beings also has great bearing on equality of women in ministry. Many women have felt that the male-oriented language excludes them, and there has been increasing interest in developing inclusive-language lectionaries and even inclusive-language Bible translations.

The Moderator of the 1984 General Assembly of the United Presbyterian Church U.S.A. had something interesting to say about this. To quote: "It is hard for some people to understand that in the English language the words for 'man' or 'men' are sometimes generic, describing the whole human race, and sometimes specifically mean 'male.' Women must decide which usage is being employed. If a woman sees 'men' written on a door, for example, she has to decide whether or not she is included in that usage. In reading the Gospel, women shouldn't have to decide, either consciously or unconsciously, whether they are included."[15]

Yet I meet more and more women who tell me: "The Bible is a book stamped MEN on the cover, and I'm tired of trying to figure out if it includes me." For these women, the generic use of the masculine does indeed obfuscate the text. This has become such an obstacle to them that they say, "Forget it—I'm not going to bother with the Bible."[16]

We who encourage people to open God's Word must be very sensitive to any possibility that our English-language translations discourage people from reading the Bible. We who have a high view of the Scripture must be very concerned about keeping our translations as accurate as possible. Evangelicals have been keenly interested in translating the Bible into so-called "native tongues," yet in translating (and paraphrasing) into our English native tongue, we have resisted using inclusive language where the text warrants it.

As a pure translation matter, the Hebrew and Greek generic terms, nouns, and pronouns relating to human beings could become much more inclusive in English and still be faithful both to the original language and to the intention of the Bible writers.

This matter of masculine language directly affects the question of women in ministry. My traditionalist friends have told me that the masculine language used about church officers indicates that women should be excluded from such posts. However, this is not a satisfactory reason for denying women full participation in church government. Why? Because throughout the entire Bible (which does indeed contain a preponderance of masculine language, when referring to human beings) women are urged to include themselves in the concepts Scripture sets forth.

In the many places where God's Word uses generic masculine language or where the masculine is used in a specific way, while still including women in the general thought, *both* women and men are encouraged to appropriate the scriptural truths. For example, women are included in the language of Psalms 1 and 119, and women are to take to heart the admonitions of the Book of Proverbs. An individual text like Revelation 3:20 is a clear case of a place in which the text uses a masculine pronoun, but where we know that women, too, can open the door to Christ and experience fellowship with Him.

So also in the matter of church officers: In 1 Timothy 3:1, Paul writes, "If anyone. . . ." In the Greek his language indicates inclusiveness. Yes, the passage does say that the overseer should be husband of one wife, but here again (as in Titus) the general thought is that the leader is to be monogamous. The overall qualifications given for a church leader apply equally well to either sex. *When we remember all the many general and specific Bible passages where women are urged to include themselves in the masculine-oriented thought, we recognize that it will be most unwise to exclude women from leadership solely on the basis of the gender of the Greek pronouns and adjective endings in 1 Timothy or Titus.*

A woman who seeks salvation would never be told: "The

Bible language is primarily masculine, so you can't ask God for His grace." Similarly a woman who has leadership gifts should not be told: "The language about church officers is masculine; therefore it excludes you."

Any who question such reasoning should consider other areas where the wording is specific but where the church has felt free to interpret the intent of the text and not adhere literally to the particular language used. For example, 1 Peter 2:17 tells us specifically to "honor the king," and that verse was used for centuries to support the divine right of kings. Today we interpret the verse broadly as meaning being obedient to civil authority, and we no longer consider monarchy the only God-ordained form of human government.

For all God's servants, theological studies and ordination are not keys to power but openings to particular avenues of service. So anyone who affirms that ministry is service and not power must avoid the trap of making a power play to control theology and church government by counting how many times masculine language is used. Any woman whose calling and gifts are commensurate with a church office has the right to challenge such a power play by asking: "As with 'sonship,' am I not included here, too?"

As we saw in chapter 9, due to our imperfect understanding, there can appear to be tension between certain passages of Scripture. Here again the truth that *all* believers (male and female alike) are "sons" and "heirs" (Romans 8:15–17; Galatians 4:1–7) appears to be in tension with seeming restrictions on women's activities as children of God (the "hard passages" and the masculine language for church officers). But the larger truth of women's equal redemption and equal inheritance rights cannot be overriden by any legalistic, gender-based role playing, as Galatians 3:26–29 so eloquently proves. Paul even uses female imagery to demonstrate this. He calls believers "children of promise," born of the free woman and declares "the Jerusalem that is above is free, and she is our mother. . . . Therefore, brothers, we are not children of the slave woman, but of the free woman" (Galatians 4:21–31). The inclusiveness and balance in Paul's imagery liberates us from bondage to stereotyped roles. Let us therefore put behind us the "new legalism" of female subordination and move out into the liberty we all have in Christ Jesus!

A Justice Issue

As we explored in chapter 5, disregard for the human rights of women discriminates because it treats women as less than human. Now we must ask: *Have traditional practices in the Christian community denied women their spiritual rights?*

Just as discrimination in the area of natural rights is contrary to God's will, so also is discrimination in the area of spiritual rights. All persons should have the right to spiritual freedom. Certainly the Bible teaches that both women and men have the right to know God, the right to act on that knowledge, the right to learn about God, and—once regenerate—the right to serve God as He calls. Discrimination is any act that restricts those spiritual rights and thus harms or diminishes a person's spiritual standing or limits a person's opportunities to serve God.

As we explored in chapters 1 and 3, there will always be more to know about the Bible. God approves of honest questioning, and the questioning process is one way we study to become approved by God. Thus God's people must be open to reexamining these questions about human relationships:

1. Is subordination of women in conflict with the human rights of women? Does it unjustly restrict both their secular and spiritual opportunities?
2. How can we reconcile subordination of women with the creation of both sexes in the image of God and their joint responsibility for the occupying and ruling of this earth? Does male dominance exalt maleness over femaleness and thus verge on male idolatry?
3. How can subordination of women be reconciled with the biblical truths of the full humanity of women, the full redemption of women, their inclusion in "sonship," the priesthood of all believers, mutual submission, and servanthood?
4. How can we reconcile subordination of women with the scriptural case histories of the many godly women who operated outside any narrow "female" role? How can it be reconciled with the actual practice of Jesus, Paul, and the New Testament church?

5. Does subordination of women go beyond Scripture by imposing extrabiblical restrictions on women only? Does it limit women to a narrow, gender-based role that discriminates against single women, prevents full use of women's gifts, and disenfranchises women within the church? Does it depend on selective exegesis to impose presuppositions on the "hard passages," in order to support human restrictions on theological education and the ordained clergy?

6. Does subordination of women divide the one family of God by focusing attention on our human sexuality (the "flesh"), rather than on our spiritual oneness as new creatures in Christ Jesus?

Christians are called upon to be doers of the truth, and any position we espouse must have integrity. So we cannot sweep these many questions under the rug of "tradition." Instead we must face them.

Therefore, before any group continues to deny women full participation in ministry, that group must ask: Are we restricting the religious freedom of our sisters in Christ? Is our position discriminatory?

In order to answer those questions objectively, some more tough—and even painful—questions must be asked: *What has our position been based upon? Custom? Feelings? A sense of male entitlement to rule? (Or even on a sense of female entitlement to be sheltered from all vicissitudes of life?) Have we been tricked into evading mutual submission and servanthood?*

When I asked my traditionalist friends these tough questions, they confronted me with one last argument: "Maybe subordination of women is wrong, but our culture isn't ready for equal partnership." My final answer was: "Is it right to allow cultural pressures to prevent you from reexamining this issue?"

Of course we must be sensitive to our surrounding culture and to other cultures. One theme in the New Testament epistles was that Christians should be as winsome as possible in presenting the Gospel to their contemporaries, and certainly we should be the same today. However, if full inclusion of women in all areas of life and service is a just cause, then rather than accommodating injustice, should we not call people to recognize justice and to act justly? Surely Christians should not conform to their culture, but should be as Christ to their culture.

This will not mean overnight change, because we must be sensitive not only to our secular mores, but also to the individual practices of the various Christian denominations. However, not to press lovingly yet forcefully for the equality and mutuality of all believers, because of fear that this may not be palatable to *all* groups *everywhere,* is reminiscent of Northerners who, before the Civil War, did not want to address the issue of slavery, for fear of alienating the South. Those interested in the ecumenical movement must not descend to making women expendable pawns in some sort of ecclesiastical game of diplomacy. Just treatment of women must take precedence over any implementation of institutional mergers.

Justice issues are not always popular, because they do threaten the status quo, but we need not worry that equality and mutuality will disrupt society. Christians must focus on the fact that we are one in Christ Jesus. In His great high priestly prayer of John 17, Christ prayed that believers be one, with a oneness that mirrors the closeness of the divine Persons of the Trinity. This is a mystery, but the ideal is plain: unity, not division. Because our goal is unity, implementing male-female partnership will not mean the end of social order or church order.

Unity in Christ will not disrupt God-given gender distinctions. Complementarity is not androgyny. Equal partnership does not erase sexual distinctions or characteristics, but does say, "Let us diverse individuals work together for the good of the one Body and so mirror the fellowship and cooperation of the Persons of the Godhead."

Such partnership will make the priesthood of all believers a reality at last. Then the salvation army will have all its soldiers on the field, free to serve wherever, however, and whenever their Commander calls.

Chapter Eleven

Saved to Serve Together

I felt tempted to bring my travels full circle by finishing my journey in New York City and rounding out this book by calling the final chapter "The Journey Ends." However, for Christians the journey never ends: We are always growing, maturing, learning more of God's truth, and finding new avenues of service. God always has some new challenge awaiting us. When we are at last with Him, we will still have all eternity to continue to explore "the unsearchable riches of Jesus Christ." No, the journey never ends, but we can look back over our journey to see the ground already covered.

Only God can meet our need for security because only our Creator has the power and authority to provide true answers to all our needs. He alone can quiet our fears of never quite measuring up, because only He can offer us complete renewal—the reality of becoming "new creatures in Christ Jesus." Only God can meet our desire for "something more" by offering us both a place in His family and the challenge and excitement of being ambassadors for Christ.

The Bible teaches us that we are each accountable for our response to God's revelation of His plan for humanity. Once we have accepted His free gift of new life, we are each responsible for how we live that life in the here and now.

Scripture encourages us to ask questions about our earthly life, so we look to God's Word for help and guidance in problem areas of human relationships. As we examine those problem areas, we must be aware that we engage in spiritual warfare and that contributing to the problems will be both humanity's fallen nature and the continuing attacks of the enemy. Evil will use any possible trick to disrupt our Christian unity, to hinder full use of our spiritual gifts, and to prevent all Christian soldiers from moving out in His Majesty's Service.

Because one of the enemy's most effective tricks is to encourage pride, we need to apply the antidote of humility. As we saw in chapters 3, 9, and 10, when we see ourselves in relation to Infinite God, we must recognize that we do not have all the answers. We do not have "the last word" on every aspect of faith and life.

Yet another symptom of our desire to "run the show" and "be in charge here" shows up in the difficult time some of us have admitting to incomplete knowledge, specially about spiritual matters. But is it so unthinkable for one of God's servants to say to another, "I'm sorry—I was wrong"?

Overburdened parents can give answers when they do not know them, because doing so retains the parental image and also stops the incessant questioning of their children (at least momentarily!). It takes a "big" parent to say, "I don't know." The same can be true of scholars and the clergy. Surely the queries of laypeople can become not only tiresome but even threatening to the self-image of the "expert." However, if exegesis of a verse like 1 Timothy 2:15 *is* tortuous, then even the experts will do well to say to the questioner, "I don't know," and wait for God to shed further light in His good time. Again, being big enough to say, "I don't know," should not be a problem, since even Peter was free to say, "There are some things in Paul's letters that are hard to understand" (*see* 2 Peter 3:15, 16).

We do indeed have new lessons to learn about God's Word, and sometimes those lessons include being honest enough to say, "I don't know," or even, "I was wrong." This is another reason why our journey never ends. No mere human being can ever say, "I have arrived at final answers to all our questions. I have no new truth to discover." No servant can say, "I have nothing further to learn from the Master."

So as with any mission, living for Christ will involve risk taking. We may well be challenged to rethink human traditions and cherished presuppositions.

Another risk in following Christ is that we may find ourselves called to unexpected kingdom posts. But servants are not to dictate to the Master, and they cannot always be sheltered. The King of kings has every right to say: "Go out into the storm of life and face the danger for Me."

Included in risk taking will be feeling the censure of those who do not understand our mission. But after Romans 14:4 warns us not to criticize our fellow servants, we read in verses 10, 12: ". . . We will all stand before God's judgment seat. . . . So then, each of us will give an account of himself to God." At that time we will answer to Him alone. When He asks us how we used the gifts He gave us, it will not be good enough to say, "Someone else told me how to use them," or even, "Someone else told me not to use them." We are individually accountable to our Lord alone, and we cannot avoid His question in Luke 6:46: "Why do you call me, 'Lord, Lord,' and do not do what I say?"

Yes, Christ challenges all believers: "Now that you are My new creatures, why aren't you My servants?" He does not ask us: "Why aren't you servants of a denomination or of a dogma or of a social system or of a cultural viewpoint?" but, "Why aren't you *My* servants?"

A Hard Teaching

In the Gospels, one of the hardest concepts for Jesus' hearers to understand was that He must be the Suffering Servant. Even His most intimate disciples did not grasp this. When Christ spoke of His coming sacrifice, Peter quickly reacted, in Matthew 16:22, by denying that Christ could ever suffer. Our Lord's rebuke was to tell Peter that he had fallen for Satan's trick of buying into human values, and Christ went on to teach: "If anyone would come after me, he must deny himself and take up his cross and follow me. For whoever wants to save his life will lose it, but whoever loses his life for me will find it" (vv. 24, 25).

The longer we hesitate about identifying with Christ the Suffering Servant, the more we are in danger of becoming like the people in John 6. They wanted easy answers, like miraculous free food, but Jesus challenged them with their deeper need for His spiritual food. He focused on the real issue: "The work of God is this: to believe in the one he has sent" (v. 29).

John tells us of the crowd's growing restlessness during Christ's great discourse on Himself as Bread of Life. Their conclusion: "This is a hard teaching. Who can accept it?" John 6:66 reports, "From this time many of his disciples turned back and no longer followed him." Jesus then asked the Twelve: "You do not want to leave too, do you?" Today if we persist in clinging to "business as usual" by ignoring the challenge of servanthood, His poignant words to the disciples will apply to us as well: "Will you also go away?"

When we hear that question, we realize that we must be open to abandoning feelings, custom, and even entrenched human tradition. We must say with Peter: "Lord, to whom shall we go? You have the words of eternal life." Peter's answer puts all these issues in perspective. Confronted with a servanthood that in many parts of the world does literally lead to losing earthly life, will we turn away? Will we look for easier answers from our friends or our denominations? Will we retreat into, "We've always done it this way"? Will we look to the sinking sand of human answers—or to the Rock of our salvation?

Peer Pressure

Sometimes it does seem very difficult to "stick our necks out." I know men who feel convinced that mutual submission between men and women is biblical, but will not say so, because they fear censure by their peer group. I know women who are reluctant to use their gifts, because it is easier to give in to peer pressure and agree, "We can only do 'women's work' in a restricted role," than to get down on their knees and struggle with "Lord, what would *You* have us to do?"

But if we feel tempted to settle for less than Christ's best for us, to whom *will* we go for answers to our problems? Remember the contrast of the false answers of legalism and patriarchalism ("Save yourself," and, "You can't change human nature") to Jesus' offer of forgiveness and complete renewal of the "real me."

Remember, too, the scenario of John 6. Jesus said, "Identify with Me by feeding on My Word; become one with Me so that My interests are your interests." The crowd's reaction? "That's too hard. We want the easy answer."

Could that be what many people are saying today? Is it too hard to think of giving up traditional roles and traditional dogmas? For us today, do we find identifying with the Suffering Servant just too hard?

As I ask these questions, I am keenly aware of two things. First, these are hard lessons that I personally am only beginning to understand. My own journey into servanthood has barely begun. Second, many of you will have disagreed with me and many of you find it painful to follow a discussion that you consider misguided or wrong. But as you and I have come this far, I thank you for your willingness to keep an open mind, and I pray that God will continue to guide us all on our journeys exploring His inspired Word.

The Bottom Line

Underneath all our questions about relationships, careers, social interaction, and cultural mores is the scriptural principle that all believers are first and foremost God's servants. So while this book has explored human relationships, its underlying theme has been servanthood.

We believers are part of God's family. Just as in human families, in God's family the most exciting acts are performed by the child who has become mature enough to willingly serve the other family members. That child has learned the very important lesson of giving up personal rights and subordinating self-interest to the larger needs of the family body. So we new creatures in Christ Jesus will find our highest joy as we advance from being self-centered Christian infants to becoming mature, adult believers who can serve as Christ's ambassadors, because His mission and our mission are now one.

In its largest sense, Christian service means bowing to the Lordship of Christ; being, following, and doing what He commands; and using the gifts He gives as He directs. Christian service is doing God's will, not man's, and carries with it Jesus' beautiful assurance: "Whoever hears the Word of God and does it, the same is my brother, and my sister, and my mother." (*see* Mark 3:34, 35).

Doing His will involves doing what He commands. In our preoccupation with perpetuating human interpretations of hierarchy and squabbling over roles, rituals, and language, have we forgotten our Lord's own commentary on His practical example of mission? After washing the disciples' feet, Jesus told them in John 13:12–17:

"... Do you understand what I have done for you? ... You call me 'Teacher' and 'Lord,' and rightly so, for that is what I am. Now that I, your Lord and Teacher, have washed your feet, you also should wash one another's feet. I have set you an example that you should do as I have done for you. I tell you the truth, no servant is greater than his master, nor is a messenger greater than the one who sent him. Now that you know these things, you will be blessed if you do them."

What was our Lord's ultimate practical demonstration of servanthood? Loving us to the end, even to death on the cross. Now He commands that we love as He loved, so we, too, must love unto the end—the end of self.

Not Self-serving, but Christ Serving

Without Christ, feminism is just another *ism* and just another power struggle, a fight for rights. So also is any philosophy of headship that promotes male "power over" women. This, too, will end up in just another fight for rights.

Hebrews 13:16 urges us "... to do good and to share with others, for with such sacrifices God is pleased." Could it be that sharing power is a sacrifice pleasing to God?

In contrast to a fight for rights and a refusal to share rights, a biblical view of human relationships incorporates giving up all sense of entitlement and yielding our rights to Christ. Only the yielded person can be the servant. Remember the example of Mary and Joseph.

The pastor of my present church, Dr. David H. C. Read, has this to say about Christ's new commandment to love as He loved: "It is still the new commandment, because it is so rarely practiced." We could say the same about a truly Christian and therefore sacrificial view of servant-leadership: "What a new concept it remains, because it has been so rarely practiced."

Serving in a Christ-like way is the antithesis of self-serving, the opposite of any desire to retain power over another or to wrest power from another. In Matthew 20:25–28 Jesus said: "You know that the rulers of the Gentiles lord it over them, and their high officials exercise authority over them. Not so with you. Instead, whoever wants to become great among you must be your servant, and whoever wants to be first must be your slave—just as the Son of Man did not come to be served, but to serve, and to give his life as a ransom for many."

Accepting Christ's call to servanthood means giving up any rights to being in a privileged position in our spiritual warfare or to being protected from that spiritual warfare. Service as Christ's ambassadors will mean the sacrifice of giving up our preconceived ideas about how we and others can best be deployed. As Oswald Chambers points out: "God puts His saints where they will glorify Him, and we are no judges at all of where that is."[1]

The Hardest Question of All

Matthew 20 and Mark 10 tell us that James and John asked Jesus to seat them at His right and His left, when He entered into the glory of His kingdom. He answered them: "You don't know what you are asking. Can you drink the cup I am going to drink?"

The fourth Gospel teaches us that Christ's glorification began at Calvary, so in a very immediate and real sense the places at Christ's right and left were even then being prepared. When He drank that cup of sacrifice at Calvary, there were two places on either side of Him—two crosses.

Christ could have said to James and John, "Yes, you can have those two places. You can be at My right and My left, nailed on those two crosses at Golgotha." How would they have responded to *that*? I think we can guess. They did not even understand the servant role of washing feet, and we know that when He was betrayed, they all fled. What a telling comment on the lessons they needed to learn about sacrifice, that Jesus was crucified between two strangers and not two disciples!

We need to see that today we, too, so often pluck at Christ's sleeve for the wrong reasons. Following Christ, being nearest to Him, is not becoming part of a power structure or getting on some spiritual "fast track." We are not saved to become "holier than thou" or "better than" other people or even to be protected from the world. Becoming a Christian is not joining an exclusive club of persons whom God will miraculously deliver from all unpleasantness. No, when we enter His Majesty's Service, we become part of a diplomatic corps whose members are all servants deployed in enemy territory.

I suggest that we would not think of excluding women from any aspect of Christian life or ministry if we really saw service as Christ sees service. Indeed, in all honesty, far fewer men might have any desire to serve Christ.

Whether professional or nonprofessional, ordained or nonordained, paid or volunteer, Christian service is not a job or a duty, but the privilege of being a sacrifice. It is the way we use our bodies, minds, and spirits to say, "Thank You," to God for His so-great salvation. In the highest sense, Christian service is a devotional act in which we use all our gifts and abilities to the glory of God. True Christian service—our whole selves on a lifelong diplomatic mission as Christ's ambassadors—will be inevitable for people who desire to glorify Christ. It will be a love offering to Him.

Yet today, like James and John, so many people pluck at Christ's sleeve: dogmatists, traditionalists, egalitarians, feminists, liberationists, all sorts of activists. They all say the equivalent of "Seat *me* nearest You, Lord; show those other people that *my* system is best." As they pluck at Christ's sleeve, thinking that places at His right and His left will bring them honor and power and worldly recognition, He looks at them—and all of us—and still asks: "Can you drink My cup? Don't you see that whoever stays nearest Me must follow Me in the closest sense—go where I go, serve as I serve? Don't you see that, loving the world as I do, I must serve it to the uttermost, because only then can I save it to the uttermost?"

So the real measure of our suitability as Christ's ambassadors (and therefore His servants) is not whether we have a collar on backwards or have a certain title or are a man or a woman. The real measure of our suitability as ambassadors for Christ will be how we answer that hardest question of all: "Can *you* drink My cup?"

A Modern Version

Let us put the question in contemporary language as we confront the cup of submission. For men: Like Barak, would you be willing to serve under Judge Deborah as your chief of state? Like Hilkiah, would you be willing to go to Huldah for God's Word? Like Josiah, would you act on Huldah's words? Like the congregation at Cenchrea, would you be willing to let Phoebe oversee your church's affairs? Like Apollos, would you be willing to learn from Priscilla?

To be even more current, would you men willingly serve in a situation where a woman was department head, editor-in-chief, committee chair, doctor in charge of a medical team, employer, Bible teacher, or church leader? Could you accept the fact that your wife's gifts might make her the more visible of the two of you? Would you dare to be a Joseph? If not, what prevents you from being willing to appear secondary in the eyes of the world? Peer pressure? Pride of place? A sense of entitlement to a preferred position?

For women: Can you drink the cup of submission? Yes, I realize full well that many of you are thinking, *That's all we've ever done,* but I would ask you: Can you now drink the cup as Christ means you to drink it? Not because you must, but because you choose to? Would you be willing to put aside your legitimate rights, if the time to exercise them is not yet right in your particular circumstances? Would you be willing to put your career on "hold," if that is in the best interests of your family or your cultural milieu? Will you work for change in a patient and loving manner, rather than sinking into anger, frustration, or bitterness? Will you commit yourself to act in a Christ-like way, even if you are in un-Christ-like situations?

For both: In order to serve us, Christ emptied Himself and became the Suffering Servant. Philippians 2:5 commands us to have the same servant attitude. Can you—both men and women—empty yourselves and drink the cup of mutual submission as a love offering to Him?

Approved by God

Our journey into truth never ends, but since this has been a book about serving God, it is appropriate that we come full circle by returning to the questions we asked in chapter 1: *How can we be approved by God? How can we become the kind of servants who will hear His "well done"?*

Paul wrote in 1 Corinthians 1:25, "The foolishness of God is wiser than man's wisdom, and the weakness of God is stronger than man's strength." In chapter 7 we saw that God chose someone weak, even foolish, in the eyes of the world, for His miraculous entrance into our world of time and space. Because Mary believed God's Word, trusted in His salvation, and was willing to be His obedient servant, her life was a spiritual success.

When all is said and done, isn't that what we want today? We know that we cannot take this world's approval with us into the next, so if we are honest we know that at the end of this life's journey we want God's approval. We want to look forward to meeting a God who is our friend, not a stranger. We want to say with Mary, "God is *my* Savior."

At that wedding in Cana, Mary had no money to give the servers so that they could buy more wine, but she had the greatest resource of all—Jesus. She could point people in need to Jesus, so she did. Later on, in the Book of Acts, we read that Peter told a crippled beggar, "I have no silver or gold, but what I have I give you—healing in the name of Jesus Christ" (*see* 3:6).

The Christ who even from the cross reached out to care for His own still reaches out to heal us today. He alone has the power to substitute His new life for the old treadmill of self-reform and societal "patch up" as people seek to erase the "if onlys" of life. Only Christ has the answer to all our needs, the solutions to all our questions about human relationships.

So we must never forget whose approval really matters. As we evaluate the part that peer pressure, custom, feelings, and culture have played in developing human traditions, we must ask: *Have we been confusing human approval with God's approval?*

They are not always the same. Remember Jesus' sobering words in Mark 7:8, 13: "You have let go of the commands of God and are holding on to the traditions of men. . . . Thus you nullify the word of God by your tradition that you have handed down. . . ." We can think of the tragic account in John 12:42, 43, where some Jewish leaders were afraid to go against tradition by confessing their belief in Christ, ". . . for fear they would be put out of the synagogue; for they loved praise from men more than praise from God."

In contrast, we can also think of the good example of the "great cloud of witnesses" (Hebrews 12:1). We can profit from the good example of Abraham, as Genesis 15:6 tells us that it was not his traditional role as patriarch that made him approved by God, but his faith. The list of people of faith in Hebrews 11 makes it clear that no role or tradition made them approved by God, but their faith did. It was not Samson's macho image and David's masculinity that God approved, but their faith. The same is true of women. It was not Sarah's female role and Rahab's feminine wiles that God approved, but their faith. Again we remember Mary: God used her female body, but her faith in Him as Savior made her approved. In the many biblical case histories where men and women were approved by God, they were people of faith—faith in God, not trust in roles or traditions.

God's World View

So as we meditate on that hardest question of all—"Can *you* drink My cup?"—we must look beyond our emotions, our cultures, and our customs and see our faith in relation to Christ's concern for the entire world. John 3:16 says that He came to give Himself for *all* people of the world.

In recent years the phrase *world view* has become a popular way of describing an individual's political, philosophical, or spiritual orientation. But perhaps a true world view is as simple as the two words themselves—*world* and *view*—and those two words must remind us that God thinks globally.

Scripture says, "God so loved the world." It does not say: "God so loved a doctrinal formulation," or, "God so loved role playing," or "God so loved some human tradition." Scripture simply and all-inclusively says, "God so loved the world," and goes on to reveal that He Himself came into our world to offer us a way back to fellowship with Him.

As we think about God's concern for *all* humanity we can paraphrase His words in Jonah 4:10, 11 to hear Him challenge us today: "You've been so preoccupied with your ideas of mission and protecting your dogmas and preserving your societal status quo and even selfishly putting your comfort first, but should not I be concerned about all those lost people?" Hear also Jesus' words in Matthew 9:37, 38: "The harvest is plentiful but the workers are few. Ask the Lord of the harvest, therefore, to send out workers into his harvest field."

We, His servants, must also have His world view. His concerns must be our concerns. We, too, must want to get all the ambassadors to their posts and all the Christian soldiers on the field.

Yes, God so loved the world, and we must resist anything that would prevent that message from being proclaimed. As His agents of reconciliation, we must be alert to any action—or inaction—that would hurt individuals in this world God loved so much He came Himself to die for it.

As we study the example of the Suffering Servant we must come to a fresh appreciation of God's grace—the wonder that while each one of us was estranged from Him, Christ died for us. When we see ourselves as simply fellow sinners for whom Christ died, we will be glad to give up all thought of being "over" or "better than" or even, for some of us, all thought of being restored to our "rightful place." When our primary role as ambassadors for Christ is seen in the light of the glory of the cross, questions of power and position become irrelevant.

So as we continue to explore these issues, may we each be committed to following Jesus' perfect example of how human relationships ought to be. May we commit ourselves to following His perfect example of sacrificial servanthood. But above all, as we study His Prospectus to find out more of what it means to live for Him, may we each bow down before Him in gratitude and love as we echo the words of Thomas: "My Lord and my God!" To Him and Him alone be the power and the glory!

Appendix I

Does Order of Creation, Redemption, and Climax Demand Female Supremacy?

(A Satire)

Alvera Mickelsen

Alvera Mickelsen is a free-lance writer and editor and former teacher of journalism at Bethel College and Wheaton College. With her husband, Berkeley, she has coauthored *Understanding Scripture* and *Family Bible Encyclopedia;* they have also been contributors to Christian magazines, including *Christianity Today*.

I am most grateful to Mrs. Mickelsen for graciously allowing her essay to be included in this book.

In light of the persistent emphasis on the assumed "order of creation" in Genesis 2, we present the following tongue-in-cheek look at the "order of creation, redemption, and climax" to establish the subordination of men to women. *We believe our case has as much validity as the historical approach that sees the subordination of women in the order of creation. The validity of both approaches, we believe, is equally nonexistent.*

In studying the early chapters of Genesis, before sin entered the world, we get a clear picture of God's intention that females should be dominant over males.

Let us first examine the order of creation that appears in chapter 1. The creation begins with chaos, darkness, and void. But God moves in an orderly way to change that chaos into a beautiful world in which human beings stand at the pinnacle. First, the light is separated from the darkness—day and night (first day). Then the waters are separated from the dry land (second day). Then the earth brings forth vegetation and plants (third day). God next creates the sun, moon, and stars (fourth day). On the fifth day He makes birds and sea creatures, and finally, on the sixth day, God creates animals and human beings. The movement clearly is from chaos to harmony and order.

Chapter 2 refines this further as it tells how God created man and finally woman—the pinnacle of his creation. This chapter indicates that God made the male as He made the animals and birds—from the dust of the ground; then He placed the male in the Garden and told Adam (the male) to give each of them names. In the process it was clear to both Adam and to God that the male was inadequate by himself for the responsibilities he had. So God said He would make for Adam a strength and power equal and corresponding to him.

Unfortunately, male translators have refused to recognize the clear force of the Hebrew word *'ezer* used here and usually translated "helper." This word appears twenty-one times in the Old Testament and is nearly always used of God as He supports humans with His superior strength or power. In this same sense, the woman "helps" the man with her superior strength and power and wisdom.

Adam clearly understood this subordinate relationship, as is seen in Genesis 2:24 (RSV), where the male says, "Therefore a man leaves his father and his mother and cleaves to his wife, and they become one flesh." This surely indicates that the male should be under the supervision of his father and mother until marriage, when he leaves them and "cleaves" (meaning "is glued to") to his wife. If God had intended the woman to be subordinate to the man, surely the Bible would say, "For this reason a *woman* leaves her mother and father and cleaves to her husband." If God had meant equality, the Bible would say, "The man and woman will each leave mother and father and cleave to each other."

The Apostle Paul verifies this interpretation of the creation account in 1 Corinthians 11:7 (RSV), where he writes, ". . . woman is the glory of man [meaning mankind]." This concept is further emphasized in 1 Corinthians 11:9 (RSV), where Paul writes, "Neither was man created for woman, but woman for man." He is obviously saying that woman was created because the man couldn't get along without her. Paul then goes on in the next verse to say, "For this reason the woman ought to have authority over her head [the man]. . . ." However, Paul seems to realize that what he says may tend to make the woman feel that she can lord it over the man, so he reminds women, "Nevertheless, in the Lord woman is not independent of man nor man of woman, for as woman was made from man [and is thus the pinnacle or glory of creation], so man is now born of woman. And all things are from God" (RSV).

Satan clearly understood God's hierarchy in the Garden of Eden, for he approached Eve rather than Adam, knowing that she was the one in charge. When she handed the forbidden fruit to Adam, he ate some of it immediately, recognizing her God-given dominance over him. When God called to Adam and asked what had happened, Adam replied, "The woman whom thou gavest to be with me, she gave me fruit of the tree, and I ate" (Genesis 3:12 RSV).

This interpretation is verified in 1 Timothy 2:13–15, where Paul reminds his readers in Ephesus that Eve was created after Adam, thus she was the pinnacle of God's creation. He also reminds them that Satan, recognizing the primacy of Eve, went to her with his temptation—not Adam. Eve, God's chosen leader, was clearly deceived by Satan, while Adam simply followed her instructions. In spite of this fact, Paul says, the woman is still the agent of salvation for all humanity (she will be saved by the birth of the child), and in that position she is expected to live in faith, love, and holiness, with modesty.

Of course, God held Adam just as responsible for the sin as Eve, since they each had the capacity to obey or disobey God.

When the punishment for sin was handed out, both Adam and Eve got a full share, but God still recognized the higher status of the woman. He told Eve that although she had so grievously sinned, she would be the instrument through which salvation would come to the world. "He [the seed of woman] shall bruise your head [Satan's], and you [Satan] shall bruise his heel." The childbearing necessary to bring salvation to the world (in the person of a divine Savior) would be given to the woman as the dominant one in the pair, but great toil would accompany it. Worst of all, a terrible "role reversal" would occur. The divine order of creation (female domination) would be reversed, and the male would rule over the female. Even the most casual observer can easily see the havoc that this role reversal has wrought. We have war, fighting, inability to communicate with nations, friends, or neighbors—all the result of the male dominance that entered the world with sin and thus reversed God's ordained order of creation.

God's own preference in roles with men and women did not

change—only the sinful acts of humans got mixed up. For example, we see that naming was the primary responsibility of women. The Bible does not say who named Cain or Abel, but it clearly says that Eve named the third child, Seth (Genesis 4:25). Rachel and Leah named all the sons of Jacob (for whom the twelve tribes of Israel were named). The only exception was Benjamin, because Rachel died in his childbirth, and Jacob changed his name.

We see the same significance in the New Testament, where the angel Gabriel appears first to Mary and announces the coming Savior. Gabriel tells Mary that she is to name the baby Jesus.

God's choice of Mary as the human parent of Jesus is another evidence that God still saw the primacy of the woman in the human race. Actually, no male played any part in the conception of our Redeemer, but God chose a woman to bear the Savior through apparently normal processes of growth within the womb. Since the birth of the Savior was miraculous anyway, God could just as easily have made Christ from the rib of Joseph, just as He made Eve from the rib of Adam. But He did not.

Instead, God fulfilled His original promise to Eve in the Garden of Eden. *Her* "seed" would bruise the head of Satan. Women were the exclusive human instruments of salvation for all humanity.

Women will continue in this role in the days ahead, as is evident in the Book of Revelation. In Revelation 12, a woman is clothed with the sun, and on her head is a crown of twelve stars. She is pregnant, and she and her offspring represent the people of God, whom the dragon (Satan) has tried to destroy from the early church to the present day. But God prepares a special place for her in the wilderness, where she is nourished during persecution. Again, God's revelation to John shows the woman in her proper, God-ordained place of leadership— the position from which she was removed when sin entered the world. This is reinforced by the fact that when Satan was thrown out of heaven, after the ascension of Jesus, he immediately went forth to make war on *the woman and her posterity*.

It is no accident that the New Testament always refers to the church as female. The church embodies the very power of God and is His instrument for the salvation of His people. The church (*ekklesia* is the feminine gender) is subject only to Christ, for through a woman the Savior came to this world. Throughout the Bible, the woman is God's instrument through which salvation comes.

Often we hear men refer to the Jewish system of preference for the first male in a family as some kind of "proof" that God ordained Adam to be dominant over Eve. The silliness of this interpretation becomes apparent when we note that God Himself usually chose the younger to be His chosen leaders. Jacob (the second-born twin) became the ancestor of the Hebrew people, rather than Esau, the first-born. When God sent Samuel to anoint a king to take the place of

Saul, He did not permit Samuel to anoint the oldest son of Jesse, as the Jewish custom would have it, but insisted on taking the *youngest* in the family. God chose Moses rather than Aaron, the older son. Jesus reinforced this principle when He said that to be great in His kingdom, a person had to become as "the youngest" (Luke 22:26 RSV). This again would point to the primacy of Eve in God's plan.

We also see the God-ordained dominance of women in God's choice of the ancestry of His chosen people. Who was the determining ancestor of the Hebrews? Was it Abraham? Not at all. Abraham had eight children, born by three different women. God's chosen instrument of ancestry was *Sarah*. Isaac, Sarah's only child, was the one through whom the Hebrews came. Ishmael, the son of Abraham by Hagar, did not count in God's plan, nor did the six children of Abraham and Ketura. Obviously, *Sarah* was God's chosen vessel for the ancestry of the Hebrews. Abraham was only the agent by whom she became pregnant.

Sarah's God-ordained leadership in the ancestry of the Hebrew nation is reinforced in Genesis 21:12. In this passage, a conflict has risen between Abraham and Sarah over what to do with Ishmael. In keeping with Sarah's ordained dominant role, God tells Abraham that he is to obey Sarah in the matter: ". . . Whatever Sarah says to you, do as she tells you, for through Isaac shall your descendants be named." We should also note that *nowhere* in the Old Testament is any wife told to obey her husband.

Some of the most crucial attributes of God are also represented as female—wisdom, for example, in Proverbs 8. Scripture often compares the love of God to the love of a mother for her child.

Simple observation of male and female traits indicates how the "role reversal" that occurred when sin entered the world has damaged all humanity. Psychological tests and biblical data show that males tend to be more aggressive than females, more eager to show how "strong" they are, less skilled in building deep relationships, less able to communicate love and feelings. Women usually have greater verbal skills, are better listeners, find nurturing easier than men find it, mature more rapidly, have greater endurance, are more willing to negotiate rather than fight. These very skills are needed in the world today, both in leadership of nations and of the church.

Men in places of leadership have brought an unending sequence of devastating wars (the natural result of the need to show who is "biggest and strongest"). Churches with male leadership have had a sad history of conflicts—ranging from the Reformation to the smallest village hamlet.

The basic purpose of the church involves nurturing and communicating the Gospel—both of which tend to fit the "female psyche" better than the male's. The failure of nations and of the church can perhaps be laid finally to the "role reversal" that changed God's ordained "order of creation," involving female leadership, to the sad state we have today.

Since the biblical teachings on this subject are crystal clear, obviously the leadership of women over men as a divine mandate can only be denied by refusing the authority of the Scriptures. There is no middle ground. Either we accept the clear teachings of female leadership and male subordination, or we deny the authority of the very Scriptures that are the foundation of our faith.

What are we trying to say in this article? That selective, propositional exegesis can build whatever case the propositional logician wants to establish. Unfortunately, big lies repeated often enough seem to become accepted, regardless of how little foundation they have. Let's stop assuming the ancient myth that "female subordination" is found in the "order of creation" and substantiated in Paul's interpretation of Genesis. Let's rather stay with sound principles of interpretation, all textual passages, and a fresh look at the new order Christ came to establish.

Appendix II
Exegetical Difficulties in the "Hard Passages"

Sanford Douglas Hull

The Reverend Sanford D. Hull is pastor of the Brookdale Presbyterian Church, St. Joseph, Missouri, and has been a contributor to the *Trinity Journal* and the *Journal of the Evangelical Theological Society*. He holds a B.A. from Amherst College and an M. Div. *summa cum laude* from Trinity Evangelical Divinity School. He was formerly instructor in classical languages at Wilbraham and Monson Academy and later held a teaching fellowship in Greek at Trinity Evangelical Divinity School. He holds a D. Min. from McCormick Theological Seminary.

I am deeply indebted to my son for compiling these exegetical difficulties.

What follows is a list of the exegetical difficulties in 1 Corinthians 11:2–16, 1 Corinthians 14:33b–36, and 1 Timothy 2:8–15, along with some solutions scholars have suggested. Claiming to be exhaustive is naive; yet an attempt has been made to be complete. The difficulties are listed in the order in which they appear in the text. Not all of course, are of equal moment. At the end we will review some proposals for reconciling these passages with one another.

1 Corinthians 11:2–16

1. How does Paul's praise in verse 2 relate to the rest of the passage? John Short detects a "hint of irony" in view of what appears to be corrective advice in the rest of the passage ("The First Epistle to the Corinthians," *The Interpreter's Bible,* vol. 10 [New York: Abingdon Press, 1953], 124.) But Walter Liefeld maintains that Paul's praise indicates the Corinthians were right in allowing women to pray and prophesy and the entire passage is basically commendatory ("Women, Submission and Ministry," *Women, Authority and the Bible,* ed. Alvera Mickelsen [Downers Grove, Ill.: InterVarsity Press, 1986], 136–137). C. K. Barrett sees in verse 2 a hint that Paul had permitted women to pray and prophesy unveiled while he was at Corinth (*The First Epistle to the Corinthians* [New York: Harper & Row, 1968], 6). Finally, W. J. Martin concludes from Paul's commendation in verse 2 that the practices Paul seeks to correct were only hypothetical ("1 Corinthians 11:2–16: An Interpretation," *Apostolic History and the Gospel,* ed. W. W. Gasque and R. P. Martin [Grand Rapids, Mich.: Wm. B. Eerdmans, 1970], 231).

2. What is the meaning of "head" (kephalē) in verse 3? The two major alternatives are "authority over" (so W. A. Grudem, "Does κεφαλη Mean 'Source' or 'Authority Over' in Greek Literature? A Survey of 2,336 Examples," *Trinity Journal* 6 NS [1], 38–59; James Hurley, *Man and Woman in Biblical Perspective* [Grand Rapids, Mich.: Zondervan, 1981], 167; and many others. TEV translates "is supreme over") and "source" or "origin" (so Stephen Bedale, "The Meaning of κεφαλη in the Pauline Epistles," *Journal of Theological Studies* 5 [2], 214; Berkeley and Alvera Mickelsen, "What Does *Kephalē* Mean in the New Testament?" *Women, Authority and the Bible,* 97–110; Barrett, *First Epistle,* 248; and others). In addition, Liefeld suggests " 'prominent' or 'honored' member" ("Women, Submission and Ministry," 139–140), and J. Massengbyrde Ford sees *kephalē* as indicating "essential complementarity" ("Biblical Material Relevant to the Ordination of Women," *Journal of Ecumenical Studies* 10 [4], 679).

3. What is the significance of the sequence of heads in verse 3? Gilbert Bilezikian perceives a chronological sequence of sources (*Beyond Sex Roles* [Grand Rapids, Mich.: Baker Book House, 1985], 138). Liefeld posits a building up to the climax of Christ and God ("Women, Submission, and Ministry," 140). George W. Knight III writes, "He [Paul] sandwiches the disputed relationship [that of man and woman] between undisputed ones to set it in proper framework" (*The Role Relationship of Men and Women,* rev. ed. [Chicago: Moody, 1985], 21).

4. Does verse 3 (and therefore the entire passage) speak of man and woman or husband and wife? The Greek words *anēr* and *gunē* can

APPENDIX II

mean either. F. F. Bruce (*1 and 2 Corinthians* [London: Oliphants, 1971], 103), Paul Jewett (*Man as Male and Female* [Grand Rapids, Mich.: Wm. B. Eerdmans, 1975], 131), and Knight (*Role Relationship*, 23) hold the former. A. Robertson and A. Plummer (*A Critical and Exegetical Commentary on the First Epistle of Paul to the Corinthians* [Edinburgh: T & T Clark, 1914], 230) and William F. Orr and James A. Walther (*1 Corinthians* [Garden City, N. Y.: Doubleday, 1976], 259) prefer the latter.

5. *Do verses 4 and following refer to a veil or long hair?* The Greek word for "veil" appears nowhere in this passage. All that verse 4 says is *kata kephalēs* (literally, "down from the head"). While most commentators conclude that this phrase refers to a veil, Hurley (*Man and Woman*, 81), Martin ("1 Corinthians 11:2–16," 233), and Isaksson (*Marriage and Ministry in the New Temple*, trans. N. Tomkinson [Lund: G. W. K. Gleerup, 1965], 169) contend that only long hair is signified.

6. *If verse 4 refers to a veil, what kind of veil is it?* Bruce suggests one that covers the entire head (*1 and 2 Corinthians*, 104; so also C. T. Craig ["The First Epistle to the Corinthians," *The Interpreter's Bible*, vol. 10, 126] and Bruce Waltke ["1 Corinthians 11:2–16: An Interpretation," *Bibliotheca Sacra* 135 (537), 50]), although Barrett thinks the veil conceals the head and upper body (*First Epistle*, 249). Orr and Walther describe a veil that simply binds the woman's hair (*1 Corinthians*, 260). Annie Jaubert, however, maintains that the type of veil would vary according to local custom ("Le Voile des Femmes (I Cor. xi. 2–16)," *New Testament Studies* 18 [4], 424).

7. *Does Paul's advocacy of veils reflect Jewish or pagan custom?* Patricia Gundry opts for a Gentile background to Paul's command (*Woman Be Free!* [Grand Rapids, Mich.: Zondervan, 1977], 66); Short ("First Epistle," 125) and Jaubert ("Le Voile," 421–422), among others, for Jewish roots; while Hurley (*Man and Woman*, 81) asserts that neither pagan nor Jewish women wore veils in Paul's day. Fritz Zerbst (*The Office of Women in the Church*, trans. A. G. Merkens [St. Louis: Concordia, 1955], 49) and Charles C. Ryrie (*The Place of Women in Church Life* [New York: Macmillan, 1958], 73) see the practice of veils for women who are praying and prophesying as distinctively Pauline and Christian.

8. *When verses 4 and 5 speak of dishonoring one's head, is "head" a literal reference to one's physical head or a figurative allusion to Christ (for the man) and man (for the woman)?* Orr and Walther, for example, hold to the literal sense (*1 Corinthians*, 260), Jewett to the figurative (*Man as*, 55 n. 5), while Waltke ("1 Corinthians 11:2–16," 51) and Morna D. Hooker ("Authority on Her Head: An Examination of I Cor. xi. 10," *New Testament Studies* 10 [3], 410–411) claim that both the literal and figurative meanings are present.

9. What does being unveiled and/or shorn signify in verses 5 and 6? The options include: (1) the punishment for adultery (W. G. H. Simon, *The First Epistle to the Corinthians* [London: SCM, 1959], 112, and many others); (2) a Nazarite vow (Isaksson, *Marriage and Ministry*, 170); (3) the rejection of one's husband's authority (Stephen B. Clark, *Man and Woman in Christ* [Ann Arbor, Mich.: Servant, 1980], 170); (4) a sign of mourning or the mark of a slave (Craig, "The First Epistle," 127), (5) a pagan rite for girls reaching puberty (Martin, "1 Corinthians 11:2–16," 233–2324); and (6) the characteristic appearance of pagan prophetesses (Bruce, *1 and 2 Corinthians*, 105) or temple prostitutes (Gundry, *Woman Be Free!* 66). Furthermore, Zerbst posits that short, uncovered hair put women "on the same level as homosexual hussies" (*Office of Women*, 55).

10. What is the meaning of "glory" (doxa) in verse 7? G. Kittel states that *glory* means "reflection" in this context ("δοκέω, etc.," *Theological Dictionary of the New Testament*, trans. G. Bromily [Grand Rapids, Mich.: Wm. B. Eerdmans, 1959]; so also Knight, *Real Relationship*, 21, and Hooker, "Authority on Her Head," 414–415). Jaubert rejects this, opting for the sense of "splendor" ("Le Voile," 422), while Liefeld, ("Women, Submission, and Ministry," 143) and Jewett (*Man as*, 56) see *doxa* as simply the giving of glory to another.

11. Why is man described as "the image and glory of God," but woman only as "the glory of man" in verse 7? Liefeld maintains that this emphasizes woman as man's glory ("Women, Submission, and Ministry," 140), but Hooker contends that image is omitted for woman because woman is the image of God and only the glory of man ("Authority on Her Head," 411).

12. What is Paul's point in verse 8? Is Paul emphasizing man's chronological priority (so W. Harold Mare, "1 Corinthians," *The Expositor's Bible Commentary*, ed. F. E. Gaebelein, vol. 10] Grand Rapids, Mich.: Zondervan, 1976], 255) or the fact that Eve was generated from Adam's rib (so Leon Morris, *The First Epistle of Paul to the Corinthians* [Grand Rapids, Mich.: Eerdmans, 1958], 153)?

13. What does exousia ("authority") mean in verse 10? The word translated "sign of authority" in NIV and NEB and "veil" in RSV is simply "authority" in the Greek text, which reads literally, "the woman ought to have authority on her head." (The difficulty of understanding *exousia* in this context is reflected by textual variants in some manuscripts.) Whereas Hooker believes that *exousia* denotes the woman's right to pray and prophesy publicly ("Authority on Her Head," 415, so also Bruce, *1 and 2 Corinthians*, 106; Jaubert, "Le Voile," 430; and Liefeld, "Women, Submission, and Ministry," 146), Clark (*Man and Woman in Christ*, 171). Craig ("The First Epistle," 128), and others maintain that *exousia* signifies the veil which is a symbol of the woman's being under her husband's authority. A third possibility, advanced by Simon (*The First Epistle*, 113) and Robertson and Plummer (*Critical and Exegetical Commentary*, 232), is that the authority is the security and dignity the veil gives to women in Middle Easter society. Perhaps the most ingenious suggestion is Kittel's: he maintains that *exousia* is a mistranslation or popular etymology of the Aramaic word "veil," which has a root similar to the Aramaic word "rule" (*Rabbinica* Leipzig: J. C. Hinrichs, 1920], 17–31).

14. Why does Paul state in verse 10 that a woman ought to have authority on her head "because of the angels"? The major alternatives are: (1) angels are the guardians of the created order as set forth in verses 3–9 (Barrett, *First Epistle*, 254; Ryrie, *Place of Women*, 74); (2) women are to follow the example of the angels, who cover their faces in God's presence, as in Isaiah 6:2 (Bilezikian, *Beyond Sex Roles*, 135; Robertson and Plummer, *Critical and Exegetical Commentary*, 233–234); (3) angels participate with humans in worship (J. A. Fitzmyer, "A Feature of Qûmran Angelology and the Angels of 1 Cor. xi. 10," *New Testament Studies* 4[1], 55; followed by Jaubert, "Le Voile," 427; and Jewett, *Man as*, 57). Other possibilities for the meaning of angels include evil spirits whom the veil wars off (J. Héring, *La Première Epître de Saint Paul aux Corinthiens* [Neuchâtel: Delacheux et Niestlé, 1949], 94–95), and the views of the Church Fathers that the angels are the "sons of God" in Genesis 6 who seduced human women (Tertullian, cited by Robertson and Plummer, *Critical and Exegetical Commentary*, 233) or human messengers (Ambrosiaster, cited by Fitzmyer, "Qûmran Angelology," 54).

15. What is the place of verses 11–12 in Paul's argument? Jewett holds that these verses are parenthetical (*Man as*, 113) and Craig concludes that they are an afterthought Paul inserted for fear that he had gone too far in stressing women's subordination ("The First Epistle," 128). Bilezikian, however, asserts that verse 11–12 are in the "climactic position" and set forth Paul's "ultimate teaching" on men and women (*Beyond Sex Roles*, 143; so also Liefeld, "Women, Submission, and Ministry," 147).

16. What is the force of plēn (NIV: "however") in verse 11? Robertson and Plummer hold that *plēn* expresses a limitation of or exception to Paul's prior points (*Critical and Exegetical Commentary*, 234), while Barrett translates "only," possibly indicating just the taking up of a new subject (*First Epistle*, 255). But Liefeld contends the *plēn* is strongly adversative, perhaps even completely reversing the previous argument ("Women, Submission, and Ministry," 146).

17. What is the meaning of "nature" (phusis) in verse 14? Possibilities include: (1) the natural world as God created it (Barrett, *First*

Epistle, 256; Knight, *Role Relationship*, 20 n. 5); (2) custom (Gundry, *Woman Be Free!* 65; Bilezikian, *Beyond Sex Roles*, 136); and (3) the Stoic notion of the law of nature (Jaubert, "Le Voile," 419). In addition, J. B. Phillips translates "natural principle," and Zerbst lists as an option "a natural feeling" (*Office of Women*, 42).

18. What is the force of the preposition anti (*NIV: "as"*) in verse 15? While most scholars opt for "in place of," which might signify that if a woman has long hair, she does not need a head covering (Barrett, *First Epistle*, 257; Bilezikian, *Beyond Sex Roles*, 244), Waltke argues for "over against" or "asking for," in which case long-haired women still need veils ("1 Corinthians 11:2–16," 55).

19. To what does sunētheia (*"practice"*) refer in verse 16? Most commentators hold that the term refers to the custom of wearing veils in worship (so Bruce, *1 and 2 Corinthians*, 106; Robertson and Plummer, *Critical and Exegetical Commentary*, 235), but Orr and Walther argue that it refers to church practice both of veiling and of being contentious (*1 Corinthians*, 261). Liefeld suggests that *sunētheia* "throws emphasis on the principles behind the headcovering rather than on the headcovering itself" and therefore use of this word indicates that Paul "does not come down . . . heavily" on the wearing of headcoverings ("Women, Submisssion, and Ministry," 148).

20. Who is meant by "we" in verse 16? Options include Paul himself (Barrett, *First Epistle*, 258), the apostles (Robertson and Plummer, *Critical and Exegetical Commentary*, 235), or even "we Jews" (Herveius, cited ibid., 235).

21. How does Paul's argument progress through the passage? Bruce (*1 and 2 Corinthians*, 103) and Richard Longenecker ("Authority, Hierarchy and Leadership Patterns in the Bible," *Women, Authority and the Bible*, 72), for example, see an orderly argument with four points: creation order, seemliness, nature, and church practice. Others, such as Barrett (*First Epistle*, 257), see in Paul's words, "judge for yourselves" (v. 13), an invitation to disagree and therefore a mitigation of earlier arguments, indicating that Paul is not laying down an inviolable rule. Still others sense that Paul's argument falls apart in the course of the passage. Craig views verses 13–15 as a rationalization and verse 16 as Paul's finally asserting his own authority because he realizes how weak his argument is ("The First Epistle," 128). J. C. G. Greig writes, "Paul is having a long-drawn-out argument with himself"; having contradicted himself in verses 11 and 12, he "gets out as well as he can" ("Women's Hats—1 Corinthians xi. 1–16," *Expository Times* 69 [5], 157). Hence Greig offers this rendering of verse 16: "We have no custom *the one way or the other*, either personally or as churches."

22. What is the problem Paul addresses in this passage? What, therefore, is the purpose of the passage? Most scholars (e.g., Hooker, "Authority on Her Head," 410) see the background as Corinthian women desiring to worship unveiled due to their sense of newfound freedom in Christ. The problem, then, is variously presented: (1) Worshiping unveiled was a violation of Jewish and/or Gentile decorum and might give Christianity a bad reputation (so Liefeld, "Women, Submission, and Ministry," 142; Craig, "The First Epistle," 124). Ryrie, while agreeing with this understanding of Paul's purpose, sees a more practical problem: Women were hindered in exercising their legitimate privilege of prayer and prophesying, because their veils covered their faces and hence muted their voices (*Place of Women*, 72–73). (2) Unveiled worship for women, a Gentile custom, was offending Jewish Christians in Corinth (Richard and Catherine Kroeger, *Women Elders . . . Saints or Sinners?* [New York: Council on Women and the Church of the United Presbyterian Church in the U.S.A., 1981], 12–13). Paul's purpose would therefore be church unity. (3) The presence in the congregation of women with their hair let down was a distraction to the men (Hooker, "Authority on Her Head," 415). (4) Coming from another angle, Zerbst calls attention to a Roman law requiring emancipated slaves to wear hats: Men with their heads covered would therefore be giving evidence of their freedom from Christ's Lordship (*Office of Women*, 39).

1 Corinthians 14:33b–36

1. Where does the paragraph begin? Barrett (*First Epistle*, 330), NAS, and Phillips take verse 33b with the preceding paragraph, with Paul's discussion of women beginning in verse 34. F. W. Grosheide (*The First Epistle of Paul to the Corinthians* [Grand Rapids, Mich.: Wm. B. Eerdmans, 1953], 341) and Orr and Walther (*1 Corinthians*, 311), among others, take verse 33b as the beginning of the paragraph, as in RSV and NIV.

2. What does Paul mean in verse 33b by "in all the congregations [or churches] of the saints"? This phrase occurs nowhere else in the New Testament. W. Harold Mare ("1 Corinthians," *The Expositor's Bible Commentary*, ed. F. E. Gaebelein, vol. 10 [Grand Rapids: Zondervan, 1976], 276) and Grosheide (*Epistle of Paul*, 341) see it as a universal statement, while Bilezikian takes it to refer specifically to the churches in Palestine (*Beyond Sex Roles*, 148).

3. Does the passage deal with wives or women in general? *Gunaikes* (v. 34) can mean either. A reference to wives is preferred by E. Earle

Ellis ("The Silenced Wives of Corinth [1 Cor. 14:34–35)," *New Testament Textual Criticism*, ed. E. J. Epp and G. D. Fee [Oxford: Clarendon, 1981], 217); Ford ("Biblical Material," 681); and Orr and Walther (*1 Corinthians*, 312). On the other hand, Mare ("1 Corinthians," 276), Knight (*Role Relationship*, 25), and others opt for women in general.

4. What does Paul mean in verse 34 by "to speak" (lalein)? Suggestions include: (1) any kind of speaking (Liefeld, "Women, Submission, and Ministry," 150; Grosheide, *Epistle of Paul*, 343); (2) the exercise of the gifts of the Spirit, such as speaking in tongues (Ellis, "Silenced Wives," 218; Mare, "1 Corinthians," 276); (3) the community's examination of prophetic messages (Clark, *Man and Woman in Christ*, 186; Hurley, *Man and Woman*, 193); (4) teaching men (Knight, *Role Relationships*, 24–25); (5) asking questions of their husbands (Don Williams, *The Apostle Paul and Women in the Church* [Glendale, Calif.: Regal, 1977], 71; Gundry, *Woman Be Free!* 69); and (6) "sacred cries of joy or mourning" uttered by pagan women in worship for *lalein* in verse 34 and private conversation among women during worship for the same word in verse 35 (Kroegers, *Women Elders*, 13).

5. To whom must women be "in submission" (verse 34)? Orr and Walther (*1 Corinthians*, 312–313) and Grosheide (*Epistle of Paul*, 343) argue that it is to their husbands that women must submit. Clark maintains that it is to men in general, for they had "responsibility . . . for the life of the community as a whole" (*Man and Woman in Christ*, 186). Liefeld suggests the possibility of submission to "the orderly principles of Christian ministry" ("Women, Submission, and Ministry," 151).

6. To what does "the law" (v. 34) refer? The major alternatives are: (1) Genesis 3:16 (so Barrett, *First Epistle*, 330; Robertson and Plummer, *Critical and Exegetical Commentary*, 324; and others); (2) Genesis 2:21ff. (Knight, *Role Relationship*, 25; and Bruce, *1 and 2 Corinthians*, 136, who also includes Genesis 1:26ff.); (3) the whole Old Testament (Hurley, *Man and Woman*, 191–192); (4) the Rabbinic tradition of women's silence in worship (Jewett, *Man as*, 114; Gundry, *Woman Be Free!* 70); (5) Jewish and pagan laws restricting public participation of women (Liefeld, "Women, Submission, and Ministry," 149).

7. If women are instructed in verse 35 to ask their own husbands at home, what are unmarried women to do? Those who believe that the passage deals with wives only have no problem here, but those who relate the passage to women in general posit that unmarried women would have to go through married women or perhaps brothers or fathers (so Robertson and Plummer, *Critical and Exegetical Commentary*, 325; Clark, *Man and Woman in Christ*, 187).

8. What is the referent for the masculine plural monous *("only") in verse 36?* Orr and Walther, for example, take it to refer to the whole Corinthian church (*1 Corinthians*, 313), whereas Bilezikian limits it to the men only (*Beyond Sex Roles*, 151).

9. Are verses 33–35 a Corinthian slogan? Most commentators understand these verses as Paul's command that women be silent, but Bilezikian (ibid., 150) and Walter C. Kaiser, Jr. ("Shared Leadership or Male Headship?" *Christianity Today* [October 3, 1986], 12-I), among others, hold that these verses quote a slogan of the Corinthians, which Paul contradicts in verse 36. Liefeld asserts in opposition to this view that verse 36 contradicts the Corinthians' disobedience of Paul's commands in verses 34–35 ("Women, Submission, and Ministry," 149).

10. Where should verses 34–35 be placed in the text? A number of manuscripts locate these two verses after verse 40.

11. What is the reason for this textual variant? G. W. Trompf believes that verses 34–35 are a later, non-Pauline interpolation ("On Attitudes Toward Women in Paul and Paulinist Literature," *Catholic Biblical Quarterly* 42 [2], 191–215), but Ellis suggests that they are Paul's own marginal note ("Silenced Wives," 218–220).

12. What problem is Paul addressing in this passage? Ellis suggests that wives were testing their husbands' prophetic speech and thus not being properly submissive (ibid., 218). Alternatively, Letha Scanzoni and Nancy Hardesty see the problem as disorderly speech in the worship service (*All We're Meant to Be* [Waco, Texas: Word, 1974], 68–69), and the Kroegers specify private conversation among women, which disrupted the service (*Women Elders*, 13). Still another option is that women were attempting to preach or at least ask questions (Robertson and Plummer, *Critical and Exegetical Commentary*, 324), and the resultant controversy embarrassed their husbands (Orr and Walther, *1 Corinthians*, 313). Bilezikian, furthermore, contends that the issue was "arrogant members competing for conspicuous ministries" (*Beyond Sex Roles*, 147). Finally, Martin believes Paul was addressing a need for soteriological symbolism in worship: Women's silence signifies that the church plays no role in salvation; Jesus has done it all ("1 Corinthians 11:2–16," 240).

1 Timothy 2:8–15

1. Where does the paragraph begin? Is verse 8 a part of the previous paragraph on prayer, leaving verses 9–15 to cover the subject of women, or is verse 8 linked to verses 9–15, all dealing with proper conduct in worship? Niv and tev choose the latter alternative, the Jerusalem Bible the former.

2. What does Paul mean in verse 8 by "holy hands"? Possibilities include: (1) ceremonial purity (Fred D. Gealy, "1 Timothy," *The Interpreter's Bible,* vol. 11 [New York: Abingdon Press, 1955], 404); (2) moral purity (Walter Lock, *A Critical and Exegetical Commentary on the Pastoral Epistles* [New York: Charles Scribner's Sons, 1924], 30); or (3) that the one praying has repented (E. F. Brown, *The Pastoral Epistles* [London: Methuen, 1917], 19) or is not angry or quarreling (Gealy, "1 Timothy," 404).

3. What is the meaning of dialogismou (NIV: **"disputing") in verse 8?** The word can mean "disputing" (so Brown, *Commentary on Pastoral Epistles,* 19; and Lock, *Pastoral Epistles,* 30) or "doubt" (so William Barclay, *The Letters of Timothy, Titus, and Philemon,* rev. ed. [Philadelphia: Westminster, 1975], 65, and Phillips's paraphrase).

4. What is the connection between verse 8 and verse 9? The Greek word *hōsautōs* (NIV: "also") in verse 9 allows the possibility that Paul wants women as well as men to pray. Some hold that only men are urged by Paul to pray in worship (e.g., Zerbst, *Office of Women,* 51; Williams, *Paul and Women,* 110; A. R. C. Leaney, *The Epistles to Timothy, Titus, and Philemon* [London: SCM, 1960], 52; and Ralph Earle, "1 and 2 Timothy," *The Expositor's Bible Commentary,* vol. 11, 360). Others maintain that women are to pray also, so long as they are properly attired (e.g., Lock, *Pastoral Epistles,* 31; Gundry, *Woman Be Free!* 76; and Aida B. Spencer, *Beyond the Curse* [Nashville: Thomas Nelson, 1985], 72–73). David M. Scholer concludes that this problem "cannot be resolved" ("1 Timothy 2:9–15 and the Place of Women in the Church's Ministry," *Women, Authority and the Bible,* 201).

5. Is Paul referring in verses 11 and 12 to wives or women in general? Zerbst (*Office of Women,* 56), Lock (*Pastoral Epistles,* 32), and N. J. Hommes ("Let Women Be Silent in the Church," *Calvin Theological Journal* 4 [1], 13), among others, prefer the former, while Knight (*Role Relationship,* 18) and Douglas J. Moo ("1 Timothy 2:11–15: Meaning and Significance," *Trinity Journal* 1 NS [1], 63), for example, opt for the latter.

6. What does the word hēsuchia (NIV: **"quietness") signify in verse 11?** Bilezikian suggests it connotes the attitude of a disciple eager to learn (*Beyond Sex Roles,* 179; so also Lock, *Pastoral Epistles,* 29; Clark, *Man and Woman in Christ,* 195; Spencer, *Beyond the Curse,* 77). But Leaney (*Epistles,* 53) and Moo ("The Interpretation of 1 Timothy 2:11–15: A Rejoinder," *Trinity Journal* 2 NS [2], 198–199), among others, hold out for absolute silence. Hommes recommends a different nuance: to "remain within the established limits" ("Let Women," 20).

7. To whom or what does verse 11 tell women/wives to submit? Among the proposals are: (1) their teachers (Spencer, *Beyond the Curse,* 77); (2) their husbands (Earle, "1 and 2 Timothy," 362); (3) men (Moo, "Meaning and Significance," 64); and (4) the constituted authority of the church (ibid.).

8. What is the force of ouk epitrepō (NIV: *"I do not permit") in verse 12?* There are two alternatives, depending on how one understands the verb tense as well as the word's meaning. Some scholars take these words as a universal prohibition (so Clark, *Man and Woman in Christ,* 199–200; Moo, "Rejoinder," 199–200; and Knight, who detects a "strong sense of absoluteness," [*Role Relationship,* 19]). Others, however, would translate these words, "I am not presently permitting," indicating Paul's personal preference with consequent local and temporal limitations (so Ford, "Biblical Material," 682; Bilezikian, *Beyond Sex Roles,* 180; and Spencer, *Beyond the Curse,* 85).

9. What does Paul mean in verse 12 by "teach" (didaskein)? More fundamentally, then, what was the nature of teaching in the church of Paul's day? Hommes ("Let Women," 10) and Philip Payne ("Libertarian Women in Ephesus: A Response to Douglas J. Moo's Article, '1 Timothy 2:11–15: Meaning and Significance,' " *Trinity Journal* 2 NS [2], 173–175) contend that teaching in the New Testament church involved a variety of methods, was done by many individuals in the context of the community, and was invested with no special authority. On the other hand, Moo argues that teaching involved authority and was restricted to certain individuals ("Meaning and Significance," 65; so also Clark, *Man and Woman in Christ,* 196). Still other positions are that teaching in New Testament times meant "formulating doctrine" (Ford, "Biblical Material," 683) or that the context limits *didaskein* in verse 12 to mean teaching false doctrine (Catherine Clark Kroeger, "1 Timothy 2:12—A Classicist's View," *Women, Authority and the Bible,* 225–226).

10. What is the precise meaning of authentein (NIV: *"to have authority") in verse 12?* This Greek word is very rare, occurring only here in the New Testament. The major alternatives are "have authority" (Moo, "Meaning and Significance," 67; Earle, "1 and 2 Timothy," 363; Knight, *Role Relationship,* 18 n. 1, among others) and "domineer" (Lock, *Pastoral Epistles,* 32; Payne, "Libertarian Women," 175; and Carroll D. Osburn, "ΑΥΘΕΝΤΕΩ [1 Timothy 2:12]," *Restoration Quarterly* 25 [1], 12, for example). In addition, Catherine Kroeger posits that *authentein* may mean "engage in fertility practices" ("Ancient Heresies and a Strange Greek Verb," *The Reformed Journal* 29 [3], 13) and Martin Dibelius suggests "interrupt" (cited by Gealy, "1 Timothy," 405).

11. Is "a man" the object of "to teach" as well as "to have authority over"? Moo ("Rejoinder," 202), Brown (*The Pastoral Epistles*, 20), and Knight (*Role Relationship*, 18) believe that it is, while Payne ("Libertarian Women," 175) and Bilezikian (*Beyond Sex Roles*, 174) conclude that it is not.

12. Is Paul prohibiting one or two things in verse 12? Moo holds that Paul forbids "two distinct, yet related, activities" ("Meaning and Significance," 65; so also Clark, *Man and Woman in Christ*, 198). But hendiadys is grammatically possible (as in Hurley's rendering, "be authoritative teachers" [*Man and Woman*, 201]), and the Kroegers put forward as a possible translation, "teach that she is superior to a man" (*Women Elders*, 16).

13. What is the place of verses 13–14 in Paul's argument? Many scholars, such as Clark (*Man and Woman in Christ*, 195) and Knight (*Role Relationship*, 19) maintain that these verses provide two reasons for Paul's prohibition in verse 12. Bilezikian argues that the two verses together form just one reason for verse 12's prohibition (*Beyond Sex Roles*, 258–260). Spencer, however, posits that the references to Eve are simply an "explanation or analogy" (*Beyond the Curse*, 89; so also Williams, *Paul and Women*, 113).

14. What is the force of the preposition gar (NIV: "for") in verse 13? Payne ("Libertarian Women," 176–177) and Scholer ("1 Timothy 2:9–15," 208) argue that it is explanatory and hence supports the view that verses 13–14 are an analogy. Zerbst (*Office of Women*, 54) and Moo ("Meaning and Significance," 70) hold that it is causative and therefore verses 13–14 provide reasons for verse 12. And Williams believes *gar* should be translated "furthermore" and is "nothing more than a continuative or connective" (*Paul and Women*, 112).

15. What is the point of verse 13? The traditional view is that because Adam was created first, men have authority over women (so Zerbst, *Office of Women*, 54). Moo objects to this, however, stating that Paul's "point would appear to be that the role of women in the worship service should be in accord with the subordinate, helping role envisaged for them in creation" ("Meaning and Significance," 68). Bilezikian takes the position that verse 13 indicates that Eve did not learn of the proscribed tree directly from God, as did Adam (*Beyond Sex Roles*, 180).

16. What kind of formation does eplasthē (NIV: "was formed") signify in verse 13? While most commentators take it to refer to God's creating Adam and Eve, Kaiser ascribes to *eplasthē* the classical sense of instruction, i.e., being formed by education ("Shared Leadership," 12-I).

APPENDIX II

17. *What is the point of verse 14?* There are three major options: (1) Women are by nature susceptible to being deceived (Earle, "1 and 2 Timothy," 362; Brown, *The Pastoral Epistles*, 20). (2) Disaster transpires when male and female roles are reversed, as when Eve instructed Adam to eat the fruit (Gealy, "1 Timothy," 406; Knight, *Role Relationship*, 19; Moo holds to both views one and two ["Meaning and Significance," 70]). And (3) Eve was untutored concerning God's command and therefore should not have taught Adam (Bilezikian, *Beyond Sex Roles*, 180; Kaiser, "Shared Leadership," 12-I, and Kenneth S. Kantzer, "Proceed With Care," *Christianity Today* [October 3, 1986], 14-I). According to the first two options, verse 14 renders women unfit for teaching, while the third option makes this verse speak against uneducated teachers. One other view may be mentioned: Zerbst posits that Paul inserted verse 14 just to show that the Fall did not abrogate the creation order set forth in verse 13 (*Office of Women*, 54).

18. *What does verse 15 mean?* This verse is extraordinarily difficult, because any adequate exegesis must not only do justice to the text itself but also reconcile this verse with Paul's clear teaching elsewhere that humans are saved by grace through faith. In a very helpful summary, Moo lists these proposals for the meaning of verse 15, along with their proponents ("Meaning and Significance," 71):

1. Despite the judgment pronounced upon woman (Genesis 3:16), Christian women will be safely preserved through the experience of childbirth.
2. Christian women will experience salvation even though they must bear children.
3. By observing her proper role (*teknogonia*) and maintaining Christian virtues, the woman will be kept from the error just mentioned (lording it over the husband and being deceived).
4. Christian women are saved through good works, figuratively represented by *teknogonia*.
5. Despite the disastrous results of Eve's deception, Christian women will be saved through *the* childbirth, the coming of the Messiah, just as was promised in the *protoevangelium* (Genesis 3:15).
6. It is not through active teaching and ruling activities that Christian women will be saved, but through faithfulness to their proper role, exemplified in motherhood.

Indicative of the difficulty of this verse, Susan Foh states, "The last verse (verse 15) in this section is a puzzle and a sort of non sequitur" (*Women and the Word of God: A Response to Biblical Feminism* [Grand Rapids, Mich.: Baker Book House, 1980], 128), and Gundry finally gives up because verse 15 is "incapable of adequate interpretation with the information we now have" (*Woman Be Free!* 75).

The next four difficulties discussed are specific exegetical issues that form part of the larger debate summarized by Moo.

19. What does the verb sōzō ("save") mean in this context? Suggestions include the word's full salvific connotation (Gealy, "1 Timothy," 407), deliverance or preservation (NIV: "kept safe"), "sanctify" (Brown, *The Pastoral Epistles*, 21), "find their place among the saved" (Scholer, "1 Timothy 2:9–15," 197), "find both physical health and a higher spiritual state" (Earle, "1 and 2 Timothy," 362), and "experience the blessings of salvation" (A. M. Stibbs, "The Pastoral Epistles," *The New Bible Commentary*, ed. D. Guthrie and J. A. Motyer, rev. ed. (London: InterVarsity Press, 1970), 1171).

20. What is the force of the preposition dia (NIV: "through")? Payne speaks of "agency" ("Libertarian Women," 180), Moo of "efficient cause" ("Meaning and Significance," 72), and Moo's first option (*see* 18) obviously gives *dia* a temporal sense ("during").

21. What is the meaning of teknogonia (NIV: "childbirth")? The primary possibilities are: (1) childbirth (C. K. Barrett, *The Pastoral Epistles* [Oxford: Clarendon, 1963], 56); (2) child rearing or motherhood [Leaney, *Epistles*, 54]; or (3) *the* childbirth, that is, the birth of Jesus (Payne, "Libertarian Women," 177).

22. What is the force of the definite article tēs ("the"), which precedes teknogonia in the Greek text? Payne holds that it is specific (ibid., 181), Moo that it is generic ("Rejoinder," 206). (It must be specific if *teknogonia* is to mean *the* childbirth.)

23. Why is the verb "remain" (meinōsin) plural in verse 15? As KJV reflects (but NIV does not) "woman" is singular from verse 11 through the first clause of verse 15. But then Paul writes, "If *they* remain." Suggestions for the subject (*they*) include: women (A. T. Hanson, *The Pastoral Letters* [Cambridge: University Press, 1966], 38), Christian women (Gealy, "1 Timothy," 406), Ephesian women (Bilezikian, *Beyond Sex Roles*, 183), women and children or women and men (Zerbst, *Office of Women*, 56), the woman's children (Leaney, *Epistles*, 54), and husbands and wives (Lock, *Pastoral Epistles*, 33; NEB suggests in a note, "If husband and wife continue in mutual fidelity").

24. Where does the paragraph end? While most commentators end the section with verse 15, Lock (*Pastoral Epistles*, 33) and Brown (*The Pastoral Epistles*, 18) carry it over to 3:1a, so that verse 15 is the "trustworthy saying."

25. What problem is Paul addressing in this passage? Among the alternatives are the following: (1) the presence of heresy, which has been variously identified as (a) a Gnostic cult of Eve (Catherine Kroeger, "1 Timothy 2:12" 232ff.); (b) two heresies within the church, a Judaizing and a libertine faction (Payne, "Libertarian Women," 185); and (c) a "proto-gnostic Jewish heresy" from outside the church, which undermined traditional sex roles (Moo, "Rejoinder," 217–218); (2) untutored women who were spreading heresy in the Ephesian church (Payne, "Libertarian Women," 185; Spencer, *Beyond the Curse*, 183–184); (3) women's rejection of traditional sex roles, giving Christianity a bad reputation (Osburn, "ΑΥΘΕΝΤΕΩ," 11; Leaney, *Epistles*, 53); and (4) alternative approaches to church order with which Paul disagreed (Clark, *Man and Woman in Christ*, 192).

How Can We Reconcile the Teaching of These Three Passages?

Paul seems to permit women to pray and prophesy in 1 Corinthians 11:5, while forbidding them to speak at all in 1 Corinthians 14:34–35 and 1 Timothy 2:11, 12. We may summarize the most significant attempts at reconciliation as follows:

1. First Corinthians 14 and 1 Timothy 2 lay down the general rule, to which 1 Corinthians 11:5 is the exception (Waltke, "1 Corinthians 11:2–16," 49; Ryrie, *Place of Women*, 76).
2. First Corinthians 11 deals with private worship, so the regulations Paul sets down for public worship in 1 Corinthians 14 and 1 Timothy 2 do not apply (Simon, *The First Epistle*, 112; Craig, "The First Epistle," 213).
3. First Corinthians 11 describes public worship, but not official services of the church, for which Paul makes the stipulation in the other two passages (Grosheide, *Epistle of Paul*, 341).
4. First Corinthians 11:5 is Paul's unwilling concession to a Corinthian practice of which he disapproves (Ryrie, *Place of Women*, 77; Lietzmann, cited by Zerbst, *Office of Women*, 50).
5. First Corinthians 11:5 is hypothetical, an extreme case that might never occur (Robertson and Plummer, *Critical and Exegetical Commentary*, 229).
6. Paul does not forbid women to pray and prophesy, but to preach and teach, because preaching and teaching constitute an exercise of authority, and praying and prophesying do not (Moo, "Meaning and Significance," 75; Knight, *Role Relationship*, 34).
7. First Corinthians 14:33b–36 and 1 Timothy 2:11–15 are specific measures Paul takes to combat particular problems in the

churches at Corinth and Ephesus, and there is therefore no need for reconciliation (Ellis, "Silenced Wives," 218; Bilezikian, *Beyond Sex Roles,* 139).

8. First Timothy 2 and 1 Corinthians 14:33b–376 are non-Pauline, and therefore no reconciliation is possible or necessary (Barrett, *First Epistle,* 332–333).

Additional Note

In 1 Corinthians 11:4, 5, women are instructed to prophesy with covered heads. Some difficult issues surround the subject of prophecy in the New Testament. Salient disputed points are:

1. What was the nature of prophecy in the New Testament Church? Some scholars see it as the equivalent of preaching today (e.g., Robertson and Plummer, *Critical and Exegetical Commentary,* 301; and W. W. Gasque, "The Role of Women in the Church, in Society, and in the Home" [*The Priscilla Papers* 2 (2)], 2). But Barrett sees prophecy as "excited, perhaps ecstatic speech" (*First Epistle,* 280), and Morris holds that there was a predictive element in New Testament prophecy (*First Epistle,* 172). Wayne Grudem, in *The Gift of Prophecy in 1 Corinthians* (Washington, D.C.: University Press of America, 1982), contends that prophecy was the reception and public communication of a spontaneous revelation from God (179) and was neither preaching (139–144) nor ecstatic (176).

2. How much authority did New Testament prophecy possess? This is pivotal in attempting to reconcile 1 Corinthians 11:4, 5 and 1 Timothy 2:12. Grudem maintains that New Testament prophecy had "authority of general content," not "authority of actual words" such as was possessed by Old Testament prophets and the apostle John as he wrote Revelation (*Gift of Prophecy,* 72). But D. E. Aune (*Prophecy in Early Christianity and the Ancient Mediterranean World* [Grand Rapids, Mich.: Wm. B. Eerdmans, 1983], 6) and R. B. Gaffin (*Perspectives on Pentecost* [Phillipsburg, N.J.: Presbyterian & Reformed, 1979], 71) reject this sharp distinction.

3. When does the gift of prophecy cease? This issue is focused on 1 Corinthians 13:8, 9 but is relevant to the application of 1 Corinthians 11:4, 5 to the church today. Chief options for the time of the cessation of prophecy are: (1) the return of Christ (Grudem, *Gift of Prophecy,* 219), (2) the completion of the New Testament canon (Grosheide, *Epistle of Paul,* 287), and (3) the maturity of the church (R. L. Thomas, "Tongues . . . Will Cease" [*Journal of the Evangelical Theological Society* 9 (1)], 81–89).

Appendix III

The Classical Concept of *Head* as "Source"

Catherine Clark Kroeger

Catherine Clark Kroeger is a chaplain and lecturer in religion at Hamilton College. She holds an M.A. in Greek and a Ph.D. in classical area studies. She was an instructor in Greek at the University of Minnesota and a contributor to various religious journals. The bulk of the material in this appendix was presented as a plenary address to the 1986 national meeting of the Evangelical Theological Society.

I am most appreciative that Dr. Kroeger has allowed me to include her paper in this book.

The concept of *head* as "source" is well documented in both classical and Christian antiquity and has been long accepted by scholars. Some evangelicals, however, have shown a reluctance to deal with the data. There has even been a contention that the understanding of the Greek word for "head," *kephalē*, as meaning "source" is of modern invention, that dictionaries earlier than Liddell, Scott and Jones do not list such a definition. We must in the first instance observe that Greek-English dictionaries are a relatively late phenomenon. The first such lexicon of classical Greek appeared in about 1819, although as usual the Germans were well ahead. To find earlier works, we must use Greek-Latin dictionaries, of which there are a great abundance. In these the definition of "source" for *kephalē* is well attested. Henry Petrina's *Lexicon Dictionarium Graecolatinum* of 1577 lists the following meanings: *caput, vertex, summa pars, apex cerni, exorium, origo* (source or origin), *statura corporis.* It would be somewhat tedious to list the entries of lexicographers over many centuries, but some are available in my footnotes.[1] Let me add one further caveat, at the risk of being insulting: a dictionary is *not* a concordance. Certain scholars feel that they can prove their point by counting the number of examples used to demonstrate a certain value in the lexicon. The function of a dictionary is to cite the various meanings and to provide at least one illustration of the usage.

Ancient Definitions of *Kephalē*

But one need not be bound to the dictionary in any case. It is far more useful to turn to the ancient authors and see how they themselves defined *kephalē.* Since the definition was important in christological arguments, they were careful to spell it out exactly. Athanasius stated, "For the head (which is the source) of all things is the Son, but God is the head (which is the source) of Christ."[2] Cyril, Archbishop of Alexandria, wrote of Adam:

> Therefore of our race he became first *head, which is source,* and was of the earth and earthy. Since Christ was named the second Adam, he has been placed as *head, which is source,* of those who through him have been formed anew unto him unto immortality through sanctification in the spirit. Therefore he himself our *source, which is head,* has appeared as a human being. Yet he though God by nature, has himself a generating head, the heavenly Father, and he himself, though God according to his nature, yet being the Word, was begotten of Him. *Because head means source,* He establishes the truth for those who are wavering in their mind that man is the head of woman, for she was taken out of him. Therefore as God according to His nature, the one Christ and Son and Lord has as his head the heavenly Father, having himself become our head because he is of the same stock according to the flesh.[3]

1. Franz Passow, *Handwörterbuch der Griechischen Sprache,* rev. ed. (Leipzig: Rost, Palm, and Kreussler, 1847). Henri (Estienne) Stephanus, *Thesaurus Graecae Linguae* (Paris: 1831–1865), ed. Dindorf Iohannis Zonarae, *Lexicon* (Leipzig: 1808) V. C. F. Rost, *Griechisch–Deutsches Wörterbuch* (Braunschweig: 1859). *See also* C. Schenkl, *Vocabolario Greco-Italiano* (Bologna: n.d.); Rudolf Bolting, *Dicionario Grego-Portugues* (Rio De Janeiro: 1941.)
2. Κεφαλὴ γὰρ, ὃ ἐστιν ἀρχὴ πάντων, ὁ Υἱός • "κεφαλὴ δέ," ὃ ἐστιν ἡ ἀρχὴ "τοῦ Χριστοῦ ὁ Θεός." Athanasius *De Synodis* anathema 26 (Migne PG 26, 740, B).
3. οὐκοῦν πρώτη γέγονεν ἡμῖν κεφαλὴ τοῦ γένους, τουτέστιν ἀρχή, ὁ ἐκ γῆς τε καὶ χοϊκός • ἐπειδὴ δὲ δεύτερος Ἀδὰμ κατωνόμασται ὁ Χριστὸς, κεφαλὴ τέθειται, τουτέστιν ἀρχὴ, τῶν δι' αὐτοῦ πρὸς αὐτὸν ἀναμορφουμένων εἰς ἀφθαρσίαν δι' ἁγιασμοῦ ἐν πνεύματι. οὐκοῦν αὐτὸς μὲν ἡμῶν ἀρχὴ, τουτέστιν ἡ κεφαλὴ, καθὸ πέφηνεν ἄνθρωπος • ἔχει γεμὴν κεφαλὴν αὐτὸς ὡς φύσει Θεὸς τὸν ἐν τοῖς οὐρανοις Πατέρα, γεγέννηται γὰρ ἐξ' αὐτοῦ κατὰ φύσιν Θεὸς ὢν ὁ Λόγος. ὅτι δὲ ἡ κεφαλὴ σημαίνει τὴν ἀρχὴν, ἐμπεδοῖ πρὸς ἀλήθειαν τῶν ἐνδοιαζόντων τὸν νοῦν τὸ κεφαλὴν γενέσθαι τὸν ἄνδρα τῆς γυναικός •

In case you have lost count, *kephalē* is defined as "source" (*archē*) no less than four times in this single paragraph. In his application of the words of Paul in 1 Corinthians 11:3, Cyril bases his argument upon this definition. Christ was begotten of the Father, who is His source, woman was drawn from man, who is her source.

Ancient Concepts of the Function of the Head

Nevertheless, literary definitions and dictionaries cannot help us at the more basic stage of inquiry: namely, the ideological basis for attaching a certain significance to the term for "head."

We must acknowledge that the ancients had varying views as to the function of the topmost bodily member. Alcmaeon of Croton believed that the brain was the seat of the leading factor,[4] but there was a decided difference of opinion on the matter. In the dispute as to whether the head or the chest is the seat of the ruling part, "Plato favored the head, Aristotle the heart, and Epicurus the chest, while the Stoics were divided."[5] The argument was a lively one; and Galen, a major medical writer of the second century A.D., goes so far as to quote a lengthy refutation of those who considered the head the ruling part of the body.[6] Philo of Alexandria, a Jewish writer of the first century A.D., wisely decided that it was best to leave to the experts the question of whether the ruling faculty lay in the brain or in the heart.[7]

Let us remember that these brilliant minds were at work upon a method that is still the basis of modern science, namely observation of phenomena and the drawing of conclusions from the data. The empirical process employs a method of trial and error.

In our inquiry, let us begin with an observation that the ancients made very early, notably that the head could produce more luxuriant hair than any other part of the body. This quality of productivity made a lasting impression. The head could produce not only hair but wetness as well. Reflection leads us to conclude that every opening in the head is capable of secreting a moist or viscous substance, such as tears, saliva, and earwax. Aristotle concluded that it was because of its moisture that the head could produce such abundant tresses and

ἐλήφθη γὰρ ἐξ αὐτοῦ. εἰς οὖν ἄρα Χριστὸς καὶ Υἱὸς καὶ κύριος ὁ κεφαλὴν μὲν ἔχων, ὡς Θεὸς κατὰ φύσιν, τὸν ἐν τοῖς οὐρανοῖς Πατέρα, γεγονὼς δὲ ἡμῖν κεφαλὴ διά τοι τὸ κατὰ σάρκα συγγενές. Cyril of Alexandria, *De Recta Fide ad Pulcheriam et Eudociam* 2.3 (ed. Pusey), 268.

4. ἐν τῷ ἐγκεφάλῳ εἶναι τὸ ἡγεμονικόν. Alcmaeon of Croton (ed. Diels) A 8 Aet. 4, 17, 1.
5. R. B. Onians, *The Origins of European Thought About the Body, the Mind, the Soul, the World, Time, and Fate* (Cambridge: Cambridge Univ. Press, 1951), 117, footnote 9. For Galen's objection to those who considered the chest to be the governing part of the soul, Galen, *On the Doctrines of Hippocrates and Plato* 2.2.20.
6. Galen *On the Doctrines of Hippocrates and Plato* 3.3–10.
7. Philo of Alexandria *On the Posterity and Exile of Cain* 137. See also *The Worse Attacks the Better*, 90.

beard. He wrote: "The head seems to be the wellspring or source (πηγή) of moisture, and therefore the hair grows, since it is due to great moisture."[8]

The head can produce other kinds of wetness as well. Those who have ever been afflicted with a head cold are well aware that from the nostrils and mouth there can issue a remarkable diversity of secretions. Sometimes they can indeed bear a likeness to human semen. This phenomenon did not escape the notice of the ancient philosophers. Many of them, including Aristotle, considered the head to be the source of human sperm. Alcmaeon of Croton, a near contemporary of Pythagoras, believed that the sperm came from the brain,[9] while Aristotle explained that the semen descended from the head through the spinal cord to the genitals and was then sent forth to produce new life.[10] We must bear in mind that these philosophers had never attended an eighth-grade movie on human reproduction or a high school biology class. They were simply making observations and drawing conclusions about all that they saw in the world around them.

Others, too, came to the conclusion that the head was the source of sperm and therefore of human life. A closely associated culture, that of ancient Rome, subscribed so strongly to this notion that sexual intercourse was occasionally referred to as "diminishing one's head."[11] The Athenians loved to tell how their patron goddess, Athena, sprang directly from the head of her father Zeus. This remarkable birth circumvented several steps in the normal process of generation.

The Head as Source of Life

The concept of head as source of life was so strongly entrenched among the Pythagoreans that they were forbidden to eat any meat from the head, lest it prove to be that of an ancestor who had become an animal in a subsequent reincarnation. This practice precluded a descendant eating the very organ from which he or she had sprung. Shortly after the New Testament period, Plutarch told of those who abstained from eating an egg just as others did from the brain "thinking it to be the source of generation."[12]

From the concept of the head as the source of generation, it followed that the father was viewed as procreator and head of the fam-

8. δοκεῖ δὲ πηγὴ εἶναι ἡ κεφαλὴ τοῦ ὑγροῦ. Aristotle *Problemata* 10 (867a).
9. Alcmaeon of Croton (ed., Diels) A13.
10. ἡ γὰρ γονή ἐστιν ἀπὸ τοῦ ἐγκεφάλου χωροῦσα διὰ τῆς ῥάχεως. Aristotle *Problemata* 57.
11. Plautus, fr 112, *Mercator*, 100 ff., 533ff (Lindsay) Statius Caecilius. 140. Livius Andronicus 28 (Ribbeck). Sextus Turipilius 112.
12. Athenaeus 2.65, ἐγκέφαλον, ἀρχὴν ἡγούμενος γενέσεως. Plutarch *Symposium* 2.3.

ily. Philo of Alexandria, a contemporary of the Apostle Paul, described Esau as head and progenitor of his race.[13] "As though he were the head of a living being, Esau is the progenitor of all those members who have been mentioned," wrote Philo. Cosmas Indicopleustes, in the sixth century A.D., called Adam the head of all people in this world, because he was their source and father. Likewise, he said, Christ was head of the church, according to the flesh, and Father of the age to come.[14] In a similar manner Theodore of Mopsuestia, who died in A.D., 428, hailed Adam as the one whom we, who are subject to passion, consider our head, for we derive our being from him. When we are made free from passion, we consider Christ our head because we, who are delivered from passion, have our being from Him.[15] We shall return presently to the notion of the oldest living male as progenitor and head of his family, especially as it applies to Roman law in the first century A.D.

Like the head, the father was the source of sperm and of life. Artemidorus of Ephesus, a philosopher of the second century A.D., wrote that the head was like one's father,[16] because just as the head (kephalē) was the source of light and life for the whole body, so a father was the source of life for his son.[17] He wrote again "The head (kephalē) is like one's parents because it is the source or cause (aitia) of one's having life."[18]

The Head as Source of Supply for the Body

The notion of the head as supplying other parts of the body with life is strange to us. Yet Aetius Amidenus Medicus wrote that in treating illness, one must always begin with the head, because it was the root and source of the entire bodily condition.[19] If ever the head was ill-disposed, then it had its effect throughout the whole body.[20]

---

13. κεφαλὴ δὲ ὡς ζῴου πάντων τῶν λεχθέντῶν μερῶν ὁ γενάρχης ἐστὶν Ἠσαῦ. Philo *On Mating With the Preliminary Studies* 61. I am indebted to Philip Payne for calling this text to my attention.

14. κεφαλή ἐστιν ὁ Ἀδὰμ πάντων τὼν ἀνθρώπων ἐν τούτῳ τῶ κόσμῳ, ὡς αἴτιος αὐτῶν ὢν καὶ πατύρ ὄντω καὶ ὁ Δεοπότης Χριστός, κατὰ σάρκα, τῆς Εκκλησίας κεφαλή ἐστι καὶ Πατὴρ του μέλλοντος αἰῶνος. Cosmas Indicopleustes *Topgraphia Christiana*, book 5.209 (Migne PG 88, 224).

15. Παθητοὶ μὲν γὰρ ὄντες, κεφαλὴν ἡγούμεθα τὸν Ἀδάμ, ἐξ οὖπερ τὸ εἶναι εἰλήφαμεν· ἀπαθεῖς δὲ γενόμενοι, κεφαλὴν ἡγούμεθα τὸν Χριστόν, ἐξ οὖπερ ἀπαθεῖς εἶναι ἐσχήκαμεν. Theodore of Mopsuestia, *Commentary on 1 Corinthians* 11.3 (Migne PG 66,888C).

16. οἷον κεφαλὴ εἰς πατέρα. Artemidorus Daldiensis, *Oneion* (ed. Teubner) 1, 2, 9.

17. ὃς καὶ τοῦ ζῆν καὶ τοῦ φωτὸς αἴτιος ἥν, ὥσπερ καὶ ἡ κεφαλὴ τοῦ παντὸς σώματος. Artemidorus Daldiensis *Oneirocritica* (ed. Teubner). 2, 7.

18. γονεῦσι μὲν γὰρ ἔοικεν ἡ κεφαλὴ διὰ τὸ τοῦ ζῆν αἰτίαν εἶναι. Ibid 1.35, 43.

19. ἡ δὲ σύμπασα θεραπεία ἀπὸ κεφαλῆς ἀρχεσθαι δεήσει αὕτη γὰρ ῥίζα καὶ ἀρχὴ τῆς ὅλης ἐστὶ διαθέσεως. Aetius Amidenus Medicus *Liber Medicinales*, ed. Olivieri (Berlin: 1950), 6.28.69. 174–175.

20. κἂν ἡ κεφαλή ποτε πάσχοι διὰ τὸ σύμπαν σῶμα καὶ τοῦ παντὸς σώματος ἐπιμελουμένους. Ibid. 8.35.9. 448.

The medical writer Aretaeus declared, "From the head is the source of life, because the head is the place of perception and the starting point of the nerves."[21] Aristotle held that the source of flow to the body was from the head,[22] but that those were wrong who said that the origin of the veins lay in the head.[23] Galen, too, condemned his teacher Pelops because he tried to demonstrate that the brain was the source of all the blood vessels.[24]

In his *Timaeus*, Plato develops a rather detailed explanation of the origin and function of the head. The gods created a receptacle for the soul, which was itself the seed, and encased it within the strong bones of the skull. The route through which the sperm should pass was well guarded by the spinal column through the neck and back.[25] In the creation of humanity, the gods had first formed a bodily member that was spherical like the universe and then placed it on top of the body, nearest to the heavens. In it, the immortal part of the soul was set, while the mortal part indwelt the chest. Thus the head became the vehicle of the soul. Other bodily members serve as attendants.[26] From heaven, whence the soul began, the divine part suspends our head or root (Κεφαλήν καὶ ῥίζαν) and causes the entire body to stand upright.[27] The apposition of "head or root" demonstrates that for Plato the rest of the body stemmed from the head and received from thence its sustenance. Archer-Hind wrote of this phrase in Plato, "as a plant draws its sustenance through its roots from its native earth, so does the soul draw her spiritual sustenance from her native heavens."[28] In the first century A.D., Philo was to echo the same thought, declaring that man drew his sustenance from heaven because, unlike the animals, his head was uplifted toward the sky.[29] In another treatise, Philo spoke of the truly virtuous, whether a single individual or a people, as being the head of humanity from which the rest may draw inspiration as limbs of the body draw life from the

21. ἀπὸ κεφαλῆς . . . ἐνθᾶδε γὰρ τῆς ζωῆς ἐστὶ ἡ ἀρχή. κεφαλὴ δὲ χῶρος μὲν αἰσθήσιος καὶ νεύρων ἀφέσιος. Aretaeus Medicus, *De curatione acutorum morborum libri duo*, ed. K. Hude (Berlin: Akademie-Verlag, 1958) 1.1.5.8.
22. Διὸ καὶ τὰ ῥεύματα τοῖς σώμασιν ἐκ τῆς κεφαλῆς ἐστι τὴν ἀρχήν. Aristotle PA 652 b.34.
23. Aristotle 665b.28.
24. παρὰ του διδασκάλου Πέλοπος ἐπιδεκνύναι πειρωμένου τὸν ἐκέφαλον ἀπάντων τῶν ἀρχὴν. Galen *On the Doctrines of Hippocrates and Plato* 6.3.26. ed., p. 378.
25. Plato *Timaeus* 73 b–74 a. ἐκ τῆς κεφαλῆς κατὰ τὸν αὐχένα καὶ διὰ τῆς ῥάχεως . . . ὃν δὴ σπρέρμα . . . εἴπομεν. 91a.
26. *Timaeus* 44c–45 a.69d.
27. ἐκεῖθεν γάρ, ὅθεν ἡ πρώτη τῆς ψυχῆς γένεσις ἔφυ, τὸ θειον τὴν κεφαλὴν καὶ ῥίζαν ἡμῶν ἀνακρεμαννὺν ὀρθοῖ πᾶν τὸ σῶμα. Plato *Timaeus* 91a.
28. As quoted in appendix on Philo, *The Worse Attacks the Better*, vol. 2 (Cambridge: Harvard Univ. Press, 1968) 495.
29. Philo *The Worse Attacks the Better*, 85.

forces in the head.[30] The head provides not only sperm, but life itself, to the rest of the body.

Two biblical metaphors also express the function of the head as being the source of coordination and supply. In the letter to the Ephesians we read, "Let us grow up unto him in all things, who is the head, Christ, from whom the entire body, fitted together and united through the supply of every ligament by the proper working of each part, produces the growth of the body for its upbuilding in love" (See Ephesians 4:15). Colossians 2:19 speaks of Christ as "the head from whom the entire body, as it is supplied through the ligaments and sinews and knit together, grows with the growth of God." In each case the writer speaks of Christ, but he uses a metaphor of what he conceives to be the function of the head. The head is seen as the point of origin for integration and growth for the body.

Head as Source of a River or Stream

But let us examine other ways in which the head was viewed as the beginning or source of something. Both Greeks and Romans considered the source of a river to be its head.[31] The *Digest* of Justinian declared, "The head is the place whence the water issues forth."[32] Homer called the innermost part of a stream its "head," and in his commentary on Homer Eusthatius explained that the river's head is that which generates the whole river.[33] Sometimes a bearded head of either man or bull was set up at a fountain or source of a river.[34] An exceptionally fine example of the river's head with the gods of the

30. κεφαλὴν μὲν τοῦ ἀνθρωπείου γένους ἔσεσθαι φησι τὸν σπουδαῖον εἴτε ἄνδρα εἴτε λαόν, τοὺς δὲ ἄλλους ἅπαντας οἷον μέρη σώματος ψυχούμενα ταῖς ἐν κεφαλῃ καὶ ὑπεράνω δυνάμεσιν. Philo *On Rewards and Punishments* 125.
31. Tibullus 1.7.23ff. Virgil *Georgics* 4.319.355.
32. "Caput est unde aqua nascitur." *Digesta* (Libri Pandetarum) 43.20.
33. Homer *Odyssey* 9.140.8.102.346. Eusthatius, on *Iliad* as quoted in Onians, 232.
34. *"Die 'tête de taureau' über dem orifice einer fontaine en einem rocher als die Acheloosmaske zu fassen ist."* Friedrich Wieseler, *"Ueber ein Votivrelief aus Megara,"* *Abhlandlungen der Königlichen Gesellschaft der Wissenschaften* zu Göttingen, Philologisch-historische Klasse, Abhandlungen, zwanzigster Band (1875), 21, 2. *"Sonst flegte man die auch im Cultus immer besonders hervorgehobene Quelle durch ein bärtiges Menschenhaupt anzudeuten,"* Ludwig Preller, *Thegonie und Götter* (Berlin: 1894) rev. Carl Robert, vol. 1, 549. See also Onians, *Origins*, 232. Ad. Michaelis *"Il dio Pan colle Ore e con Ninfe su rilevi votivi Greci,"* *Annali dell' Instituto di corrispondenza archaeologica*, Vol. 35 (1863), 292 f. esp. 317, lf 333. C. Friederichs, *Berlins Antike Bildwerke*, 1, 392. Kekeulé, *Die Antike Bildwerke im Theseion zu Athen*, 192, 80. O. Jahn, *Berichte der sächs: Gesellschaft der Wissenschaften*, 1851, 143 ff. Furtwängler, *Sammlungen Sabouroff I, Skulpt* tables 27, 28. Fr. Marx, *Interpret, hex. (Ind. lect. hib. Rostock* 1888/9), 8ff. Panofka, *"Ueber den bärtigen, oft hermenähnlich gestützen Kopf der Nymphenreliefs,"* *Abhandlungen der Akademie der Wissenschaften zu Berlin* (1846). Fröhner, *Notice de la scupture antique du Louvre*, vol. 1, 289. Heydemann, *Die Antike Marmorbildwerke zu Athen*, 533. Schöne Griech, *Reliefs aus Athen*. Sammlungen, 58. Matz, *Bull. d. lust. arch* (1870), 68, *Götting. ge. Anz.* (1873), 334. 28.

Pantheon seated around it.[35] It dates from the fourth or third century B.C. and had been set up at the origin of a stream at Megara on the Isthmus of Corinth.

The term *kephalē*, like the Latin *caput*, is applied to the source of a river. A Persian king caused a poem lauding the sources (*kephalai*) of the Tearos River to be inscribed on a stone. The quotation is preserved both by Herodotus[36] and in the collection of poems known as the Greek Anthology.[37] Some have complained because "sources" is in the plural, but Herodotus tells us specifically that the river arose from thirty-eight springs. How could the origins of the stream be anything but plural? That the term could also be used in the singular is demonstrated by Galen, in the late second century A.D. He was discussing the tributary system of rivers. A river that arose from a single spring was larger at its source (*kephalē* in the singular) than it was later.[38] Whirlpools in a river might arise from the waters being heated at the source (*kephalē* in the singular).[39] Philoponus, in the sixth century A.D., explained that a river, when it rushed upon a rock, might divide and become two streams, even though it had but a single source (*kephalē*).[40] In other words, when a writer referred to headwaters in the plural, he used the plural *kephalai*. When he referred to a single source, he used the singular *kephalē*.

The concept of *kephalē* as beginning might refer to other things beside the starting point of a river. Plato uses *kephalē* to mean the beginning of a story or argument, and *akephalos* (headless) as an adjective to define a myth or argument without beginning.[41]

The Head of a Deity as Source

A line of poetry occurs several times in ancient Greek religious material known as the Orphic writings. It runs:

35. Friedrich Wieseler, "*Ueber ein Votivrelief aus Megara*," 11–39.
36. Herodotus 4.91.
37. Τεάρου ποταμοῦ κεφαλαῖ ὕδωρ ἄριστόν τε καὶ κάλλιστον παρέχονται πάντων ποταμῶν. *Anthologia Graeca* 9.703.2.
38. ποταμὸς δὲ οὐδεὶς ἐκ μιᾶς ὁρμωμενος πηγῆς ἐλάττονα τὴν κεφαλὴν ἔχει τῶν ἐφεξῆς. Galen *On the Doctrines of Hippocrates and Plato* 6 3.21.4 (ed. De Lacy) vol. 2, 378.
39. συμβαίνει δ᾿ αὐτοῖς ταῦτα μᾶλλον. ὅταν ἡλιοωθῶσιν, ἤ πως ἄλλως θερμάνθῶσι τὴν κεφαλήν. Galen *De locis affectis libri vi* (ed. Kühn) 8.202.9
40. ὁ εἷς ποταμός, ὅταν ἀντικρούμη εἰς πέτραν, εἰς δύο διαιρειταῖ, ἕος ὄντος τοῦ ἐπέκεινα τῆς πέτρας, οὕτω καὶ ἐπὶ τούτων κεφαλὴ μὲν μία ἀνάλογος οὖσα. . . . Philoponus *Gen. Anim.* 14.3.1.
41. Plato *Gorgias* 505; *Laws* 6.752 A. *Phaedrus* 264 C. Olympiodorus wrote: in his commentary on the *Gorgias*, βούλεσθε κινήσω τὸν λόγον, ἵνα κεφαλὴν ἔχῃ ὁ μυθος ἢ οὐ κεφαλὴ δὲ τοῦ μύθου το ἐπιμύθιον • αὐτὸ γὰρ τὸ ἀληθὲς τὸ κεκρυμμένον ἐν τῷ μύθῳ διδάσκει δ᾿ ἐχρὴν καὶ τοὺς ποιητικοὺς ἔχειν, καὶ οὐκ ἂν ἡπατώμεθα εὐθέως τὴν ἀλήθειαν μανθάνοντες ἔδει οὐν᾿μὴ ἐᾶσαι ἀκέφαλον τὸν λόγον. Olympiodorus (ed. Teubner) 161.4. 176.

Zeus was born first, Zeus last, god of the bright bolt:
Zeus is the head, Zeus the middle, from Zeus are all things
made.[42]

The various quotations of the same line are valuable because the
terms "head" (*kephalē*) and "source" (*archē*) are used interchangeably,
so that the line sometimes runs:

Zeus the beginning, Zeus the middle and Zeus the end.

The interchangeability of the two words *archē* and *kephalē* is in itself
significant. Apparently the ancient authors considered the two terms
synonymous in this context.[43]Four times Zeus is called head, *kephalē*,[44]
and three times *archē*, source or beginning.[45]

The famous singer Orpheus was considered a seer and prophet, and a significant body of literature is attributed to him. Orphic
concepts were closely associated with Pythagoreanism and pro-
foundly influenced Greek philosophical and religious thought. Interestingly enough, when the body of Orpheus was dismembered, the
severed head continued to sing and, to the initiates, to prophesy his
famous utterances.

A series of funerary statuettes from southern Italy demonstrate the
Orphico-Pythagorean belief that at birth the soul leaves the bosom of
the goddess Persephone and rises through her head to the earth
above.[46] These representations date from the third and fourth centu-

42. Ζεὺς πρῶτος γένετο, Ζεὺς ὕστατος ἀργικέραυνος.

Ζεὺς κεφαλή, Ζεὺς μέσσα • Διος δ' ἐκ πάντα τελειται. Otto Kern, *Orphicorum Fragmenta*,
vol 2 (Berlin: Weidman 1963) 21 a. 2. 168, 201. (Trans. M. L. West, *The Orphic Poems*
[Oxford: Clarendon Press, 1983], 89.)

43. "Sie verstanden also das Wort κεφαλή hier also Anfang, ja setzten, beeinflusst von
der Aion-Theologie, das Wort ἀρχή dafür ein.... Plato ... sagt (Leg. IV 715 e) dafür
ἀρχήν τε καὶ τελευτὴν καὶ μέσα. Wer sich für die Schreibung der Verse auf ihn beruft,
müsste folgerichtig auch ἀρχή für κεφαλή schreiben." Riuchard Reitzenstein and Hans
Heinrich Schaeder, *Studien zum Antiken Synkretismus aus Iran und Griechenland*,
Darmstadt: Wissenschaftliche Buchgesellschaft, 1965, 80–81.

44. Proclus *Commentary on Plato's Timaeus* 2. 95.48 (V.322). Pseudo-Aristotle *On the
World* 7. This treatise was attributed to Aristotle in antiquity. It appears actually to be
a late Stoic work but to be based upon an earlier Stoic source (Kern, 1922), 21 a).
Eusebius *Preparation for the Gospel* 3.9. Derveni Papyrus col. 13, line 12. Text in S. G.
Kapsomenos. 1964b:21. Stobaeus *Eclogue* 1.23.

45. Proclus *Theol.* 6.8.363. Plutarch *de Comm. Notion.* 31.385, *De Def. Orac.* 48.379.T.9.
Anonymous in *Vit. Arat*, 273 Petav Otto Kern, *Orphicorum Fragmenta*, vol. 2 (Berlin:
1963). *Fragmenta Veteriora* 21, 91 (Adnotat Scholiasta) 451, Bekker Scholion on Plato
Laws 4.715e.

46. Frederike van der Wielen-van Ommeren, "Polychrome Vases and Terracottas from
Southern Italy in the J. Paul Getty Museum," *Occasional Papers on Antiquities, 3. Greek
Vases in the J. Paul Getty Museum 2*. Malibu, 1985, pl. 176–177. A. Oliver, Jr., "The
Reconstruction of Two Apulian Tomb Groups," *Antike Kunst*, Suppl. 5 (1968), esp. 19,
n. 99. Cf. E.P. Biardot, *Explication du symbolisme des terres cuites grecques de destination*

ries B.C. and were found in tombs, especially in the area of Canosa. At death the soul is shown descending beneath the bosom of the goddess through the crown upon her head. Thus her head is both the source and the end of life. Like Zeus, Persephone, queen of the dead, is head and middle and end.

The Father as Source of the Son

If pagan deities were regarded as the source of the soul and of all life, what were the implications in Christian theology? Saint Basil wrote that because the Son had the Father as His one source, it was said that God was the head of Christ.[47] Athanasius declared that the Son had been begotten before the ages, not as though He were unbegotten of the Father but that He had the Father who begot him as His Source. He then quotes the words of Paul, "The Head of Christ is God."[48] Twice in his *Theology of the Church*, Eusebius interpreted the Apostle Paul's statement that God is the head of Christ as meaning that God was His source.[49]

> The great apostle teaches that God is head of the Son and the Son of the church, for in one place he says, "God is the head of Christ," and in another, speaking of the Son, "and he gave him as a head over all things to the church, which is his body." Surely then he would be author of the church and head, and the father author and head of him. Thus the one God is father of the only begotten Son and the one head of Christ. Since there is one source and head [*kephale* and *arche*], how would there be two gods, when that one alone claims as father no one higher nor any other causative principle?[50]

funéraire, Paris, 1864, pl. no. 44. Pindar *Frag.* 133, Sandys = Plato *Meno* 81 b-c. Kaibel, *Corpus Inscr. Gr. Ital. Sic.*, 481, a,b,c. 641, 1, 7. See also Kuntz, *Persephone: Three Essays on Religion and Thought in Magna Graaecia* (Oxford: Clarendon Press, 1971), passim.

47. διά τε τὴν κατὰ πάντων ἀρχὴν, καὶ διὰ τὸ μίαν ἔχειν εαυτοῦ ἀρχὴν τὸν Πατέρα· "Κεφαλὴ" γὰρ "Χριστοῦ ὁ θεός." Basil *Theologus* (Migne PG 30.8U.23).

48. τὸν δὲ υἱὸν γεγεννῆσθαι πρὸ αἰώνων καὶ μηκέτι ὁμοίως πατρὶ ἀγέννητον εἶναι καὶ αὐτόν, ἀλλ' ἀρχὴν ἔχειν τὸν γεννήσαντα πατέρα. Κεφαλὴ Χριστοῦ ὁ θεός. Athanasius *De Synodis Armimini in Italia et Seleuciae in Isauria* (ed. Opitz) 26.3.35.

49. ἐπεὶ καὶ αὐτὸς. ὁ υἱὸς ἀρχὴν ἐπιγράφεται τὸν αὐτοῦ πατέρα. "κεφαλὴ γὰρ Χριστοῦ ὁ θεὸς" κατὰ τον ἀπόστολον. Eusebius *De Ecclesiastica Theologia* 2.7.1

50. καὶ κεφαλὴν δὲ αὐτοῦ μὲν τοῦ υἱοῦ τὸν θεόυ, τῆς δ' ἐκκλησίας τὸν υἱὸν ὁ μέγας ἀπόστολος διδάσκει, πῆ μὲν λέγων 'κεφαλὴ δὲ τοῦ Χριστοῦ ὁ θεός,' πῆ δὲ περὶ τοῦ υἱοῦ φάσκων 'καὶ αὐτὸν ἔδωκεν κεφαλὴν ὑπέρ πάντα τῇ ἐκκλησίᾳ, ἥτις τὸ σῶμα αὐτοῦ.' οὐκοῦν τῆς μὲν ἐκκλησίας αὐτὸς ἀρχηγὸς ἂν εἴη καὶ κεφαλή, δὲ αὐτοῦ ὁ πατήρ. οὕτως εἰς θεὸς ὁ τοῦ μονογενοῦς υἱοῦ πατήρ, καὶ μία ἡ καὶ αὐτοῦ τοῦ Χριστοῦ κεφαλή. μιᾶς δὲ οὔσης ἀρχῆς τε καὶ κεφαλῆς, πῶς ἂν γένοιντο θεοὶ δύο, οὐχὶ δὲ εἷς ἐκεῖνος μόνος ὁ μηδένα ἀνώτερον μηδὲ ἑαυτοῦ αἴτιον ἕτερον ἐπιγραφόμενος. Eusebius *De Ecclesiastica Theologia* 1.11.2–3.

APPENDIX III

Man as Source of Woman

If the church fathers understood the headship of the Father to be that of source or causative principle, what are the implications in the male-female relationship? When the Bible speaks of man as the head of woman, does it mean "source" or "chief, boss"? Let me point out that in the New Testament era *kephalē* rarely had the sense of boss or chief as it does in English and Hebrew.[51] Early commentators on 1 Corinthians 11 who understood the Father to be Head (that is, source) of the Son, also understood Christ as the source of man, and man as the source of woman. Cyril of Alexandria, Greek Father of the fifth century noted that Saint Luke had looked beyond Adam and indicated the Creator God to be the Source and Origin of every man. He wrote, "Thus we say that the *kephalē* of every man is Christ, because he was made through him and brought forward to birth. . . . And the *kephalē* of woman is man, because she was taken from his flesh and has him as her source. Likewise, the *kephalē* of Christ is God, because He is from Him according to nature."[52] Theodore of Mopsuestia held that just as Christ was considered head of all who had been born anew in Him, so the woman has man as her head "since she had taken her being from him."[53] This concept of woman being taken out of man is repeated twice in 1 Corinthians, so that it would seem to define the sense in which man is woman's head. But let us consider for a moment the implications in the ancient world.

The Pagan View of Women

We are speaking of a world that did not know Jesus Christ and did not know the Hebrew Scriptures. The world of Greek religion was one in which women had been made as a sneaky trick of the gods in order to compensate for man having gained possession of fire.[54] The purpose in the gift of woman to man was simply to get man into trouble. Although there were a number of accounts of how woman had been made, in each case she was made of a substance inferior to that of the man. Her mind was "a thing apart,"[55] incapable of the

---

51. *See* Berkeley and Alvera Mickelsen, "The 'Head' of the Epistles," *Christianity Today* (20 February, 1981), 20–23; *see also* their essay "What Does *Kephale* Mean in the New Testament?" *Women, Authority, and the Bible*, ed. A. Mickelsen, Downers Grove: InterVarsity 1986, 97–110.

52. ἀρχὴν τῷ ἀνθρώπῳ τιθεὶς τὸν ποιήσαντα Θεόν. οὕτως εἶναί φαμεν παντὸς ἀνδρὸς κεφαλὴν τὸν Χριστόν • πεποίηται γὰρ δι᾽ αὐτοῦ καὶ παρήχθη πρὸς γένεσιν . . . κεφαλὴ δὲ γυναικὸς ὁ ἀνήρ, ὅτι ἐκ τῆς σαρκὸς αὐτοῦ ἐλήφθη, καὶ αὐτὸν ὥσπερ ἔχει τὴν ἀρχήν. κεφαλὴ δὲ ὁμοίως Χριστοῦ ὁ Θεός, ὅτι ἐξ αὐτοῦ κατὰ φύσιν. Cyril of Alexandria "*De Recte Fide ad Arcadiam et Marinam*" in Cyrilli *Opera* 1.1.5 5(2).63 (ed. Pusey), vol. 7, pt. 1, 182.

53. ἐπειδὴ ἀπ᾽ ἐκείνου τὸ εἶναι εἴληφεν. Theodore of Mopsuestia, *Commentary on I Corinthians* (Migne PG 66.888 C).

54. Hesiod *Theogony* 568–601; *Works and Days* 55–89.

55. Semonides *On Women* 7.

spiritual or intellectual perceptions of man. One account declared man to have been made of a divine substance, women of the dirt of the earth.[56] A rather imaginative (and nasty) poet divided women into categories. Some were made from the sow, some from the bitch, others from the high-stepping mare or the unstable waves of the sea.[57] From these she derived her nature, which was closer to animals than to that of man.

With this perception of their ground of being, it is not surprising that women were held in low esteem. Aristotle declared that the bravest woman was more cowardly than the most craven male and that the most virtuous woman was crass in comparison to the basest male.[58] The Greeks quite frankly expressed their opinion that women were not fit to associate with civilized folk.[59] This in turn had profound effects upon society, including the matter of sexual preference.

The Ideological Basis for Homosexuality and the Christian Answer

Sexual preference was a topic of lively discussion in the ancient world, and no less than five of these debates have survived in literary texts. In most of these debates, love for women comes off second-best. Plato held that the truly noble soul was masculine and would seek another male as the object of its love. Lesser spirits might be content to bestow their affection within the women's quarters.[60] One debate, from a period slightly later than the New Testament period, was decided by a judge in favor of homosexuality, because of the moral inferiority of women. He announced: "Therefore let the obligation to marry be universal, but let the love of boys be reserved only for the wise, because perfect virtue flourishes least of all among women."[61] To declare that man was the source of woman, that she was bone of his bone and flesh of his flesh was to give woman a nature like man's own. She was no longer of the substance of the animals, but of man. She was a fit partner, his glory and his image. ". . . Neither is the woman independent of the man nor the man of the woman in the Lord; for just as the woman is from the man, so man is from the woman, and all things are of God" (see Corinthians 11:11, 12). This was a positive affirmation of heterosexual marriage.

Photius, synthesizing the work of earlier Greek fathers, wrote: "For Christ is the head of us who believe, as being partakers in one body with him and being made by him, for all of us who share one body

56. Hesiod Works and Days 89.
57. Semonides On Women 83–93.
58. Aristotle Politics, 1254b, 1259b, 1260a.
59. Euripides, Hippolytus, 1.640–650; Xenophon Oeconomicus 7.5–10.
60. Plato Symposium 180, 192.
61. Lucian Erotes 51.

have him as head. But the head of Christ is the Father, as procreator and progenitor and of like substance with him. And the head of the woman is the man because he is her procreator and progenitor and of like substance with her."[62]

The Pattern of the Roman Family

But how may we interpret this notion of man as head of woman, when we come to Ephesians 5? Here I believe we need to return to our notion of the procreator as the head of the family and to provide a sketch of the social system of the New Testament period, even though space limitations require that it be brief. Under Roman law, only one individual in each family was held accountable for the entire unit of men, women, children, and slaves. The assigned person to answer to the Roman government was the oldest living male progenitor.

It did not matter whether the son or even the grandson was a grown man and might be living in a separate house—under Roman law the oldest living male agnate was the head.[63] Just as the head is the most conspicuous member and the one by which the whole body is identified, so all other members were officially listed below the head. This individual was responsible for the moral conduct of the entire *familia,* and one of his prerogatives was that of establishing and maintaining the religion of the family. Obviously this would take the power of choice away from a young man who had become a Christian. It was possible for him to break away from the family and to become a person in his own right, but it meant bucking the tide in a system based upon veneration of one's ancestors.

In the New Testament era a woman seldom had the opportunity to stand before the law in her own right. Ordinarily she must be officially attached to father, husband, son, or uncle. If these were dead, a tutor or guardian might be appointed by the court.

When a woman was given in marriage into a family, her legal relationship to her husband was that of a daughter to a father. In this way, he became her head. Of course her husband might not be head of the family, if his father, grandfather, or even great-grandfather were still living. This could mean that even though the husband was a Christian, the wife was legally bound to older, pagan members of his family.

---

62. κεφαλὴ μὲν ἡμῶν τῶν πιστῶν ἐστιν ὁ Χριστός, ὡς συσσώμων. . . αὐτῷ γεγεννημένων . . . δι' αὐτὸν γὰρ ἅπαντες ἐν σωμα χρηματίσαντες κεφαλὴν ἔχομεν αὐτόν. ʽκεφαλὴ ἐν δὲ του Χριστου ὁ . . . πατὴρ ὡς γεννήτωρ καὶ προβολεὺς καὶ ὁμοούσιος αὐτοῦ. κεφάλη δὲ γυναικὸς ὁ ἀνήρ, ὅτι καὶ αὐτὸς γεννήτωρ αὐτης καὶ προβολεὺς καὶ ὁμοούσιος' ὑπάρχει αὐτῇ. Photius, "Commentary on 1 Corinthians 11:3," *Pauluskomentar aus der griechischen Kirche aus Katenenhandschriften Gesammelt,* ed. K. Staab (Munster: Aschendorff, 1933) 567.1 ff.
63. Dionysos of Halicarnassus *Roman Antiquities* 2.26.1–4.

Marriage "Without Hand"

By the first century A.D., a form of marriage had come into vogue in which the woman was not even an official member of her husband's household. The system devised by the Emperor Augustus was called *sine manu*[64] or marriage without hand. It provided that both the woman and her dowry remained under the jurisdiction of her father's family, although the husband was entitled to the income from the dowry. The woman lived in her husband's house, but must return to her own family for at least three nights each year. If she failed to observe the three nights away from her husband's roof, the marriage changed to one of permanence, in which she was a member of her husband's family.

Her own relatives, however, were interested in retaining control of her property and saw to it that she returned to them for the required time. The woman remained in the husband's household as an interloper and alien, still committed to the gods of her own family. Furthermore, she could be removed by her family and married off elsewhere any time they chose. A husband could be compelled to do the father-in-law's will by threats of taking back his wife.[65] This had moral implications that could create serious problems for a young Christian husband with a pagan father-in-law.

The system did not contribute to the stability of marriages, as Augustus had supposed it would, but quite the opposite. A social historian declared, "The only enduring relationship a married woman had was the one with her blood relatives."[66] Writing about 7 B.C., Dionysius of Halicarnassus observed that divorce was rare in early Roman days, because women looked only to their husbands and had no other recourse, while husbands knew that the wives belonged to them in a permanent relationship.[67] Thus *sine manu* marriage came to be recognized as a threat to the permanence of marriage.

In the middle of the first century A.D. an initial attempt was made to abolish the destructive elements in *sine manu* marriage and to render a woman a full member of her husband's household.[68] By the second century A.D., enough legislation had been passed so that this form of marriage fell into disuse. Nevertheless, during the New Testament era, this was the most common form of marriage throughout

---

64. An extensive bibliography on women and Roman marriage is available in *Women in the Ancient World: The Arethusa Papers,* ed. John Peradotto and H. P. Sullivan (Albany: SUNY Press, 1984), 334–337; 357–362. Especially helpful is Sarah B. Pomeroy's "The Relationship of the Married Woman to Her Blood Relatives in Rome." *Ancient Society 7,* 1976, 215–227.
65. Apuleius *Apology* 77.
66. Sarah B. Pomeroy, "The Relationship of the Married Woman to Her Blood Relatives in Rome," 220.
67. Dionysus of Halicarnassus *Roman Antiquities* 2.25.4.
68. Gaius *Institutes* 1.157.171.

the Roman Empire. Remember that both Ephesus and Corinth were Roman cities. We must recognize that the first effort to do away with the automatic guardianship of a wife by her father's family was made in the reign of Claudius (and therefore during the ministry of the Apostle Paul). I believe that there are important implications. A woman could have a greater element of choice.

The Christian Pattern of Marriage

For Christians it was expedient to be their own persons, *sui iuris*, as it was known legally. They were to look beyond their fathers according to the flesh and acknowledge Christ as their head. When it came to marriage, the household was to be free from family restriction and directly accountable to God; and the Apostle Paul applied the quotation from Genesis: "Therefore shall a man leave father and mother and cleave unto his wife."

An Alternative Definition of Submission

Now I suggest that just as the husband was asked to leave his family, the wife was being asked to leave hers and attach herself to her husband, to be identified with him. *Hupotassō*, the word often translated "submit," also means to attach one thing to another or to identify one person or thing with another. I believe that the wife was asked to identify herself with her husband and to join herself to him rather than to remain part of her father's family. The word *hupotassō*, ordinarily translated "submit" or "be subject," has many different meanings, as even a very conservative dictionary will tell you. *Hupotassō* may imply "to join one thing to another," "to relate one thing to another in meaningful fashion," "to identify one thing with another."[69] It may also signify to classify one thing in terms of another.[70] A meaningful relationship with the known provides an understanding of the unknown.

If we look at Romans 8:20, we discover a statement that says creation was made subject (*hupotassō*) to vanity. Our theology does not permit us to believe that futility or vanity is the governing principle of this world. In this verse, we must find another translation for *hupotassō*. One scholarly suggestion is that it be rendered "creation was *brought under the influence of* vanity." We might also say that the world *is identified with* frustration and meaninglessness, but ultimately God has a divine plan by which it will come to perfect fulfillment (Romans 8:21).

69. Polybius (second century B.C.) *Histories* 3.38.4.
70. 3.36.6–7;18.15.4.

EQUAL TO SERVE

Consider also Luke 2:41–51. The young Jesus has been taken to the temple at Jerusalem to make His bar mitzvah, by which He will become a man in the eyes of the law. The temple in those days was a glorious one, with a cult that attracted worldwide admiration. Two of the most brilliant scholars in the story of Judaism, Hillel and Shammai, were at their zenith. One could hear them teaching daily in the courtyards of the temple. When it was time to go home after the ceremony, Jesus remained at the temple, rather than attaching Himself to the party of friends and relatives who were journeying back to the everyday world at Nazareth.

When Mary and Joseph find their son, He is in the midst of a vigorous debate among the scholars, and He is surprised that His parents do not understand that now He belongs to the world of His Father. Then, Luke continues, He returned to Nazareth and was subject unto them (*hupotassō*). That Jesus did not always do just as His family said is obvious from the later Gospel accounts. That He left the sphere of influence in the temple and identified Himself instead with the lives of everyday people is also obvious.

I believe that the theology of Saint Paul called for an independent family unit in which the wife was fully integrated to the husband and both committed to Christ. For neither was the woman without the man nor the man without the woman in the Lord.

A Concept Opposed to Wife Battering

A major concern in the establishment of "marriage without hand" had been the fear that the husband might abuse the wife. This, I believe, is the reason why each of the so-called "household codes" calls upon the husband to love his wife and to care for her. Although the notion of husband as the head is often quoted nowadays as a justification for domestic violence, this is not the thrust of the New Testament passages. The headship image was to make both husband and wife part of the same body, dependent upon each other for their very existence. The husband was to view her not as attached to another family, but tenderly, as part of his own body, bone of his bone and flesh of his flesh. "And no man ever yet hated his own flesh."

The Status of Jesus Christ, the Son of God

Although I am deeply concerned with the biblical status of women, one other matter concerns me more: that of the status of Jesus Christ. There are those who argue for a subordination within the Godhead so that they may affirm the subordination of women. Their understanding of headship enables them to assign subordinate positions both to women and to the Son of God. Saint John Chrysostom said it far better than I when he observed that there were heretics who seized upon the notion of headship and derived from it a concept of the Son

282

as somehow less than the Father. The heretics would argue that although the Son is of the same substance as the Father, He is under subjection. No, said Chrysostom, had Paul intended to demonstrate subordination, he would have chosen slave and master rather than wife and husband. The Apostle intended to show equality. Chrysostom asked, How then should we understand head? and answered, understand it in the sense of "perfect unity and primal cause and source."[71]

Subordinationism has led again and again to a downgrading of Jesus Christ, to Arianism and Unitarianism. It has been repeatedly condemned as a heretical doctrine by those who have defended the doctrine of a Triune God equal in goodness, power, and love. Before you embrace a doctrine of headship that implies subordination, think again of the warning of John Chrysostom and of his definition of headship as implying perfect unity and first principle and source. I believe that this understanding will produce a healthy doctrine of the Trinity and of the family.

71. Κεφαλὴ δὲ γυναικὸς ὁ ἀνήρ • κεφαλὴ δὲ Χριστοῦ ὁ Θεός. Ἐνταῦθα ἐπιπηδῶσιν ἡμῖν οἱ αἱρετικοὶ ἐλάττωσίν τινα ἐκ τῶν εἰρημένων ἐπιροοῦντες τῷ Ὑιῷ ἀλλ' ἑαυτοις περιπίπτουσιν.... Τί οὖν δεῖν ... λαβεῖν; ... λαβεῖν δὲ ἕνωσιν ἀκριβῆ, καὶ αἰτίαν καὶ ἀρχὴν τὴν πρώτην. John Chrysostom, Commentary on the First Epistle to the Corinthians, Homily 26 (Migne, PG 61.214, 216).

Notes

Chapter 2

1. *Columbia*, 11 (April, 1986), 5:46.

Chapter 3

1. *New York Times* (May 5, 1986).
2. *Daughters of Sarah* (May/June, 1986), 31.
3. *Newsweek* (June 10, 1985).
4. *The Daily Walk* (September, 1985), 15.
5. *Webster's New Collegiate Dictionary* (Springfield, Mass.: G. & C. Merriam, 1974), 422.
6. *See* For Further Reading.
7. *Christianity Today* (February 6, 1981).
8. Oswald Chambers, *Daily Thoughts for Disciples* (Grand Rapids, Mich.: Zondervan, 1976), 215.

Chapter 5

1. A comprehensive treatment of patriarchy is found in historian Gerde Lerner's book *The Creation of Patriarchy* (New York: Oxford Univ. Press, 1986).
2. *Webster's New Collegiate Dictionary* (Springfield, Mass.: G. & C. Merriam, 1974), 840.
3. The position of women in Islamic countries was highlighted at the United Nations Decade for Woman Conference (Nairobi, 1985). The *New York Times* (July 25, 1985) reported that Saudi Arabian women were "conspicuously absent . . . perhaps because Saudi women are not allowed to travel without a male relative or because Saudi's strict interpretation of Islam imposes restrictions on women that would have made it hard to defend women's equality. Saudi women are not allowed to drive a car, mingle with men or leave home without covering their heads, arms and legs." While Egypt is more liberal, an article in *U.S. News & World Report* (December 12, 1985) stated: "Any limitations of a man's rights is bitterly resented in this traditionally male-dominated society. Resentment is fueled by the housing shortage. 'Why should I give up my apartment, which I paid for, if I divorce my wife?' asks an ex-Army officer. 'It goes against God's law.' "

In Muslim countries men may have four wives and may divorce a wife at will. Daughters are entitled to only half the inheritance due sons (*New York Times*, June 10, 1985). In the United Arab Emirates brides are still purchased, and women consider a higher price as marital security: A husband will be less likely to divorce a costly wife (*Time*, September 9, 1985). However, the husband may take as many concubines as he pleases.

Women's educational and vocational opportunities are severely restricted where a *purdah* (seclusion of women) is practiced by strict Muslims. In present-day Iran a Muslim woman risks arrest if she appears on the street with more than her eyes showing.

In addition many Muslim women struggle with an underlying fear of physical abuse. The Quran says, "The man has authority over women because Allah has made the one superior to the others" (Sura 4:34) and goes on to invest the man with the right to use corporal punishment on his wife or wives. (*See also* material cited in Valerie Hoffman's article "The Christian Approach to the Muslim Woman and Family," *The Gospel and Islam: A 1978 Compendium*, ed. Don McCurry, MARC, 919 W. Huntington Dr., Monrovia, CA 91016.)

4. Exodus 21:20 tells a master that "the slave is his property," but the church today feels free to consider that text as limited to a certain historical era.

5. The Jerusalem Bible contains a prayer attributed to Esther, words found in the Greek text of the Old Testament, although not in the Hebrew. A particular part of this prayer gives us possible further insight into Esther's feelings about her "promotion" as "she besought the Lord God of Israel in these words":

"You have knowledge of all things,
and you know that I hate honours from the godless,
that I loathe the bed of the uncircumcised,
of any foreigner whatever.
You know I am under constraint,
that I loathe the symbol of my high position
bound around my brow when I appear at court;
I loathe it as if it were a filthy rag
and do not wear it on my days of leisure. . . .
Nor has your handmaid found pleasure
from the day of her promotion until now
except in you, Lord, God of Abraham."

6. Phyllis Trible, *Texts of Terror* (Philadelphia: Fortress Press, 1984).

7. Oswald Chambers, *Daily Thoughts for Disciples* (Grand Rapids, Mich.: Zondervan, 1976), 111.

Chapter 6

1. In thinking of the Exodus period, we must not forget the defiant Hebrew midwives (Exodus 1:15–21) or the fact that Moses' own life was preserved by the courageous actions of his sister, mother, and wife.

2. *The Wycliffe Bible Commentary* has a significant comment about this incident: "Discrimination on the ground of sex was foreign to the spirit of the Old Testament. . . . Restriction of women, e.g., to a separate court in the Temple, arose only with the perversions of inter-Testamental Judaism." *The Wycliffe Bible Commentary* (Chicago: Moody Press, 1962), 418.

3. Some have argued that the fact the Twelve were men mandates only

males as leaders, reasoning that if Jesus had wanted to include women, He would have done so. However, logic demands that this argument restrict leadership to Jewish males, because if Jesus had wanted to include Gentile men, He would have done so. Yet proponents of male leadership feel free to say that excluding Gentiles from the Twelve was a concession to Jewish culture, insuring Jesus a more receptive audience. Isn't it possible that excluding women from the Twelve was another concession to first-century culture—as well as to decorum?

4. Aida Besançon Spencer, *Beyond the Curse* (Nashville: Thomas Nelson, 1985), 113–117.

5. Paul includes the names of many women in his list of friends and co-workers found in Romans 16:1–16, and the Greek indicates that these women were prominent in ministry. Again, Dr. Spencer's book gives us insight into this question, including interesting material about Junia (Romans 16:7), who was considered by such Church Fathers as Origen, John Chrysostom, and Jerome to be a significant leader in the early church. Ibid., 101.

6. Ibid., 109–112.

7. Again, although many translations do not make it clear, in the Greek, the language in these verses is inclusive and refers to both men and women.

8. Oswald Chambers, *Daily Thoughts for Disciples* (Grand Rapids, Mich.: Zondervan, 1976), 219, 220.

Chapter 7

1. Oswald Chambers, *Daily Thoughts for Disciples* (Grand Rapids, Mich.: Zondervan, 1976), 233.

2. We can reverently speculate that she was probably familiar with the sad case history in Genesis 16, which warns of the folly of ignoring God's scheduling.

3. Donald Davidson, quoted in Herbert Lockyer, *The Women of the Bible* (Grand Rapids, Mich.: Zondervan, 1967), 99.

4. Chambers, *Daily Thoughts*, 239.

Chapter 8

1. Thomas Hardy, *The Darkling Thrush and Other Poems by Thomas Hardy* (Topsfield, Mass.: Salem House, 1985).

2. R. V. Krafft-Ebing, *Psychopathia Sexualis*, 10th ed. (London: Rebman Ltd., 1899), 16.

3. Patricia Gundry's book *Heirs Together* contains an excellent chapter titled "What Is Marriage?" 31–40. *See* For Further Reading for this and other books by Gundry.

4. In addition, Gilbert Bilezikian points out: "Beyond concern for the emotional welfare of Adam, the creation of the woman stemmed from ontological necessities rooted in the very nature of God. Femaleness was also an aspect of the *imago Dei*." Gilbert Bilezikian, *Beyond Sex Roles* (Grand Rapids, Mich.: Baker Book House, 1985), 216, note 7.

5. Louis Auchincloss, *The Embezzler* (New York: Dell Pub., 1966), 24.

6. *Webster's New Collegiate Dictionary*, 1974 edition, 414.

7. *See* Aida Besançon Spencer, *Beyond the Curse* (Nashville: Thomas Nelson, 1985), 34–42; and Gilbert Bilezikian, *Beyond Sex Roles* (Grand Rapids, Mich.: Baker Book House, 1985), 54–57.

8. One reason women want to control their sexuality is because historically only women have been tied to the result of sexual intercourse. Only women bear the "fruit" or visible evidence of sexual union, but to allow men to disassociate themselves from an act in which they fully participate places an unfair share of responsibility for the issue of that act on women alone. It also encourages irresponsibility in men, which ranges from "he's only sowing wild oats" to the extreme of rape. But in a truly Christian union *both* partners must assume responsibility for their sexual actions. In a truly Christian union neither partner controls that action. I suggest that if men assumed their rightful share of responsibility, which includes a fair share of nurturing their offspring, we would hear little talk of women "controlling" reproduction. The thoughtless "hit and run" of the unwed father, the insensitive impregnating of a wife unready for motherhood or already overburdened with children, the cruel aggression of the rapist have driven women to the extreme of demanding *sole* control of the issue of what was intended to be a joint function—a union of the two becoming one.

9. Small children were also part of this broad work force, as they still are in many underdeveloped countries today. Even in northern Europe and North America, until the nineteenth century, formal educational opportunities were only available to a favored few; therefore young children were not in school, but occupied themselves with observing adult work and then beginning to help adults with tasks necessary to support daily life.

10. Possibly because small girls have been encouraged to play with dolls, it has seemed natural for some men to think of child care as an extension of a "play" activity rather than recognizing that child care is not "playing," but a bona fide career.

11. Dr. William Spencer's essay showing how his family has implemented shared marriage, parenting, and ministry appears in *Beyond the Curse* (*see* For Further Reading).

12. Evelyn Bence, *Leaving Home: The Making of an Independent Woman* (Wheaton, Ill.: Tyndale House, 1986), 24.

Chapter 9

1. Some traditionalists feel that their interpretation of the order of creation is also supported by Paul's references to creation in 1 Timothy 2:13, 14. However, his precise point there is not uniformly agreed upon as clear, as Appendix II, "Exegetical Difficulties in the 'Hard Passages,' " demonstrates. *See also* Roger Nicole's discussion of some of the difficulties in 1 Timothy 2:8–15. ("Biblical Authority and Feminist Aspirations," *Women, Authority, and the Bible*, ed. Alvera Mickelsen [Downers Grove, Ill.: InterVarsity Press, 1986], 47–48, note 1.)

2. Both Gilbert Bilezikian and Aida Spencer give detailed examinations of *'ēzer*. Their books are listed in For Further Reading.

3. Some have appealed to Adam's naming of woman (Genesis 3:20) as indication of his dominance. An examination of the logical difficulties in that position can be found in Gilbert Bilezikian, *Beyond Sex Roles* (Grand Rapids, Mich.: Baker Book House, 1985), 220–223, note 16.

4. In studying Scripture we begin with the process of *exegesis*, that is, extracting the meaning from the text and hopefully making that meaning clear. Then we go on to *hermeneutics*, the science of interpreting the text, while *biblical theology* constructs ideas and concepts about God as these appear in the text, and finally *systematic theology* categorizes those concepts.

This whole sequence depends on that first step, exegesis, arriving at a clear meaning for the text. But what if that first step is not possible? Remember that the Bible is a translated book, and as with any translation, there can be difficulties. Special problems occur when you deal with ancient languages and cultures, because there are often no easy ways to check the meaning of an unknown word or even completely to understand what known words say. So when it is not at this time possible to extract a clear meaning from some verse or passage, we have what scholars call an "exegetical crux." You can see what happens next: Whenever there exists an exegetical crux, or hard place where the meaning of the passage is unclear, interpretations will vary, and these interpretations can result in sincere differences of opinion in matters of theology.

5. *See* Roger Nicole's comments, "Biblical Authority," 48, note 1.

6. For example, in studying 1 Corinthians 11:2–16, it is helpful to know that in Corinth only a "loose" woman went unveiled in public (*see* Patricia Gundry, *Woman Be Free!* [Grand Rapids, Mich.: Zondervan, 1977], 63–69; and Richard and Catherine Kroeger, "Sexual Identity in Corinth," *The Reformed Journal* [December, 1978]). In studying 1 Corinthians 14:33–36, it is helpful to be aware not only that some pagan worshipers spoke in tongues, but that others—especially women—considered excessive wailing honoring to their gods. (*See* Richard and Catherine Kroeger, "Pandemonium and Silence at Corinth," *The Reformed Journal* [June, 1978].) Certainly in his instructions to the Corinthians, Paul would have wanted to be sure the early church avoided any suggestion of immorality or paganism.

As for background relevant to 1 Timothy 2:8–15, the entire letter contains many admonitions against heresy, so it will be important to try to discover what sort of heresy might have existed in ancient Ephesus. If indeed there was an Eve cult that taught a reversal of the Genesis creation account, Paul's words in 1 Timothy 2:11–14 could take on a new shade of meaning. His prohibition against women spreading such a cult would be obvious. (*See* Catherine Kroeger, "1 Timothy 2:12—A Classicist's View," as found in *Women, Authority and the Bible;* and Aida Besançon Spencer, "Eve at Ephesus," *Journal of the Evangelical Theological Society* [Fall, 1974]. Additional material about Ephesus appears in *The Biblical Illustrator* [January, 1981].)

7. Clark Pinnock, *Biblical Revelation* (Chicago: Moody Press, 1971), 175–207.

8. Unfortunately the popular *The Living Bible* paraphrase has imposed such presuppositions on its rendering of 1 Corinthians 11:10 and 14:34. To Paul's words in 11:10 about female head covering, this paraphrase inexplicably adds "as a sign that she is under man's authority," although no such words occur in the original Greek. To Paul's words in 14:34, about women's silence, this paraphrase gratuitously adds about women "for they are subordinate to men." Footnotes indicate that these comments have been added to the text, but the average reader may not pick up on the fact that no such language occurs in the original manuscripts. Such additions reinforce traditionalist presuppositions, but do so at the high cost of debasing the text.

9. Berkeley and Alvera Mickelsen, "What Does *Kephalē* Mean in the New Testament?" *Women, Authority, and the Bible*, 97–132.

10. *See* Appendix II and Gilbert Bilezikian, *Beyond Sex Roles*, 137–139.

11. For a more detailed look at this problem, see Bilezikian, ibid., 157–162.

12. Although many English translations do not make this clear (nor do their man-made subtitles and paragraph breaks), in the Greek there is no equivalent of a period after verse 21. Verse 21 is connected grammatically with the succeeding verses. In addition, in the Greek there is no verb in verse 22, but the verb is understood from verse 21. This is further evidence that injunctions to wives and husbands must be taken as a whole and must begin with verse 21. Don Williams has a helpful chapter on the cohesiveness of this passage in his book *The Apostle Paul and Women in the Church* (Van Nuys, Calif.: BIM Pub., 1977), 87–94.

13. Patricia Gundry gives a full-length discussion of mutual submission in her book about Christian marriage, *Heirs Together* (Grand Rapids, Mich.: Zondervan, 1980).

14. Chambers, *Daily Thought for Disciples* (Grand Rapids, Mich.: Zondervan, 1976), 220.

15. Paul also feels free to use feminine imagery for himself, as in 1 Thessalonians 2:7, 8.

16. Bilezikian, *Beyond Sex Roles*, 207–214; and Aida Spencer, *Beyond the Curse* (Nashville: Thomas Nelson, 1985), 138–179.

17. Although these passages do not specifically exhort government rulers, we know from Romans 13:1–4 that the ideal state is to be God's servant, too, using God's delegated authority to reflect God's justice.

Chapter 10

1. Even groups that teach a restricted role for women practice allowing women to use their gifts to serve both men and women. As we explored in chapter 6, these groups permit it because they say that there is a male authority figure in charge of the gathering, and his presence provides some sort of imaginary "umbrella" under which these women may exercise their gifts. To me, this is specious reasoning. If a woman addresses a committee, class, or audience of any sort, she acts and speaks with authority if she is faithful to God's Word. She does not need some sort of intermediary to transmit that authority to her.

2. Some people have told me that if a male authority figure is absent, women must restrict use of their gifts. However, if women need some sort of male, human overseer, then we must conclude that they are unreliable or incapable and thus inferior. The only other alternative would be a role playing of the strictest order, with women only interacting with other women. This would return women to the nunnery and would deprive the Christian community of the enrichment half its members have to offer.

3. Even Old Testament ordination set apart the priests to *serve*. In Exodus 40:13 God said of Aaron: ". . . Consecrate him so that he may serve me as priest." This is reiterated for Aaron's sons. Have we corrupted the call to service so that priests (or ministers or pastors) have become rulers of the people rather than servants of God?

4. *See also* Walter Liefeld and Ruth Tucker, *Daughters of the Church: Women*

and Ministry From New Testament Times to the Present (Grand Rapids, Mich.: Zondervan, 1986); and Della Olson, *A Woman of Her Times* (Minneapolis, Minn.: Free Church Press, 1977).

5. This preoccupation seems especially puzzling in view of the fact that some great preachers of former years, such as Dwight L. Moody, were not ordained. Many, like John Bunyan, Charles Haddon Spurgeon, Henry A. ("Harry") Ironside, and A. W. Tozer, had no formal theological training of the sort required today, but were largely self-taught.

6. Visual representations of God have sometimes been great art, as in the case of paintings and sculpture produced by the Renaissance masters. These representations have also been aids to worship for many Christians. However, I suggest that such representations have done theological damage by reinforcing the idea (particularly in the case of God the Father) that God is a larger-than-life male figure. I also suggest that it is no accident that no contemporary visual representations of the Incarnate Christ have been preserved (if indeed any were made). The current preoccupation with the Shroud of Turin shows how we yearn to reduce God to a form we can understand.

7. C. S. Lewis, *That Hideous Strength* (New York: Macmillan, 1971), 316.

8. C. S. Lewis, *God in the Dock* (London: William Collins Sons, 1979), 93.

9. Lewis states, "We are dealing with male and female as the live and awful shadows of realities utterly beyond our control and largely beyond our direct knowledge," ibid., 93, 94. As with his presentation of male-female relationships in *Perelandra* and *That Hideous Strength*, Lewis's reasoning makes women a shadow or image of a lesser and possibly nondivine reality. His words do not indicate that he considers women fully created in the image of God, and his writings also suggest a pantheon, with a super-male divinity figure and a lesser feminine goddess or semidivine female figure.

10. Hannah Whitall Smith, *The God of All Comfort* (Chicago: Moody Press, 1956), 69.

11. G. Campbell Morgan, *The Gospel According to John* (Westwood, N. J.: Fleming H. Revell, n.d.), 47.

12. *See also* the author's article in *Women, Authority and the Bible*, ed., Alvera Mickelsen (Downers Grove, Ill.: InterVarsity Press, 1986), 22–27.

13. Sadly, some radical feminist thinkers have become more in tune with paganism than with orthodox Christianity. Some, like Mary Daly, have even labeled themselves post-Christian.

14. Why should childbearing make women subordinate in function or mean that their humanity is in some way different? Why is not the situation reversed so that women are thought superior, because they bear children and thus carry on the race? When will we see that our sinful natures have tricked us into these competitive ways of thinking and that in reality we need each other (not "one without the other") and that who bears the child is not a mark of functional inferiority or superiority?

15. Quoted in *Presbyterian Layman*, 84 (July/August, 1984): 3.

16. Our concern about this issue must not only be because of the language barrier some people feel, but because persons who consider that Bible language excludes them have themselves begun to change the text. Increasingly changes are made where the text does not warrant them, and some of those changes result in very questionable theology. When, in frustration and even desperation, these ad hoc revisions of Scripture make language about God

inclusive, at least two basic theological trends become visible: God is depersonalized, or God is mythologized. In extreme efforts to eliminate masculine language, either all masculine language for God is thrown out (and with it the wonderful closeness of the parental imagery that lies at the heart of what it means to be a child of God), or else feminine imagery is added or substituted. The result is not only a strange anthropomorphic dualism within the first member of the Trinity, but in effect the Trinity becomes a Quartet.

It should be the theologian's task to work on the issue of appropriate language for God; but as a purely textual matter, the generic terms relating to human beings could become more inclusive and still remain faithful to the original texts. The longer we evangelicals delay working on this issue, the more decisions others make about it, and they are often uninformed choices and even unorthodox ones.

Chapter 11

1. Oswald Chambers, *My Utmost for His Highest* (New York: Dodd, Mead, 1964), 223.

For Further Reading

Bence, Evelyn. *Leaving Home: The Making of an Independent Woman.* Wheaton, Ill.: Tyndale House, 1986.

Bilezikian, Gilbert. *Beyond Sex Roles: A Guide for the Study of Female Roles in the Bible.* Grand Rapids, Mich.: Baker Book House, 1985. (This book is especially valuable for the extensive bibliography that presents sources for material from a wide variety of perspectives.)

Boldrey, Richard and Joyce. *Chauvinist or Feminist? Paul's View of Women.* Grand Rapids, Mich.: Baker Book House, 1976.

Gundry, Patricia. *Woman Be Free!* Grand Rapids, Mich.: Zondervan, 1977.

Gundry, Patricia. *Heirs Together: Mutual Submission in Marriage.* Grand Rapids, Mich.: Zondervan, 1980.

Gundry, Patricia. *The Complete Woman.* New York: Doubleday, 1981.

Gundry, Patricia. *Neither Slave nor Free: Helping Women Answer the Call to Church Leadership.* New York: Harper & Row, 1987.

Hassey, Janette. *No Time for Silence: Evangelical Woman in Public Ministry Around the Turn of the Century.* Grand Rapids, Mich.: Zondervan, 1986.

Hesthenes, Roberta, and Lois Curley, eds. *Woman and the Ministries of Christ.* Pasadena: Fuller Theological Seminary, 1979.

Kroeger, Richard and Catherine. *Women Elders . . . Sinners or Saints?* New York: United Presbyterian Church, 1981.

Liefeld, Walter, and Ruth Tucker. *Daughters of the Church: Women and Ministry from New Testament Times to the Present.* Grand Rapids, Mich.: Zondervan, 1986.

Malcolm, Kari Torjesen. *Women at the Crossroads.* Downers Grove, Ill.: InterVarsity Press, 1982.

Mickelsen, Alvera, ed. *Women, Authority, and the Bible.* Downers Grove, Ill.: InterVarsity Press, 1986.

Oelthius, James. *I Pledge You My Troth.* New York: Harper & Row, 1976.

Olson, Della. *A Woman of Her Times.* Minneapolis, Minn.: Free Church Press, 1977.

Spencer, Aida Besançon. *Beyond the Curse.* Nashville, Tenn.: Thomas Nelson, 1985.

FOR FURTHER READING

Storkey, Elaine. *What's Right with Feminism.* Grand Rapids, Mich.: Wm. B. Eerdmans, 1985.

Swartley, Willard. *Slavery, Sabbath, War, and Women.* Scottdale, Penn.: Herald Press, 1983.

Williams, Don. *The Apostle Paul and Women in the Church.* Van Nuys, Cal.: BIM Publ., 1977.

Index

Abigail,
  as "exception," 127; gifts of, 210; and role playing, 113; wife of David, 92, 95; wisdom of, 111

Abortion, 48, 49, 50, 66, 173, 174

Abraham,
  as "exception," 142; and God's justice, 31; good example of, 243; insensitivity to women, 101; and Sarah, 88–89, 249; selfishness of, 145; worst-case scenario, 88, 104

Ambassadors of Christ,
  believers as, 67, 74, 106, 150, 207, 237, 239–241; equality as, 72, 188, 219; and God's call, 126, 210, 212; and Good News, 104; mission as, 176, 244; as servants, 144; unity as, 124, 208

Approval,
  God's, 22, 24, 28, 31, 133, 140, 176, 242; need for, 21, 27, 76–77

Authority,
  and church, 25, 213, 261; delegated by God, 153, 157; divine, 16–20, 73, 140, 212, 233; and "hard passages," 185, 247, 254–256, 261, 288; and headship, 197; of husband, 42, 185; and *kephalē*, 193, 194; male over female, 141, 182, 192, 193, 196, 197, 262, 289; need for, 15–16, 18, 76; parental, 132; positions of, 55; religious, 45; of Savior, 24, 141; Scripture as, 44,

60, 61, 209; source of, 211–213; women in, 211

Bathsheba, 94
Bible study, 25, 29

Career,
  child care as, 165–166, 167, 287; commitment to, 176; and competition, 178; controlling, 179–180; and marriage, 147, 157, 163–164, 170, 171, 173; and married women, 36, 160, 174; and parenting, 175; race and, 125; and single women, 148–150; as spiritual matter, 177; volunteerism as, 37, 105, 106, 175; women's limited options, 105, 106

Child care,
  as career, 165–166, 167, 287; needs, 48, 49, 50; nontraditional, 167; programs, 167, 213; providing, 165–166, 174; and role playing, 106, 107; and Scripture, 168; and traditionalist views, 160; vs. parenting, 162–164, 175

Church,
  and authority, 25, 213; and Bible interpretation, 229; and careers, 177; compared to wife, 196, 197, 198, 205; early, 230, 248, 261, 286; and "hard passages," 257, 258, 265; and patriarchy, 55; and relationships, 44, 177, 179, 180,